OVERSTREET'S NEW WINE GUIDE

CELE-BRATING THE NEW WAVE IN WINE-MAKING

OVERSTREET'S NEW WINE GUIDE

BY DENNIS OVERSTREET
WITH DAVID GIBBONS
PHOTOGRAPHS BY
CATHERINE LEUTHOLD
DESIGN BY SUBTITLE

Clarkson Potter/Publishers
New York

ALSO BY DENNIS OVERSTREET

WINE SECRETS

Published by Clarkson Potter/Publishers,
201 East 50th Street, New York, New York 10022.
Member of the Crown Publishing Group.

Random House, Inc. New York, Toronto, London, Sydney, Auckland
www.randomhouse.com

CLARKSON N. POTTER, POTTER, and colophon are registered trademarks of Random House, Inc.

Photographs printed at B Lab, Inc.

Printed in the United States of America

Library of Congress Cataloging-in-Publication Data
Overstreet, Dennis.
Overstreet's life with wine: celebrating the new wave in winemaking/by Dennis Overstreet with
David Gibbons; photographs by Catherine Leuthold.
Includes index.
1. Wine and winemaking. I. Gibbons, David Scott, 1957–   . II. Title.
TP548.O748   1999
641.2'2—dc21   99-13373
                  CIP

ISBN 0-517-70784-5 hardcover
ISBN 0-609-805185 paperback

10 9 8 7 6 5 4 3 2 1

First Edition

have many people to thank because here are so many who participated in making this book happen, either by submitting to interviews, allowing me to taste their wines, dine in their establishments, partake of their wine lifestyles or to simply soak up their inspiration. Although some are not mentioned here by name, I raise a glass and salute every one of you and I apologize to all those I have inadvertently left out:

Our friends in France, including Mr. and Mrs. Jean-Eugene Borie, Château Ducru-Beaucaillou; Petrus Desbois of Château Saint-Georges for his friendship, hospitality and understanding; Madame Mae-Elaine de Lancquesaing, Château Pichon Lalande; Count Alexandre de Lur-Saluces, Château D'Yquem; Corinne Mentzelopoulos, Château Margaux; Mr. and Mrs. Bernard Nicholas of Château La Conseillante, consummate hosts.

Our Italian wine colleagues, among them Daniele Cernilli, editor of *Gambero Rosso,* and his lovely wife, Marina Thompson; Marc de Grazia, wine guru and Italian exporter *par extraordinaire;* Bruno and Bruna Giacosa and Dante Scaglione; Silvio Jermann; Francesco and Filippo Mazzei and

Tammy; the entire Scavino family for their warm hospitality.

And in America, Scott Carney, Master Sommelier, The Tonic Restaurant & Bar, New York City; Roger Dagorn, Master Sommelier, Chanterelle, New York City, and chairman, Sommelier Society of America; Professor Bipin Desai, Dr. Dick Fleming, Greg Gorman and Wolfgang Grunwald, friends and collectors; Andrea Immer, Master Sommelier, Windows on the World; Thomas Keller, chef, The French Laundry, Napa Valley; Fran Kysela, importer and Master Sommelier, Winchester, Virginia; Leonardo Lo Cascio and his staff at WineBow, including Antoinette Tumino and Alessandra Bezzi; Rob McDonald, Old Bridge Cellars, San Francisco; Professor Ann C. Noble of UC-Davis; Jorge Ordonez, importer of fine Spanish wines; Alfred Portale, executive chef, and John Gilman, Sommelier, of Gotham Bar & Grill, New York City, for allowing us to sit in on their tasting seminar with Josh Wesson; Renzo Rapacioli, Barolo Restaurant, New York City; Koerner Rombauer, his son K.R., and the rest of the staff and family at Rombauer Vineyards; Neal Rosenthal; my good friend Piero Selvaggio, a force in fine wines and proprietor of the best Italian restaurant in America, Valentino of Santa

Monica, Tony Soler; Margaret Stern and Kate McManus of Margaret Stern Communications; Al Stewart and his beautiful wife, Kris; Larry Stone, Sommelier, Rubicon Restaurant, San Francisco; and John Thoreen, The Wine Tutor.

Special thanks to Ted Lemon for providing invaluable insights into the art of winegrowing, and also to his wife, Heidi who was equally charming and helpful.

An extra-special thanks to Alfred and Michel and the entire Tesseron family and staff at Château Pontet-Canet for their gracious hospitality.

Kudos to my loyal, dedicated and hardworking staff at The Wine Merchant, Beverly Hills. Thanks to our customers who, over the years, have made this wonderful wine adventure possible.

Hats off to my "production team" for their valuable contributions: writer and general factotum Dave Gibbons; editor Pam Krauss and her wonderful assistant, Chloe Smith; photographer Catherine Leuthold; agent Bob Markel; and Roger Vergnes of Copperplate Press.

And most of all, thanks to Chris for all her help in each and every way.

WINE IS BOTH
AN ADVENTURE AND
A LIFESTYLE

CONTENTS

INTRO WHAT IS THIS NEW REVOLUTION ALL ABOUT?

IT'S ABOUT CROSSING NEW WORLD SCIENCE WITH OLD WORLD TRADITIONS . . . MOM-AND-POP OPERATIONS WITH FAXES AND CELL PHONES . . . TENTH-GENERATION WINEMAKERS WITH PH.D.S AND STAINLESS-STEEL FERMENTERS. IT'S ABOUT THROWING OUT HARD-AND-FAST RULES AND TAKING A FEW CHANCES, DRINKING RED WINE WITH FISH AND WHITE WINE WITH SPICY FOODS . . . TECHNOLOGY IN BORDEAUX AND *TERROIR* IN CALIFORNIA, FRENCH OAK BARRELS IN NAPA AND AMERICAN ONES IN COONAWARRA.

The New Wine Revolution is about wine as entertainment and wine as adventure, about doing away with mystery and pretension. It's about artisans on the Internet, a cottage industry in the information age, winemakers with mud on their boots and tickets on the Concorde, million-dollar consultants who hand-sort grapes at harvest and small producers who earn world renown by standing the old hierarchy on its ear.

It's about wines that whisper and wines that shout. And because of all these things, it's about a world where there are more great wines coming from more different places than ever before.

The New Wine Revolution is both a lifestyle and an attitude, a casual expertise, an effortless enjoyment, subtlety without obfuscation, hedonism without excess, serious (but not too serious) fun for grown-ups and, finally, one piece of a bigger puzzle wherein the finer things in life become part of one's everyday experience.

My first book, published years ago, was entitled *Wine Secrets*. I was letting readers in on the mysterious secrets of wine, giving them a glimpse into a special, privileged world of celebrities and high-flying haute connoisseurs that most people only dream about. Today we've moved beyond that elitism. The world of fine wines is no longer an exclusive club. Not everybody can afford—or is willing to pay—$35 to $3,500 for a bottle of fine wine; the good news is they don't have to. With a little effort at self-education, by tapping into the huge worldwide network of information about fine wines, anyone can and should take pleasure in their myriad delights. There are no more secrets. But there are whispers.

There is a Chinese proverb that says "A whisper is louder than a shout." I always apply this to the marketing of wines. The whispers are the wines of subtlety, balance, finesse and longevity. They're the wines you have to ask about, the wines from the smaller producers that aren't always immediately available. It takes a little more effort to hear the whispers. You have to seek out a bartender at a special wine bar, a wine maven on the Internet or launch a personal search out in the wine market, but these efforts will be rewarded. For me, the search and the thrill of discovery are among the primary pleasures of the New Wine Revolution.

Ted Lemon is one of my favorite winemakers for the new millennium; he makes the kinds of wines I'm holding up as the new standard. "Ours is a society that is dominated by shouting," Ted told me. "Whether it's in television, in the news, in the wine press, you are heard when you are screaming. We don't want to make wines that scream. We're interested in making wines that have balance, elegance and length. They're not wines that are going to be heard in a noisy bar-room. They are not really wines that are made for a tasting of twenty-five or thirty-five wines."

Wines of subtlety don't have to be wines of snobbery, and to appreciate those subtle wines all you need is a desire to enjoy, a sense of smell and taste and the patience to listen. Some of the most exciting wines are those that begin quietly and just stay with you, gradually building to a glorious crescendo, a long, delicious finish. They don't overwhelm your palate with a big splash of fruit concentrate.

I'll admit sometimes there's nothing wrong with a shout. One distinguished Napa Valley producer, Larry Turley, makes a Petite Syrah that's like a four-hundred-pound sumo wrestler coming at you. That's what I call a shout. It's fun. It's a wine for a special occasion, not for casual, everyday consumption. It's what I call a "dayglo" wine: everything is exaggerated with fluorescent flavors and laserlike intensity. It's probably not right for a quiet evening at home, but it will stand up to the spicy cuisine and the high-wattage atmosphere at Chef Wolfgang Puck's famous Spago restaurants.

More often today when you do hear the shouts reverberating around the wine world, they're exclamations of enthusiasm, the news of great wines being spread far and wide. They're yelps of glee. The goal of this book is to encourage you to listen to the whispers, pop some corks, taste the wines and celebrate all the sensational flavors and aromas of the New Wine Revolution.

LIKE SO MANY OF MY ILLUSTRIOUS COLLEAGUES IN THE WINE INDUSTRY, I'M VERY EXCITED ABOUT WHAT I CALL THE NEW WINE REVOLUTION. WITH THIS BOOK, I INVITE READERS TO JOIN THAT REVOLUTION AND TO MAKE WINE A PART OF THEIR LIFESTYLE.

"Great sites are not just a dime a dozen and they never will be."
—Ted Lemon, Littorai

"What we have now is a higher level of consistency and a higher level of proficiency in winegrowing."
—Tony Soter, California winemaker and consultant

WHISPERS

"The people who pay incredible attention to detail are the ones who are successful. They're the Tony Soters and the Heidi Barretts, and on the vintner they're there when they're trimming, they're there when they're leaf pulling."
—Koerner Rombauer, Rombauer Vineyards, Napa Valley

"The winemaker is a custodian of the flavor. I tell everyone it's 75 percent artistry, 25 percent science."
—Mark Aubert, Napa Valley winemaker

"The essence of sophistication is simplicity. I found this out in the airplane business. If you don't really understand the problem, that's when you come up with the complicated solutions."
—Tom Jones, Moraga Vineyards, Bel Air

"The revolution is not just in California. It's in France. It's in Burgundy. It's in the Rhone Valley as well as in Italy."
—Michael Bonaccorsi, Master Sommelier

"We're all fortunate to be sitting here. There are new wines and winemakers and new areas popping up all over. It's really an exciting time to live in the wine industry."
—Chuck Wagner, Caymus Vineyards, Rutherford

"Making wine is really the art of man working with nature, and there aren't many things more exciting than that."
—Bill Harlan, Harlan Estate, Rutherford, California

"Tchelistcheff said years ago that a big wine is like a great historical personage. It always has a small defect that makes it unique."
—Attilio Pagli, international consulting enologist

"Your colleague is not a competitor. If he makes a good Barolo or Barbaresco, he's just increasing the demand for these wines."
—Angelo Gaja

SOIL

TERROIR

SOUL

PEOPLE, PLACES AND WINES

Over the years, the wine business has given me so much pleasure and sustenance. Like many people involved with wine, I'm lucky to be able to combine my passion with my profession. Being a purveyor of fine wines has always been a wonderful vocation, but what amazes me is the crescendo of excitement over the last decade, all the new labels, producers, winemakers and varietal blends. This book is about the New Wave of Wine, how it began, the questions, the answers, the assumptions, the changes that have taken place in tastes and attitudes and what is yet to come.

In the mid-nineties I expanded my business, which enabled me to explore new areas of fine wines. Exploration is exciting and rejuvenating; it gives me a chance to put my hand on the pulse of the industry. I try to spend as much time as possible meeting the people who make it happen and trying their wines. In these pages, you will encounter many of these people and learn about their delicious wines.

As a retailer for more than twenty-five years, I am bursting with enthusiasm and excitement over this revolution. For many months, my wife, my staff, my co-author and I have conducted numerous and extensive interviews to uncover the fascinating story of how potential disaster has led us to the rebirth of winemaking in every aspect, and how more world-class wines than ever before are being delivered to the consumer's dinner table. As we spoke with friends and colleagues in the industry—the winemakers, proprietors and producers, consultants, and collectors whose voices you'll hear throughout this book—there was one common note that we heard over and over: "This is the most exciting time to be in the wine business." The second adventure is happening.

Every day, more and more consumers are experiencing the revolution, experimenting with different varietals and matching different and exotic cuisines with wines. The restaurant sector is integral to this revolution. More sophisticated wine bars are opening every year; restaurant wine lists are offering more interesting and better selections all the time.

The purpose of this book is not just to expose everyone who enjoys wines to the New Age of Wine, but to encourage them to make their own discoveries, to make wine part of their lives. Wine is art, science, food and a lifestyle all in one.

Where are the new wines of distinction and who are the new personalities in wine? I went looking for them, and everywhere I looked I was struck by the superior energy and commitment of cutting-edge winemakers, producers, importers and distributors, restaurateurs and sommeliers. Many of them are featured in these pages. You'll encounter names such as Asteroid, Screaming Eagle, Point Rouge, Valandraud and The Bride. They are the ones raising the standards. You'll see them exhibiting a commitment to one goal: making the best wines they can—and in many instances at great personal and professional sacrifice. They're all pushing the envelope in their own way.

ROADSIGNS
NOT MAPS

This book is meant to help readers recognize and enjoy the finest wines in the world. I want to inspire you to partake of the simple pleasure of having a good, affordable bottle of wine in the comfort of your home or in your favorite casual cafe. I want you to be able to seize the wine list in any four-star restaurant and, without feeling the slightest bit intimidated, make an informed choice. I'd like to spur you on to become a collector of the finest, rarest wines, precious liquid produced in infinitesimal lots. I'd like to inspire in every wine lover the spirit and commitment that, for collectors, transforms "You can't have it" into "I'm going to get it."

Collecting $200 bottles of wine isn't for everybody. As proprietor of The Wine Merchant, Beverly Hills, I do have a few "high-end" clients. For those who are twenty-four years old and making $10 million a picture, what's wrong with buying a bottle of 1961 Château Petrus for $10,000 and sharing it with a couple of friends? Meanwhile, the rest of us can capture the same pleasures by sharing a good bottle of wine for a fraction of that price.

Wine, especially today, is a fascinating journey, a global quest for the best. This book provides fundamental knowledge, inspiration and highlights. It is not an encyclopedia or an atlas. In the information age, one of the greatest challenges is focus. Part of what I want to give readers is a series of wine benchmarks. The best way to learn is by example. I can tell you how to do it over and over, but if I show how it's done, things start to come into focus. This is how I teach my wine-tasting classes: just sit down and pop some corks, start a conversation and see where it

takes us. No lectures, no prescriptions. Just a few basic tools followed by some concrete examples so you can begin to judge for yourself. Whether you are a beginner, a longtime wine lover or a connoisseur, I believe this book will be a welcome addition to your portfolio of wine experiences, to your appreciation of the people, places, aromas and flavors in the world of fine wines.

I'll put up a few road signs, but it's your adventure. I want you to have the thrill of discovery. I'll be your Wizard of Oz, supplying a few bells and whistles, but you have to find your own way to the Emerald City. It's what I try to do at The Wine Merchant. It's about creating an aura around wines, a total experience that both entertains and builds confidence.

The best wine producers don't make wines to please certain powerful critics or to conform to a specific standard; they make them to express the unique character of the grape and the vineyard. By the same token, I can't tell you what to like. I can, however, give you a few hints about what *I* like, and that should be enough to get you started. Then I'll point you in the right direction and say, "Explore, enjoy, there's no getting lost."

There is a certain self-confidence that arises when you can recognize something good and appreciate it for what it is. This book will take you to that "comfort zone" vis-à-vis wine. If you liked a certain wine before you read this book, you're going to learn *why* you liked it.

The purpose of this book, then, is to share the excitement of the new wine adventure, to celebrate its pleasures, to demystify the science of wine and to make the ever-widening world of premium wines more accessible. And never to lose sight of the target, which is to appreciate and enjoy the best wines in the world.

The Medoc region of Bordeaux: the estuary of the Gironde is in the distance (top left); world-class vineyards crowd the highway (bottom).

WHY DRINK WINE?

Wine is the world's most intriguing beverage. It begets an endlessly fascinating conversation that involves mathematics, science, art, music, opinion, romance, speculation, desire and many different emotions. Each and every wine has a story to tell, and I think that's why so many enthusiastic, articulate people of depth and character are attracted to it. It's a topic that's been discussed and debated throughout history. It's been validated countless times as a subject of art and appreciation.

I've found that the opening and sharing of wine brings a broader sense of enjoyment and understanding to life. It represents one of the most sophisticated, interesting hobbies. Wine is a catalyst for camaraderie, travel and adventure; it is exciting and stimulating, inspiring and challenging. It is a subject of incredible depth and range, yet it is also amazingly accessible. All you really have to do is plunk down $10 or less and pop the cork.

Wine is made to be appreciated and celebrated. Wine is not water. Neither is it mere alcohol. A martini is a martini. All right, martini drinkers might argue that if you use Bombay Gin or if you triple distill your vodka or make it from potatoes there's a real distinction. That's fine. I don't have to agree with it, though. In fact, I think gin and vodka are basically just efficient delivery systems for alcohol. If you want a quick buzz, then have a slug of hard liquor. I urge all the martini drinkers to try two distinct glasses of fine wine. Swirl them, sniff them, taste them. If that's not an eye-opener, a burst of flavor, a delicious hint of the myriad possibilities of aroma and taste, then you should go back to your martinis.

You drink a glass of water to quench your thirst. You drink a martini to unwind after a rough day, to forget about the headaches and the hassles. You drink a glass of wine to relax, too, but also to stimulate your senses, to savor a new taste.

CELEBRATING THE NEW WINE REVOLUTION

Celebrating the New Wine Revolution is about being a wine lover, period. There are very few other requirements. If you want to take it to the max, become a connoisseur with a vast collection; that's great, but that's not what it's all about. It is about adopting the European model, making everyday wines part of a healthy lifestyle and marking special occasions with special wines.

The New Wine Revolution is about a unified vision: the best of the New World and the Old. It's about integrating wine into your lifestyle. As Americans, we have the resources to do it. Sometimes we simply lack the knowledge and the confidence. Loving wine and knowing about it can be part of a well-rounded life. It is only one piece of the puzzle, but in my opinion it will vastly improve your enjoyment of everything else. Wine is one of life's great pleasures. It is a catalyst; it's not the be-all and end-all. It's a vehicle for enjoyment, an ancient and revered handicraft, a fascinating interplay between nature, science and art.

In these pages, you'll learn some of the fundamentals of how to taste wines; to acquire the best, whether in a wine shop or restaurant; start a cellar, serve the wines and pair them with foods. It's my goal to share with you the best wines the world has to offer, the most individual, expressive wines, and to show how they express their individuality. In the appendix, you'll find a selection of them and then, I hope, you'll want to go out and try them. Cheers.

—Dennis Overstreet, Beverly Hills

Chapter One

THE NEW WINE REVOLUTION

WINE TAKES TIME. THE PROGRESS OF THE VINES DEMANDS IT. THERE IS ONLY ONE HARVEST A YEAR, ONLY ONE CHANCE TO IMPROVE LAST YEAR'S OUTPUT, TO INNOVATE, TO LEARN FROM MISTAKES. THE SINGLE-VINEYARD WINEMAKER HAS MAYBE TWENTY-FIVE OR THIRTY SUCH CHANCES IN A CAREER.

Wine production combines art and commerce. It requires a subtle, interpretive hand. The old adage "If it ain't broke, don't fix it" applies. Unless a new method represents a definite improvement, don't expect it to last very long—another good reason for the slow pace of change in the wine business. Until the second half of the twentieth century, wine was for thousands of years made using essentially the same methods. Then came the systematic study of enology and the advent of German and American technology.

The modern wine era, from the first revolution to the new wave, is no more than the blink of an eye in the context of world history. Yet I'm convinced it will go down as a watershed in the production of premium wines.

REFLECTIONS ON HISTORY

California, my native state, has an obsession with change. We've got to have the latest and the greatest of everything. The First Wine Revolution started in California, as did the New Age of Wine. Each time, the rest of the world jumped on the bandwagon. There's a reason for this.

If California is always ripe for innovation, then the opposite is true of Europe—particularly France, the wine mecca—where the burden of tradition weighs heavily on contemporary vintners. You don't rearrange the paintings in the Louvre. If someone has the strength of character and the skill to change Bordeaux, more power to them, but it's not likely. My friend Alfred Tesseron, the dynamic proprietor of Château Pontet-Canet, adjacent to Château Mouton-Rothschild in the Pauillac region of Bordeaux, has done experimental bottlings from particular parts of his vineyard. These wines, in my opinion, unequivocally blow Mouton off the map. They would definitely create a ripple in the marketplace. But when I asked him why he didn't launch a separate brand, he shrugged and replied, "I can't. Pontet-Canet is Pontet-Canet."

For so long, California was a winegrower's paradise awaiting the creation of an industry. It was a land of incredible opportunities, which is not to say it didn't demand courage, vision and hard work. Early efforts by pioneers, many of them of European stock, laid a foundation for the first American wine revolution.

Robert Mondavi, who founded his winery in 1966, brought technology and marketing savvy to the making and purveying of fine wines, starting a revolution that eventually swept the world. Robert Parker, Jr., came along with his 100-point rating system and made the rarefied air of wine connoisseurship accessible to anyone willing to subscribe to his magazine. Suddenly, the United States became a market for the world's best wines. The vineyards of California—and soon of Oregon—began to produce wines to rival the greatest old French names. Americans had reached a major plateau.

Mondavi and the rest of the founding fathers, including the likes of Warren Winiarski and Andre Tchelistcheff, mined the best grape sources, invested in the latest machinery, made superior wines and marketed them with "classy" advertising. This American success story reached its apex in 1976, appropriately the U.S. Bicentennial, when two Napa Valley wines, Château Montelena Chardonnay and Stag's Leap Cabernet, beat the world's best in the now-legendary Paris blind tasting organized by British wine expert Steven Spurrier.

This initial wine revolution was driven by our Jeffersonian optimism: As Americans, we could accomplish anything we set out to do. The underlying principle was one of manipulation—science conquers nature: "Just give us the grapes, we'll manufacture the product, create the market, build an industry." The science that fueled this first revolution came largely from the University of California at Davis and Fresno State, where the systematic study of enology began in the 1950s.

By the mid-1960s, technology had begun to change the wine industry. Scientific analysis and modern, hygienic production methods were applied in the winery. Wines were sold with TV ads—who doesn't remember Orson Welles solemnly intoning "We sell no wine before its time" on behalf of Paul Masson? The wine press—*The Wine Spectator,* Parker's *Wine Advocate* and other publications—became an independent publicity and marketing engine for the industry.

Blue blazers, dark suits, and serious wine talk at Château Pontet-Canet in tradition-bound Bordeaux.

Fran Kysela, a distinguished importer and distributor of premium wines who is also a master sommelier recalls, "Wine for many years was sort of a cottage industry. No one really understood the science of winemaking. Thankfully, California really investigated that. Back in the fifties, sixties and seventies at UC-Davis, they figured out how to make wines that were fresher, brighter and tasted better. And that science has been adapted all over the world. Before, winemaking was more mystical. You'd crush the grapes, or they'd be foot-trodden, then you'd throw them in a barrel, walk away and come back a month later. It was the same technique year in and year out. The quality of the vintage determined the wine."

I started my business in 1972. My timing was fortuitous; California was a sleeping giant about to awaken. Little did I know that more than twenty-five years later I'd be writing a book to say that this uprising was merely a blip on the screen of a much greater occurrence in wine history: an international wine renaissance that would be building momentum well into the new century.

Preparing for a luncheon at Château Margaux.

When I started out, wine was still largely shrouded in mystery. People didn't know how to bring it into their lives. At that time, there were about twenty-five wineries in California producing serious wines; by the mid-eighties there were hundreds, and with them came a lowering of standards. It was a boom that inevitably succumbed to the mass-market mentality. Complacency and greed set in.

Then came the little pest that changed the world. It was a turning point, as big an event in wine history as the meteor that destroyed the dinosaurs was in natural history. Until then, the wines were good but undistin-

guished. Everyone was making Monterey Jack cheese. They used the same yeasts, the same recipes. They were all just "California Chardonnay" or "California Cabernet." They were "food wines"—pleasing but generic.

Beginning in the late sixties, Beaulieu, Mondavi, Jordan, Heitz and Stag's Leap emerged as wineries of distinction, setting the standards. Then phylloxera struck, realigning an entire industry. As the new plantings gradually became widespread, new names came to the forefront: Viader, Harlan Estate, Aruajo Estate (Eisele Vineyard), Maya (Dalla Valle), Colgin, Screaming Eagle, Bryant Family.

> **"I think it's a great time to be part of the wine world. So much is going on. There seem to be great scientific resources available to make wine as good as possible. Trying to fuse those with the ancient tradition of winemaking is a very exciting prospect."**—Scott Carney, Master Sommelier

These and others like them are synonymous with the new revolution. Their wines have moved us from an era of outstanding production to a new level of excellence, one step closer to perfection.

Phylloxera gave our industry the opportunity to change its approach to winemaking completely. The gradual destruction of California's vines led the winemakers straight back to the vineyards. It forced the entire industry to reconsider basic planting decisions and encouraged growers to experiment with different grape varieties such as Sangiovese, Tempranillo, Grenache, Mourvèdre, Viognier and Albariño. Viticulture, the science of growing vines, jumped onto a fast track. There was a vast number of new rootstocks and different methods of planting, trellising, training, pruning and harvesting grapes. Managers were faced with decisions on how close to plant the vines, which direction to plant them in, how to train them, which clones to use, which varieties to plant where and even how to ensure proper air circulation among the vines.

The idea of mass management of vineyards was disappearing. Vineyard managers, owners and winemakers started asking questions. Why were two vines from adjacent rows producing varied crop quality and quantity? A new vision was emerging. In the second revolution, winemakers nurture each vine individually, treating it as a significant piece in the giant puzzle. Organic farming is no longer merely for the fruits and nuts. Through microbiological research, vineyard managers have realized that pesticides kill more than just the pests.

The new revolution has also changed practices inside the winery. The most dramatic change has been the step backward from manipulation. The big step forward has been toward meticulous selection and elimination, starting in the vineyard and continuing in the harvest, the crush, the fermentation, the barrel aging and finally to the blending and bottling. Marco Cappelli of Swanson Vineyards and Su-Hua Newton are just a few who are looking at the barrels as far more than a mere aging vessel. Su-Hua braves the damp cold winters of France every year to bid for choice oak trees at the barrel auctions. Marco personally oversees the aging of the oak and the toasting of every barrel used for Swanson's wines.

Today, winery owners are not exclusively concerned with how much profit they can put into their bank accounts. Instead, they focus on where the money can best be spent to improve their wines—in the vineyards, in the people managing these vineyards, in the research and lab analysis, in the equipment that makes use of technological advances with minimal disturbance of nature.

The second wave is defined by an integrated approach to making the finest wines in the world: *terroir* meets technology (more on this in the next chapter). There is a new optimism, a renewed quest for the Holy Grail, for a wine of perfection. Science and art and an understanding of history have come together to create a unified vision that looks ahead to the twenty-first century yet harks back to an earlier age of artisans.

"It's sort of like Hegel's theory of history," says Scott Carney, a cutting-edge master sommelier. "There's a thesis, an antithesis and then a synthesis. The whole *terroir* notion that was held so dear in France was the thesis and then the Americans kind of came in with the sword of science and said, 'We can do whatever we want. Forget the *terroir*, we'll make every flavor on this block of land.' Now both sides are quietly accepting that each had something to offer."

THE SECOND WINE REVOLUTION BEGAN, LITERALLY, UNDERGROUND. ALTHOUGH A NEW GENERATION OF WINEMAKERS WAS EMERGING, IT WAS THE TINY PHYLLOXERA BUG THAT WAS THE SPARK.

Phylloxera devastated the vineyards of France in the late nineteenth century, when wine producers had nowhere near the scientific resources they have today. What began in the 1860s as a mysterious plague was eventually attributed to a tiny pest.

After much study, the French discovered that certain native American rootstocks were genetically resistant to phylloxera. These vines produced inferior grapes, but it was possible to graft healthy bud wood from the noble French grapevines onto it. Ironically, it would be American vines that saved the French wine industry.

The plague struck again in the late twentieth century, this time in California, marking the end of the First Wine Revolution and the beginning of the new age. The story of phylloxera in Cal-

ifornia is a classic case of blind optimism, expediency and denial that infected an entire industry—the best and the worst of America's wine revolution. Yet this crisis has been turned into a triumph by California's winegrowers.

Phylloxera is an insect that eats the roots of grapevines, gradually destroying their ability to produce grapes. It is the grapevine's equivalent of malignant cancer—an incurable, fatal, degenerative disease. Once it's discovered only one thing is certain: The vine will eventually die. The winegrower ultimately has no choice but to uproot and replant.

In 1958, the University of California-Davis, which was quickly becoming the world's leading authority on the science of wine, recommended a rootstock called AXR-1 as the best choice for California's North Coast. It pro-

duced both quantity and quality and was considered a low risk for phylloxera. It fueled the booming premium wine industry; more than two thirds of Napa Valley's vineyards were planted on it in the 1960s and 1970s.

AXR-1 is a hybrid of Aramon, a high-yielding vine popular in southern France in the late-nineteenth and early-twentieth centuries, and *Vitis rupestris,* a native American wild vine that does not produce wine grapes. (A hybrid combines two species whereas a cross is between members of the same species.) Aramon is part of the premium-grape species *Vitis vinifera,* of which Cabernet Sauvignon, Merlot and most other "noble varieties" are members. AXR-1 was introduced in France in 1879, the first of a series of hybrids developed in response to the phylloxera plague. But it succumbed to

PHYLL

A PLAGUE AND A PHOENIX RISING

the pest several times in the early twentieth century, and by the end of World War I, it became clear that it was not resistant.

Colonies of tiny yellow mites were discovered in the dug-up roots of a sick Napa vineyard in 1980, but scientists at UC-Davis were slow to recognize the problem. Ignoring the lessons of history and avoiding the obvious conclusion, they used incomplete data to hypothesize that a new strain of the bug was attacking only certain AXR roots.

Throughout the mid-1980s, many growers, in a state of confusion or denial, continued to plant on AXR. Nurseries and growers charged ahead while the experts hesitated to put up clear warning signs, and in some cases even continued to recommend AXR. As late as 1988, "the University," as it's called in the business, was pro-ceeding cautiously in the face of mounting evidence.

"We can blame UC-Davis," says Bill MacIver of Matanzas Creek Winery in Sonoma, an organizer and spokesman for small wineries, "but if we had known enough, if we hadn't been Americans—Americans can do anything; that's our attitude—we would have gone to France, we would have studied the literature, we would have found this letter that was written in 1955 to UC-Davis that said AXR is not phylloxera-resistant. They tried to tell us that far back. We didn't do our homework."

Since normal life expectancy for a vine is twenty-five to thirty years in this part of the world, vineyards planted in the early seventies would have been replanted by the end of the century regardless of disease. Phylloxera merely accelerated the process.

Ultimately, more than 24,000 acres would have to be replaced in Napa. Grower Volker Eisele estimates replanting alone cost him $1.5 million; it delayed plans for expansion. By 1996, Eisele's output was cut to a third of the anticipated level; he doesn't expect to reach full production again until at least 2005. Even he sees a positive effect of this "avoidable crisis": "We will clearly have vastly improved vineyards. No doubt about it."

Most California winemakers—even those hit hardest by the plague—see it as an opportunity to correct past mistakes, well beyond the obvious one. Phylloxera was a lesson of history ignored through the prism of science and optimism erected by the First Wine Revolution. It was also the catalyst that forced a handful of America's most important winegrowers to leap ahead into the new age. The world followed.

OXERA

> **"Nobody has invented anything. We all copy each other. There's something to learn from everybody. You listen, you taste, you learn."** —Elio Altare, Barolo winemaker

In many cases, it is the sons and daughters of the First Wine Revolution who are fueling the new wave. Heidi Peterson Barrett's father, Dick, was part of the First Wine Revolution as a young Ph.D. in the 1960s; she's now a top winemaker and consultant in Napa. Chuck Wagner represents the third generation of Napa Valley grape farmers whose Cabernet wines are consistently at the top of their class—worldwide. He figures the Rutherford district of Napa Valley, where his grapes grow, may earn status as an appellation by the time he retires. In the great winegrowing regions of Europe, by comparison, three generations would constitute overnight success.

In the Rhône Valley of southern France, sons like Philippe Belle, a Ph.D. enologist, are taking over from fathers like Albert, who built a state-of-the-art winery when Philippe was away at college, and taking the wines of a famous appellation like Crozes-Hermitage to new heights. In the Côte-Rôtie, sons Jean-Luc and Jean-Paul Jamet have taken the reins from father Joseph and are working similar wonders in a renowned appellation. Some of the new revolutionaries are young, some are old. Some of them are scientists, some are farmers.

A retired aviation chief produces excellent wines in his own backyard, a gem of a vineyard only half a mile from the freeway in the posh Bel Air section of Los Angeles?

Yes, truth is stranger than fiction; the New Wine Revolution is full of dynamic personalities with powerful dreams and visions devoting their prodigious energies to turning out great wines.

Bill Harlan, a real estate developer with a two-hundred-year vision, looked to old tea boxes and nineteenth-century engravers' art to inspire the label for his superb estate-bottled Bordeaux-style wine out of Rutherford in the Napa Valley. Dick Grace, an ex-marine and Wall Street trader, treks the Himalayas and explores his spiritual side through Buddhism, gaining inspiration to make superb wines in his pristine little winery in St. Helena, Napa Valley. Clarke Swanson, a banker with a keen sense of marketing, conducts experiments in his vineyards, making excellent wines with eight or nine varieties of grapes. You have the flying enologists from all over—Michel Rolland from France, Dr. Richard Smart from Australia. You have visionaries like Sir Peter Michael who've made their fortunes elsewhere and entered the wine business with dollars and ambition to spare. They come from all corners of the globe, but they come with one common goal: to make the best wine possible from their precious plots of land.

In the United States, European-style appellations, official government-sanctioned production zones called AVAs

A few of my favorite winegrowers (look for their wines in the appendix): Top row, left to right: Mark Aubert; Elisabetta Foradori; Elio Altare; 2nd row: Volker and Liesel Eisele; Giuseppe Mazzocolin; Alfred Tesseron; 3rd row: Heidi Peterson Barrett; Marco Cappelli; and Koerner Rombauer.

The revolution is everywhere: a young vine-yard worker in the Friuli region of Italy.

(American Viticultural Areas) are cropping up. The New Wine Revolution is about globalization. Appellations, vineyard designations and the concept of *terroir* are applied to a New World wine mecca, California. Meanwhile, varietals, blended wines and "invented" ones—all New World concepts—are being exported back to the ancient growing regions of Europe. While traditionalists might say the old order is being turned upside down, it's really about different wine cultures learning and borrowing from each other.

Winemakers the world over have entered the information age. They congregate, they communicate, they promote a free flow of information and ideas. Gone are the days when everyone guarded their secret formulas, when winemakers were afraid to discuss mites in their vineyard or bacteria in their must for fear of bad press. After phylloxera, the walls came down and people started talking. Young winemakers shared opinions about yeasts and pests; everyone started solving everyone else's problems.

Yet even though attitudes and technology have brought about enormous change, the New Wine Revolution is not about tearing down the old; it's about building on a foundation. It's also about opening new regions to the production of great wines. Australia and California are on a par now with the great vineyards of Europe, ready to blast off into the twenty-first century. New areas are under development—Chile, Argentina, Eastern Europe, South Africa. Not so long ago in the history of wine, the statement that New Zealand produces among the best Sauvignon Blancs *in the world* would have, at the very least, raised some eyebrows. Now it's a given. Plus, the wines are delicious and affordable. When a great California winemaker like Paul Hobbs or great European houses like Rothschild or Torres establish outposts in Argentina and Chile, these become regions to watch.

At the end of the twentieth century, we're planting the vines, building the wineries, making good wines great and great wines even greater with a view to the next two hundred, five hundred even one thousand years. They are wines for the new millennium.

Because of all these sweeping changes, now more than ever is the time to drink wine and to make it part of your lifestyle. Yes, it's a very exciting time to be alive in the world of wine, to take advantage of all the new opportunities. Open a bottle today and taste a great moment in wine history. Taste the *terroir,* the clean winemaking, the character and the consistency. Taste the new viticulture, the ripe, juicy fruit and the explosion of flavors. It all adds up to perfect balance and a transcendent wine-drinking experience.

> "You look at certain large wineries and say, 'They're making wine every bit as good as they did twenty years ago.' Well, guess what? That's not good enough anymore. I want to do business with producers whose wine is better this year than last year and was better last year than the year before that."—Michael Bonaccorsi, Master Sommelier

PIERO ANTINORI
AND THE ITALIAN WINE REVOLUTION

IN ANY LARGE SUCCESSFUL ORGANIZATION THERE'S ALWAYS A DANGER OF COMPLA-CENCY CREEPING IN AND IT USUALLY STARTS AT THE TOP. NOT SO AT ANTINORI. HERE IS A COMPANY WITH A LEADER WHO HAS THE COURAGE AND THE IMAGINATION TO MOVE FORWARD. PIERO ANTINORI BELIEVES THAT INNOVATION IS THE GUARANTEE OF CONTINUED SUCCESS, AND HE'S BEEN ABLE TO PUT THAT BELIEF INTO PRACTICE.

The Marchese began his career in the late sixties. He traveled around Europe and to California, learning as much as he could about quality winegrowing. Based on his own experimentations, he began to lobby against the traditional practice of blending between 10 and 30 percent white grapes into Chianti, which was mandated by law. Change was slow to come. The first Chianti Classico DOC in 1967 perpetuated the old rules. In 1984, Chianti was upgraded to a DOCG, with a 3 to 5 percent white grape quota for Chianti Classico wines. Finally, in 1995, it became legal to produce a Chianti Classico with 100 percent Sangiovese grapes.

Antinori also created the revolutionary super-premium table wines Tignanello and Sassicaia. He felt Sangiovese was a noble variety, capable of yielding world-class wines. "Until then Italian wines, even Chianti, were considered more folkloristic," he says, "a straw bottle to have with spaghetti and guitar- or mandolin-playing."

Looking to Bordeaux for inspiration and expertise, Antinori hired Emile Peynaud to consult with their enologist Giacomo Tachis. Together they helped introduce Cabernet Sauvignon for blending with Sangiovese. Aged in small oak barrels and utilizing malolactic fermentation, this approach was unknown in Tuscany at the end of the sixties. Their goal was to produce a wine with Tuscan personality that could gain international recognition. It was an anomaly, a "table wine" called Tignanello that was more expensive than the top Chiantis. First released

in 1975, it aroused curiosity and, to Antinori's surprise, attracted a following even among tradition-bound high-end native consumers. Then it made a huge splash in America and elsewhere abroad. The rest is history. Antinori's vision had launched the Italian wine revolution. Over the next twenty years, his fellow countrymen all gradually came to share that vision.

In the early 1960s, with the demise of the sharecropping system, thousands of acres of vines were planted in Tuscany with little regard for clonal selection, site selection, planting orientation, density and so forth. It was a situation similar to California's rush to plant on AXR-1, the rootstock that turned out to be vulnerable to phylloxera. Beginning in the 1990s and into the new millennium, those vines are coming due for replacement. Given the new knowledge, this is a great opportunity to correct past mistakes.

Marchese Antinori believes the Supertuscans and other premium table wines, which incorporated international grape varieties such as Cabernet, have served their purpose of improving Italian wines across the board. "I am still prepared to go ahead," he says. "That's a very refreshing and stimulating feeling. I think that although we have made much progress—and I repeat something that I always hear from my old friend Bob Mondavi—we are just at the beginning. We have a long way to go. There are some very exciting areas to explore." In the coming decades, he envisions a renaissance of Italy's indigenous grape varieties.

"The danger of the abuse of new oak is that it will standardize wines worldwide. This is a negative for high-quality wines. Personality is for me one of the crucial factors." —Marchese Piero Antinori

Chapter Two

WINE GROWING

SOME OF THE INS AND OUTS OF THE WINEMAKING PROCESS ARE SO TECHNI-
CAL THEY HAVE NO PLACE IN A "LAYMAN'S" BOOK. MANY OF THE PROCESSES
ARE STILL NOT FULLY UNDERSTOOD. DO WE NEED TO KNOW ALL ABOUT WINE-
MAKING IN ORDER TO APPRECIATE A FINE WINE? DO WE NEED TO KNOW HOW
TO PRODUCE OR DIRECT A MOVIE TO ENJOY WATCHING ONE? NOT NECESSAR-
ILY. SO FEEL FREE TO JUMP AHEAD TO CHAPTER 3 AND POP SOME CORKS.
LATER, IF YOU START TO WONDER ABOUT "MALOLACTIC FERMENTATION" OR
"AGING IN SOME PERCENTAGE OF NEW FRENCH OAK" OR "CLOSE SPACING IN
THE VINEYARD," COME BACK HERE TO FIND OUT MORE.

In the New Wine Revolution, you'll often hear the term *winegrowing.* The moment a seed is sown or a particular clone of a particular grape variety is grafted to a particular rootstock, the miracle begins. To create the finest wines in the world, the winemaker painstakingly oversees every aspect of viticulture (vine growing) and viniculture (winemaking).

The French have a word for it: *elever,* which means "to raise." It is the same verb used to describe the raising of children—that's the kind of commitment it takes. They treat their wines with loving care, applying equal measures of traditional wisdom and modern technology.

Farmers like the Wagners of Rutherford use computers and the Internet to obtain the latest weather forecasts. At the same time, they'll tell you only a fool or a newcomer thinks he can actually predict when it's going to rain. A winemaker like Patrick Ducornau, French *Vigneron* of the Year in 1996, invents a process called microxygenation in an "obscure" corner of southwestern France (Madiran) and his technology is in turn adopted by some cutting-edge colleagues in California.

There's a synthesis of the old and the new, the foreign and the familiar. We're seeing many trends—globalization, talent-pooling, cooperative competition—that are benefiting the entire industry. Young Americans are serving apprenticeships in Europe and elsewhere. French winemakers are visiting California for a new perspective. Ted Lemon trained in Burgundy, Gary Galleron in New Zealand, Heidi Peterson Barrett in Germany and Australia, Marco Cappelli in Italy, France and Australia—to name just a few examples.

PRECIOUS LIQUID FROM THE FRUIT OF THE VINES

WINES ARE MADE IN THE VINEYARD

For years, the French have held sacred the notion that each winegrowing site is unique and can produce wines of distinction, provided its caretakers do their jobs. *Terroir* is a complex of geographical and climatic elements, each one making an incalculable contribution. In a great growing site, all the aspects of *terroir*—climate, micro-climate, soil composition, the amount of light exposure during July and August, the sheltering effect of a certain crest or ridge in the landscape, drainage patterns, the predatory spiders who eat the pests that threaten the vines—conspire to ripen the grapes perfectly, giving them the potential to become great wine. The whole of *terroir* is greater than the sum of its parts. It's like the old real estate cliché: The three most important factors are location, location and location. And some locations are simply superior to others.

If you talk to the genuine winemakers, you'll hear it over and over again: "Wines are made in the vineyard!" Every great winemaker is a "terroiriste."

Without great grapes, you can't make great wine. Without great *terroir,* you can't grow great grapes, although you can make *bad* wine with good grapes. I think it was Hugh Johnson who once wrote that wine is very little more than water drawn up from the ground through a grapevine. He may not have mentioned Mother Nature's contribution—plenty of sun, cool nights, a sprinkling of rain now and again—but like all truisms about wine, it gets back to *terroir.*

A fine wine doesn't just taste good, it has a distinct character; it is an expression of its *terroir.* This distinctness is what makes wine the most fascinating of all drinks. If all fine wines tasted pretty much the same, what would be the point?

The concept of *terroir* has not been proven by science, but it's demonstrated all the time in the great wines of the world. Certain plots of land, sometimes as small as an acre or two, can and do produce superior wines. The proof is in the glass. There are so many elements of *terroir* that it is a concept impossible to define. Flavor scientists have established direct links between certain flavors or aromas and the chemical compounds found in wine. Like the geneticists who are mapping the human genome, they may some day be able to create an aroma atlas to predict which *terroir* will produce what types of flavors. That day is a long way off, though, and in the meantime wine lovers will continue to revel in the challenges and pleasures of detecting unique tastes in fine wines—*terroir* in the glass.

Taste the difference between a New Zealand wine made from Sauvignon Blanc grapes and its cousins from Bordeaux or the Friuli region of Italy and you'll be experiencing *terroir.* Compare a Pinot Noir from Carneros near Napa and one from the Russian River Valley over in Sonoma: same grape, different *terroir,* subtle variations in taste. If you're lucky enough to sample three of Marcel Guigal's Syrah-based wines from three adjacent vineyards in the Côte-Rôtie of the Northern Rhône Valley—La Landonne, La Mouline and La Turque—you'll see they are all superb—and they are all different. The difference is in the *terroir. Vive la différence!*

At some point, winemakers realize that better technique can only take them so far, that all those communes in Bordeaux and little villages in Burgundy have superior wines of unique character for a reason. They bow to the sacred notion of *terroir.* If it was ever cast aside in the wake of the First Wine Revolution, then we've come full circle and realized that it is the absolute key to producing fine wines.

TERROR

Producers of inferior wines sometimes try to appropriate superior place-names, for example slapping a label with the word *Napa* onto a bottle of blended wine of mixed provenance. Even if they're from the same grape, blending different lots of wine from different places blurs character. It is a gross violation of the credo of *terroir*, a perverse marketing gimmick. *Caveat emptor*.

THE RUTHERFORD DUST SOCIETY: *TERROIR* BECOMES OFFICIAL

The fundamental fact is that European wines have always derived their names from their place of origin, reflecting an understanding of *terroir*, while New World wines have been named after their principal grape variety. Wine made from the Pinot Noir grape in Burgundy is named after the commune Morey-St.-Denis if that's where the grapes were grown, whereas Pinot Noir from the Willamette Valley of Oregon is called Pinot Noir. Wine made from Sangiovese grapes in Chianti country south of Florence, Italy, is called Chianti whereas in California it's called Sangiovese. In the New Wine Revolution, New World producers are acknowledging the importance of *terroir* by including the specific growing sites on their labels. Use this as a rule of thumb: If you can't pinpoint where a wine comes from, then it has to be suspect.

More often than not, producers of fine wines bottle separate lots from each of their vineyards. Jean-Marc Joblot in Givry, which is in the Côte Chalonnaise area of Burgundy, has several so-called vineyard-designated wines, including Clos de la Servoisine and Clos de Celliers aux Moines (*clos* being the local word for an enclosed or specially marked off vineyard), but his label does not indicate that the wine is made from Pinot Noir.

The Rochiolis of the Russian River Valley in Sonoma County, California, label their vineyard-designated wines as Pinot Noir with subheadings of West Block, Little Hill Block, Three Corner Vineyard and so forth.

Terroir is officially acknowledged when the government, or whatever organization regulates a given wine marketplace, gives the nod to certain winegrowing regions of distinction. In the major winegrowing countries of Europe—France, Italy, Germany and Spain—this also involves some sort of ranking system. France has three national categories: *Appellation Contrôlée* (AC), which denotes superior wines from areas where there are strict criteria and controls; *Vin de Pays*, wines from areas with less strict criteria; and *Vin de Table*, simple table wines. These categories are reflected as quality guarantees printed on bottle labels—DOC or DOCG in Italy, DO in Spain and QmP in Germany. In France, within each major winegrowing region, there are also delineations and rankings of specific vineyard sites or *crus* (growths) as first, second, third and so on.

One of the first and most famous official delineations of *terroir* in the modern era was the 1855 Bordeaux classification, which ranked sixty-one chateaus as first through fifth growths and was modified only once, in 1973, to declare Château Mouton-Rothschild a first growth. Long before the Bordeaux classification, monks in the Middle Ages sought to classify every site for winegrowing. They were extremely precise, especially in Germany where there were over 10,000 appellations. (This number was reduced to a more manageable 2,700 in 1971.) There are thousands of appellations in countries like France, Italy and Germany, reflecting the breadth and depth of their winemaking traditions. In the United States, AVAs (American Viticultural Areas) have been recognized by the BATF (Bureau of Alcohol, Tobacco and Firearms) only relatively recently; they began in the early eighties and there are now more than fifty of them. With all due respect, the BATF is a large ponderous government bureaucracy that may understand mapmaking but doesn't know much about fine wines. It should be designating AVAs only in consultation with a wide array of wine experts.

In Napa and Sonoma Counties, the so-called North Coast growing region of California, AVAs are no more specific than Russian River Valley, Napa Valley and so forth. As we enter the twenty-first century, however, new, more precise appellations such as Rutherford and Chiles Valley will be recognized. The top producers in these areas are too smart to start bragging that they've earned world-class appellation status, but they're working hard toward it. In Rutherford, for example, the rumblings began in the late seventies and early eighties when Andre Tchelistcheff detected a characteristic he called "Rutherford Dust" in the wines; a group of local vintners subsequently founded the Rutherford Dust Society to promote the area's wines as distinct and superior.

It took centuries to establish legitimate appellations in Europe. Now, in New World regions such as California, New Zealand, Australia and South America, it's happening within a decade or two, a very exciting prospect. Estates like Matanzas Creek, Peter Michael, Harlan, Volker Eisele, Viader and their equivalents are moving at warp speed relative to the rest of wine history. And they are definitely here to stay.

I REMEMBER, YEARS AGO, WHEN I WAS ABOUT TWENTY-FIVE AND JUST GETTING STARTED AS A WINE MERCHANT, I WENT TO VISIT THE GREAT BURGUNDIAN PRODUCER LOUIS LATOUR. HE WAS AN OLD MAN, BENT OVER, STRUGGLING A BIT WITH HIS FOOTING, AS HE SHOWED ME THE VINEYARD WHERE HE GREW THE GRAPES FOR HIS CORTON-CHARLEMAGNE, CONSIDERED ONE OF THE GREATEST WHITE WINES IN THE WORLD. HE BENT DOWN SLOWLY AND SCOOPED UP A HANDFUL OF DIRT. "SMELL THIS," HE SAID. "THIS IS WHAT MAKES MY WINE GREAT." I PICKED UP A HANDFUL, TOOK A GOOD WHIFF OF THE AROMA. THEN HE TOLD ME TO GET DOWN ON ALL FOURS. I THOUGHT THAT WAS A LITTLE STRANGE, BUT WHO WAS I TO ARGUE WITH THE GREAT LOUIS LATOUR? "LOOK!" HE SAID. "LOOK AT THE DIRT? WHAT DO YOU SEE?" DIRT, I THOUGHT. "DO YOU SEE ANY ANTS?" "NO," I SAID. "NO ANTS." "PRECISELY," HE SAID. "ANOTHER REASON MY WINE IS GREAT. NO ANTS. DROUHIN NEXT DOOR, HE HAS ANTS. BUT I DON'T HAVE ANY ANTS. DROUHIN'S ANTS CRAWL UP AND EAT THE SUGAR OUT OF HIS GRAPES, WHICH IS WHY HE CAN'T MAKE SUCH A GREAT WINE AS THIS."

IN HIS OWN WAY, MONSIEUR LATOUR HAD EXPLAINED TO ME THE CONCEPT OF *TERROIR*.

My good friend Petrus Desbois assessing *terroir* near his family winegrowing estate, Château St.-Georges.

MARC DE GRAZIA
ITALIAN WINE GURU

ONE OF THE GREAT FORCES IN ITALY IS ITALIAN-AMERICAN MARC DE GRAZIA, WHO WAS BORN AND BRED ON THE EAST COAST OF THE UNITED STATES BUT HAS BEEN BASED FOR MANY YEARS IN FLORENCE. SINCE 1980 HE'S BEEN IN THE EXPORT BUSINESS AND HAS WORKED CLOSELY WITH HIS INDEPENDENT PRODUCERS TO GROW AND MARKET PREMIUM VINEYARD-DESIGNATED WINES. IN MANY CASES, HE HAD TO CONVINCE THEM TO INVEST IN NEW EQUIPMENT, TO ADJUST THEIR TECHNIQUES AND TO LEAVE BEHIND THE OLD-STYLE TANNIC RED WINES OR OXIDIZED WHITE WINES THAT WERE THE NORM FOR GENERATIONS. SOMETIMES HE WOULD MERELY SEEK OUT THE PRODUCERS WITH THE BEST *TERROIR* AND THE INNATE INTELLIGENCE AND DRIVE TO MAKE THE MOST OF IT. MORE THAN ANYTHING, HE CONVINCED THEM THE TIMES WERE CHANGING AND THE INVESTMENTS WOULD PAY OFF—IN BETTER WINES, IN INTERNATIONAL RECOGNITION AND, EVENTUALLY, IN PROFITS THEY DID.

Typical of a dedicated wine revolutionary, Marc simultaneously took on the roles of gadfly and midwife: nurturing yet always questioning. He pushed his producers, challenging them to try other fine wines and aspire to the highest standards. De Grazia has about thirty Barolo producers, each one with its own distinct style. He bristles at the suggestion that they are trying to achieve an international style. "We're trying to recuperate the vineyards as much as possible," he says.

Marc also has an impressive roster of high-quality producers elsewhere in Italy. He's been instrumental in the revival of traditional white wines such as Soave and Orvieto. He also represents a fine group of winegrowers in Tuscany. Marc doesn't believe in the DOC classification system; he's a *terroiriste.* What matters to him first and foremost is the *cru,* the quality of the vineyard site, followed by the ability of the winegrower to express that quality.

Marc de Grazia can be brash and opinionated; he's also personable and generous. More often than not, he's right. Can he change the Italian wine scene? Maybe not in our lifetime, but he's certainly having an effect. The bottom line is if you see "A Marc de Grazia Selection" somewhere in the fine print on the label of a wine bottle, you ought to find a way to pop that cork.

WHAT MAKES A GREAT WINEMAKER?

Winemaking is micromanagement; it requires mastery of a mind-boggling array of variables as well as impeccable judgment.

Great winemakers possess an uncompromising commitment to quality. They adopt whichever techniques make the best wines, often at great personal sacrifice. Fine wines are handcrafted by small, artisanal workshops. The pride and care of "boutique winegrowing" is nearly impossible to maintain on a large scale. (There are only a few notable exceptions, such as Mondavi with their Opus wines or Antinori with their "Supertuscans.") It takes a special commitment to sustain small enclaves like these in a corporate context, where there's always pressure to produce quantity over quality.

Great wines are not made by recipe. They are made by winemakers who supervise every step from first budding of the vines in the early spring, through ripening, harvest and crushing of the grapes and then careful fermentation and aging. It's a sophisticated taste-and-adjust approach. They rely on their palates and their experience to detect what's in the grape and the *terroir*. Then, as unobtrusively as possible, they bring the wine to the point where it can express that character.

Judgment, patience, courage, passion, risk-taking, attention to detail, constant supervision, minimal interference with maximum care, a discerning palate, a subtle understanding —all are important qualities of a superior winegrower. Great winemakers adapt to the conditions of each vineyard and vintage. They maintain a constant hands-on presence in the vineyard and in the winery. It's equally important, however, for them to know when to keep their hands off.

A great winemaker is a curator, an interpreter, not a creator. Like a great orchestra conductor, the winemaker coordinates all aspects of the performance. And just as a great editor allows the quality of the writer's prose to shine through—not the editor's marks—so the only acceptable goal for the winemaker is to express what's in the grape and the *terroir*. It is his responsibility to bring out the character of the fruit and to achieve a balance of the various taste components in the wine—not to show off his technique.

Superior winegrowers have an intuitive sense of *terroir*. They can walk a plot of land and tell you whether it's a place that will grow great wine grapes. Even before the science, before all the soil samples and the pH tests, the land tells you something. It doesn't have to be Bordeaux or Burgundy, Napa or the Rheingau, but the message has to be loud and clear.

Bob Long, one of my favorite winegrowers in Napa Valley, produces a superb Chardonnay from his hillside vineyards outside of St. Helena. He talks about the contours of the land, how a great growing site just looks right. It's a subtle assessment of microclimate, exposure, the lay of the land and other factors that come with experience.

The same type of instincts come into play at the harvest. A maker of fine wines can examine those grapes, taste them quickly and tell you whether that vintage is going to produce a good, or possibly even a great, wine. All the scientific measures and techniques are just tools that supplement the gut instincts of the enologist.

A superior winegrower never ceases to learn, whether it's through formal study or everyday observation. They are masters of the art; they are also students of the science. They can judge which numbers make sense and which don't, which techniques work and which don't. "Probably

TED LEMON:
A STAR ON THE RISE

ONE OF THE MAIN REASONS I'VE STAYED IN THIS BUSINESS FOR SO LONG IS WINE'S ENDLESS CAPACITY TO SURPRISE AND AMAZE. JUST WHEN YOU THINK YOU'VE SEEN IT ALL, SOMETHING HAPPENS TO MAKE YOU WANT TO STAND UP AND SALUTE.

I first met Ted Lemon and his wife and business partner Heidi for dinner at Pinot Blanc, my friend Joachim Splichal's restaurant in Napa Valley. I had heard a few whispers about this young winemaker being one of the ones to watch. Soon after we sat down, he opened a bottle of his Littorai 1993 One Acre Pinot Noir from Anderson Valley. I was well aware that 1993 was generally considered a mediocre year. I don't mean to sound jaded, but about a week before I'd shared a bottle of 1985 Romanée-Conti La Tache at home with my wife, Chris—a little blind taste test just to make sure she was still paying attention (and of course she was). It was a special wine and it punctuated a workaday week with an exclamation point. I took one good whiff of Ted's 1993 Pinot and I knew right away it was something special. That wine was every bit the equal of its distant French cousin. It was an eyepopper. The subtlety, the softness, the sweet perfume of its fruit . . . just a whiff and you felt a surge of excitement at discovering a fabulous wine.

Ted Lemon began his winegrowing career in his early twenties, and after two decades he's still going strong. Winegrowers, like some of their best wines, get better with age, and their careers can last forty to fifty years. I like Ted's trajectory, and I like the fact that his Holy Grail is the perfect Pinot Noir. If wines like DRC's La Tache are the world standard and Williams & Selyem's Sonoma Pinots the California standard, then Ted's Littorai is on par with the best.

Ted grew up just outside New York City and fell in love with France and French wines as an exchange student during high school and college. He went on to complete a winemaker's degree at the University of Dijon, the ancient capital of Burgundy. He did apprenticeships with a number of prestigious French producers, including Domaine Dujac in Morey-St.-Denis, where he worked under owner Jacques Seysses, who later recommended him for the job of winemaker at Domaine Guy Roulot & Fils in Meursault. Tragically, the founder and proprietor, Guy Roulout, died of cancer in November 1982 at the age of fifty-two, weeks after completing the harvest. Guy's son Jean-Marc decided to pursue a career in theater, so his mother, Madame Genevieve, broke tradition and hired Ted, who was working for Josh Jensen at Calera Winery in Hollister, California, at the time. At the age of twenty-six, Ted was the first American ever hired as a chief winemaker in France.

Ted chose to return to Burgundy because, of the two great red winegrowing regions in France, it was there that the winemaker was traditionally also the vineyard manager, whereas in Bordeaux the two functions had mostly been separated. "I had an intuitive belief that vineyard technique had to be the key to producing great wines," he says. By 1985, Ted was back in California as founding winemaker at Château Woltner on Napa's Howell Mountain. In the early 1990s, he branched out into consulting; among his clients are Franciscan Estates, Pine Ridge and Clos Pegase. He also distributes Domaine Dujac wines in the United States through his company Druid.

He and Heidi own and operate Littorai, which produces Pinot Noir and Chardonnay from carefully selected sites in California's northern coastal region. They started their company in 1992 with a three-month scouting trip of the West Coast in search of special winegrowing sites. The company name is the plural of a Latin word meaning coastal areas, and its philosophy, a model of premium winegrowing, is stated as follows:

> We use the word "coasts" with intent for we are convinced that the geology and microclimates of the extreme western portion of the continent north of San Francisco are so diverse as to create a series of unique terroirs, each with its own characteristics. The word "Littorai" reminds us that wine, this noblest agricultural product, arises from the interaction of place (vineyard), time (vintage) and man. It is this complex interaction which makes wine so endlessly fascinating. . . . We concentrate entirely on producing fine Pinot Noir and Chardonnay. As we find vineyards which have exciting potential, we will add them to the family and vineyard-designate them if they are truly unique. If there is nothing new to excite us, we simply won't grow. By the same token, if we are dissatisfied with the quality of fruit from a given vineyard in a given year, we simply will not produce it. . . . This philosophy requires that our clients understand, as we do, that fine wine is not a commodity. We cannot simply invent more of it to satisfy demand. Indeed, that is what distinguishes it from its less expensive brethren.

the most important place I get knowledge is standing next to the fermenter and tasting," says Ted Lemon, who trained in traditional methods in France. Ted also reads many scientific journals both in English and French.

Most modern wineries have labs and they take science pretty seriously. Matanzas Creek, for example, has two winemakers, one of whom has a background in biochemistry. The trick is to know when too much science can get in the way.

"There are certain high-tech wineries that are simply oversaturated with technical data," says Ted Lemon. "I see this all the time in my consulting." To the extent it's possible, testing a wine objectively in the lab for the level of tannins and other compounds doesn't ultimately tell us much about the wine's quality. That judgment is left up to subjective tasters.

Flexibility and patience, the ability to make small adjustments or none at all, are key to the winemaker's art. "You're not following a formula," says Mia Klein, who works with Tony Soter. "You're tasting and you're listening to what the grapes are telling you."

"I don't tell the wine when it needs to go to bottle, the wine tells me," says Mark Aubert of Peter Michael Winery. "I think Californians have a tendency to move a little too fast. I tell everybody the superhighway can just pass us by. If you want to get off at this exit and come into this winery, fine. Winemaking has always been a very slow, methodical process. It's amazing how when you leave things alone to evolve, you see much better quality."

Great winegrowers possess the courage and commitment to be highly selective. They have to be willing to throw out between a quarter and a half of their precious fruit at the harvest if it's not up to snuff. If the fruit is accepted but the resulting wine is not up to standard, the winegrower has to be prepared to "declassify" an entire vintage to uphold the label's reputation. This wine will not necessarily be discarded—many quality producers bottle second-tier brands. (The Bordeaux châteaus have been doing it for years.) They can also sell the wine off in bulk to less demanding producers, who might include it in regional blends.

At Etude, Tony Soter has a reputation for unloading high-quality rejects. In 1988, he sold his entire vintage of Napa Cabernet in bulk. In Pinot Noir production Tony typically budgets 20 to 25 percent for rejects each year. (Imagine a factory that had to reject a quarter of its output as defective!) These are difficult decisions economically, but they're about something much more important: maintaining quality.

Great winemakers invest in techniques and equipment to assure maximum quality. They seek out only the best oak barrels, for example, in which to age their wines. It's not always a matter of passing the excess cost on to the consumer. Certain appellations or vintages may not justify prices high enough to cover such costs. The quality winegrower, nevertheless, assumes that risk.

Robert Kacher, a U.S. importer of fine French wines, pushes each one of his growers to be highly selective. He helps them buy special equipment such as *triage* tables. At a cost of roughly $15,000 each, these tables feature a slow conveyor belt about fifteen feet long that allows for careful sorting of grapes before the winemaking process beings. Three workers stand on either side of the machine, weeding out inferior grapes. Kacher reflects: "When I started in Burgundy, you didn't throw away 25 percent of Chambertin-Clos de Bèze [a top vineyard].

A SEASON AT CHÂTEAU LATOUR

AT CHÂTEAU LATOUR IN THE MEDOC, THEY ARE VERY MUCH AT THE MERCY OF MOTHER NATURE. IN 1996 THERE WERE A FEW SCARES, BUT IN THE END ALL WAS WELL: LEAVES APPEARED MARCH 23 FOR MERLOT AND APRIL 2 FOR CABERNET SAUVIGNON. FLOWERING TOOK PLACE FROM MAY 18 UNTIL MAY 28; IT WAS EARLY AND FAST, WHICH LED TO SOME *COULURE* IN THE OLD MERLOT VINES. (*COULURE* IS THE TERM FOR DAMAGE TO THE DELICATE FLOWERS THAT TURN INTO GRAPE CLUSTERS; IT CAN STUNT FRUIT DEVELOPMENT.) JULY AND AUGUST WERE HOT AND HUMID; EVEN THOUGH THE VINES WERE PROGRESSING WELL, THERE WAS SOME CONCERN ABOUT ROT. BEGINNING IN LATE AUGUST, THE WEATHER TURNED SUNNY AND DRY, ALLOWING FOR PROPER MATURITY. HARVEST WAS FROM SEPTEMBER 17 UNTIL OCTOBER 2.

> **"[Helen Turley] knows that if she's ever going to make anything of quality, she's not going to make it in the cellar. It's not her winemaking that's turning those grapes into a good wine. It's her shepherding of great fruit from the vineyard into the bottle and intervening as little as possible along the way."**
>
> —Michael Bonnacorsi, Master Sommelier

You used to be able to sell the wine on the appellation. People paid $600 to $900 a case for it because they were buying the label. Now, if we don't have wine in the bottle that we think Chambertin-Clos de Bèze should represent, then we've got a problem."

A great winemaker must have a superior palate, but with a qualification. It's a palate more attuned to tasting grapes off the vines or young wines in the barrel and then extrapolating. A winemaker from Napa Valley might have a tough time competing in a blind tasting against the worldly palates of a group of master sommeliers, but certainly no one could touch her knowledge of her own wines at various stages of development.

Whether it's a small mom-and-pop operation like Randy and Debbie Lewis of Lewis Cellars or Ted and Heidi Lemon of Littorai or a family business handed down from generation to generation like the Wagners of Caymus in Rutherford or the Rochiolis of Russian River Valley, teamwork is an important part of fine winemaking. As in sports, the teams that succeed not only have the best individual players, they also have the best team chemistry.

At Moraga, it's proprietor Tom Jones and vineyard foreman Roberto Quintana, with support from consultants like Danny Shuster and from winemaker Tony Soter. At Harlan, it's Bill Harlan and his team—flying consultant Michel Rolland, vineyard consultant David Abreu, winemaker Bob Levy, marketing chief Don Weaver, vineyard manager Jerry Schlink and a host of other workers. At Swanson Vineyards, it's proprietor Clarke Swanson, winemaker Marco Cappelli, managing director Michael Updegraff and others.

Often, "teamwork" is a matter of the dynamic between proprietor and winegrower. At Peter Michael Winery, you wonder how they could produce such consistently great wines with an absentee owner until you talk to winemaker Mark Aubert about how he's earned the trust of proprietor Sir Peter Michael. "Peter let us decide the fundamentals. He's not a winemaker by education or experience. He's a visionary. He knows what great wine should taste like. The Europeans are wonderful. They have long-term vision. Peter knows Eric Rothschild, and Eric told him that it takes one hundred years. Peter was not surprised by that at all. This is for his children, and his children's children."

At Matanzas Creek, proprietors Bill and Sandra MacIver are a husband-and-wife team that runs the business side. Winemakers Bill Parker and Susan Reed are complementary teammates on the winemaking side—he with expertise as a cellar master and she as lab chief. The collaborative spirit spurs them all on to keep the business fresh and to strive to make better wines every year.

CONSULTING WINEMAKERS such as Tony Soter and Mia Klein or Helen Turley or Heidi Peterson Barrett are like high-priced free agents. They have several advantages over the single-vineyard winemaker. First, they participate in more harvests, gaining more experience faster. They've simply tried more wines; they have better perspective. High-flying international consultants like Michel Rolland from Bordeaux or Attilio Pagli from Italy often have clients on four continents—Europe, North America, South America and sometimes Australia. Once they've established their reputations, they're the ones choosing the clients, not vice versa. When I asked Tony Soter what he looks for in a client he replied that the key factors were integrity, the money to invest and the patience to wait for their wine dream to come true. Minimum wait? Five to ten years.

WINEMAKING ACCORDING TO TONY SOTOR

I ASKED TONY SOTER, ONE OF THE TOP CONSULTING WINEMAKERS IN AMERICA AND A LEADING FIGURE IN THE NEW WINE REVOLUTION, TO DESCRIBE THE QUALITIES OF A GREAT WINEMAKER. HE THOUGHT ABOUT IT FOR A WHILE AND CAME BACK WITH: "VIGILANCE, INTUITION, IDEALISM, PATIENCE AND A FACILITY WITH THE MATERIAL WORLD." THEN I ASKED HIM TO EXPLAIN HIS PHILOSOPHY OF GRAPE GROWING AND WINEMAKING. "I OWE IT TO MY CLIENTS AND TO MY OWN ARTISTIC INTEGRITY NOT TO JUST REPRODUCE A CERTAIN TYPE OF WINE. BELIEVE IT OR NOT, I COULD MAKE WINES FROM DIFFERENT PROPERTIES MORE SIMILAR THAN DISSIMILAR DEPENDING ON TECHNIQUES. YET IF YOU TASTE THE GRAPES AND SPEND SOME TIME ON THE PROPERTY YOU GET A FEEL FOR WHAT THE STRENGTHS AND THE SALIENT CHARACTERISTICS ARE AND THEN TRY TO CAPTURE THAT."

Tony also spoke about his development as a winemaker. "I'd say the first ten years is wine technology in its crassest form and the next ten years is grape growing. Then you really have the foundation. Then you can talk not about whether we're making good or sound or commercially acceptable wine, but whether we can start making wines of real character and breeding and personality, the kind of wines that really evoke the 'wow' response in a consumer.

"If you become reasonably competent as a winemaker you run into an awareness of your limitations. This sounds like a truism, but you really are only as good as the potential in your raw materials. The question in my mind in the mid-1980s was how do I take this winemaking act and turn it toward influencing the quality of the raw materials? I started to think with boots that have dirt on them instead of wine stains, to be out in the field and try to bring the raw materials up to their maximum potential. That's a search for site, a search in plant physiology. It involves a lot of sensitivity to the climate and the plants you work with, trying to get an idea of what the functional variables are and what you do to bring high-quality grapes to the winery."

THE ART OF WINEGROWING

GROWING THE GRAPES: VITICULTURE

Winegrowing is an ancient art that, while it is now regarded more as a science, is still pursued with a reverence toward its lore and a recognition that every small step not carried out by hand, under the supervision of a responsible, knowledgeable artisan, contributes immeasurably to the diminution of the final product. Anybody who appreciates the kind of focus necessary for successful gardening or for gourmet cuisine has an idea as to what it takes to be a winegrower of distinction. Yet this is gardening on a grand scale, cooking that takes years.

The practical aspect of winegrowing begins with an assessment of the growing site. Then comes selection of the proper vine or vines, followed by an application of the most sophisticated agricultural techniques with an ever-so-light touch. All the hard work and patience that goes into a growing season culminates in the nerve-racking decision of when to harvest the grapes; regardless of whether every other procedure is implemented flawlessly, fruit that is not perfectly ripe does not make good wine.

Once the grapes are brought into the winery, the winemaker takes over, adjusting the dials in a series of crucial decisions concerning their processing, fermentation and aging so they can become fine wine. In the case of red wines, how long do they soak in their skins, when does fermentation begin and how long does it continue? In any case, what is the proper method of fermentation? How should the wine be aged? Can it benefit from resting in oak barrels? How much exposure to oxygen does it need? Will any additional refining enhance its appeal?

Here is a step-by-step outline of the winegrowing process, with the aim of giving you, the reader, a glimpse into the "mystery" of how grape juice becomes wine.

Choice of Variety, Rootstocks and Clones

What is it about the climate, the soil, the lay of the land —in short, the *terroir*—that suggests a certain variety of grape will thrive? The winegrower's first job is to assess the location and decide what to plant. Each grape variety has its own quirks and preferences. Pinot Noir, for example, is an early-ripening variety that can thrive in cooler climates such as Burgundy, Oregon or certain foggy valleys in California's northern coastal region. Chardonnay, another early-ripening variety, can thrive in cooler climates, but it also buds very early and can be susceptible to spring frosts. Cabernet Sauvignon and Nebbiolo ripen later and work best in hotter climates such as Italy, California's Napa Valley and Australia.

In places like California, where the tradition of premium winegrowing is less than half a century old, there is still a lot of misplanting. Much of this is the result of a "band-wagon mentality": "If the market's going crazy over Merlot, then let's plant more Merlot." Planting according to the latest fad can be dangerous because it can take ten years to produce fine wine. By the time the wine reaches the marketplace, a new fad has arrived and the grower is stuck with a mediocre product that's out of style. The vintner who plants the right variety for his or her *terroir* and follows through with proper noninterventionist tech-

A steep hillside vineyard in California.

"Every famous wine in the world, every wine we all love to drink, comes from an identifiable piece of property where you can go out and say, 'Here it is.'"

—Volker Eisele, Eisele Family Estate, Chiles Valley

niques is the one who will eventually succeed. Patience and perseverance are essential; there is no avoiding them.

The rootstock is the portion of the vine planted in the ground, the clone is the portion that produces the grapes. Clones are like different branches of a family. You might hear, for example, that Swanson Vineyards in Napa is growing Sangiovese from the Biondi-Santi clone; this means that the California vines are genetically related to the ones in the great Tuscan vineyard that produces those famous Brunello di Montalcino wines. They are descended from a common ancestor. (If you hear it's a "suitcase clone" it means that somebody smuggled it in in their luggage.)

Rootstocks are selected according to a number of criteria, including vigor, soil content, phylloxera resistance, and ripening cycle. Vigor means the amount of energy a vine puts into producing vegetation—roots, shoots, canes and leaves. It is also often used by winegrowers to describe the characteristics of a vineyard: A "high-vigor site" is one rich in soil nutrients that will support big, bushy vines with a lot of fruit. Low-vigor describes a smaller, tougher vine that directs more of its energy into producing the fruit and less into the leaves and wood. Most high-quality grape varieties tend toward low vigor. They do better in rocky soil with good drainage that is relatively low in nutrients. These cause them to produce less fruit with more concentrated flavors.

The vine's ripening cycle is important in certain European climates as well as in a place like Oregon, where late-season rains can dilute flavor and/or promote moisture-related problems such as rot in slow-ripening varieties.

Typically, the winegrower considers a pool of about fifteen rootstocks, choosing several that are compatible with the selected clones and the soil type. For insurance against potential problems—disease, incompatibility—a twenty-acre vineyard might be planted in equal blocks of three or four different clones of a given variety on top of two or three similar rootstocks.

Planting Orientation

After selecting the best rootstocks for a given location, the winegrower must determine the proper placement and orientation of the vines. In the winter, when the vines are dormant, frost is no problem, but it is in the early spring when their fragile buds and shoots are beginning to emerge. Warm air rises and cool air flows down, making frost a danger on the valley floors. For this reason, vines are planted on hillsides wherever there's a threat of frost damage.

Row orientation in more northerly or cooler climes is generally north-south to maximize sun exposure on the east and west sides of the vines. In a warmer climate like California, this might not be the case.

Traditionally, hillside vineyards have been planted in terraces running across the slopes. More recently, if drainage is good and erosion can be controlled, they have been planted in rows running straight up- and downhill. In premium winegrowing you hear a lot about "hillside vineyards" and "exposure," which refers to the way the vines are oriented vis-à-vis the sun, which in turn affects the ripening of the grapes, the thickness of their skins and so forth.

Density

Density of planting is measured by the distance between plants and the distance between rows. An example of lower-density planting of vines would be "nine by twelve," which is twelve feet between rows and nine feet between plants along each row. Higher density would be "five by five"—five feet between rows and between plants in a row. Higher-density farming incurs higher onetime costs because there are more vines to plant per acre and also higher yearly costs since conventional (bigger, more efficient) farm machinery simply can't fit between the rows. Straddle tractors, those gangling machines that look like props for a Steven Spielberg film and are often used in European premium high-density vineyards, are very expensive.

In winegrowing, there's a trade-off between quality and efficiency. Lower-density planting means there are fewer vines per acre producing more fruit per vine of a lesser quality at lower costs. High-density planting means there are more plants in the vineyard with less fruit per vine of a higher quality.

Density is also measured in plants per acre or hectare. (The hectare is a metric measure—100 square meters—equivalent to 2.471 acres.) Premium growers tend to increase planting densities. At the distinguished Chianti estate Fattoria di Felsina outside of Siena, they went from 3,200 plants per hectare (about 1,300 per acre) in the old regime to 5,600 (over 2,200 per acre) to reduce yields per plant. At Château Latour, St.-Julien, one of Bordeaux's original first growths and perennially one of the top wines in the world, the density is 10,000 vines per hectare (over 4,000 per acre).

Trellising

Structures made of metal or wood and wires prop the vines up and train them to grow in a certain way, exposing the leaves and bunches to the appropriate amount of sun.

There are many different types of trellis systems. A traditional vertical trellis forces the plants to grow straight up and the canopy or leaf covering to grow naturally up and out from it, like the hairs on our heads, with the bunches of grapes hanging from the vine shoots.

WHAT IS "METER-BY-METER" PLANTING?

IT'S ONE OF THOSE CATCHWORDS OF PREMIUM WINEGROWING THAT SIMPLY REFERS TO ALLOWING ONE METER BETWEEN ROWS AND ONE METER BETWEEN VINES. BECAUSE IT HAS BEEN PRACTICED IN THE CLASSIFIED-GROWTH VINEYARDS OF BORDEAUX, FOR EXAMPLE, THERE IS A TENDENCY TO THINK OF IT AS *THE* SECRET FORMULA FOR SUCCESS. BUT THERE'S NO MAGIC IN IT. IT JUST HAPPENS TO BE THE MOST SUCCESSFUL CONFIGURATION FOR THE PARTICULAR SOIL AND CLIMATE CONDITIONS OF THAT REGION.

A contrast of old and new: aged vines (above); a straddle tractor (below).

Premium growers throughout Italy, especially in Piedmont (Barolo and Barbaresco country) and Tuscany (Chianti country) use a type of vertical or "cordon" training system in which wires held up by stakes run the length of rows. This trains the vines to grow their leaves in a neat "panel" six to eight feet high and hang their fruit toward the bottom, thereby providing good leaf exposure for photosynthesis and good bunch positioning for long, slow ripening.

In Bordeaux, a similar system is employed, although the vines are much shorter due to a cooler climate and less-fertile soil. In parts of Italy you can see another traditional—and picturesque—training method, called a *pergola* or *tendone,* where large wooden stakes are erected in a post-and-lintel or Y shape, which makes the vines grow in a kind of bushy overhead canopy with the grapes hanging down from it.

The traditional method of head pruning—propping the vines up with individual vertical stakes—also produces a picturesque effect. In winter, the dormant vines resemble gnarled miniature trees, a vision right out of *The Hobbitt,* which is why in Italy they call this system *alberello* (literally "little tree").

Split canopy systems like the Geneva Double Curtain, so called because it was invented at Cornell University's Agricultural Experimental Station at Geneva, New York, separate and spread the vines' shoots in a Y, U or T shape, rather than a simple vertical panel, creating more buds, leaves and ultimately grape bunches per vine, which is appropriate in a high-vigor site.

In the end, there are probably as many different trellising systems as there are recipes for meat loaf, the point being that each winegrower needs to find what works best for his or her particular *terroir.*

Yield: Stressing the Vines

One concept we hear a lot about is "stressing the vines," the idea of forcing them to concentrate their energy on producing the ripest, most flavorful grapes. The bottom line in grape growing is yield: How much crop does a vineyard produce? The premium winegrower is concerned with quality not quantity, which means smaller grapes, lower yield, more flavor and concentration. Less is more.

There are parameters for each vineyard site, and variations for each vintage. In Europe, the regulations governing appellations not only specify where certain wines can come from but the proportions of each grape variety permissible in the blend and even the allowable yields. Angelo Gaja's vineyards in Piedmont, for example, all yield less than three tons per acre, well below their legal maximums.

One of the great misconceptions about premium winegrowing is that vines are forcibly stressed. Not true. A good winegrower does not fight Mother Nature. Planting high-vigor vines in a fertile site and then trying to manipulate them by excessively cutting them back or starving them does not work. Stressing the vines, practiced in high-vigor sites, is actually more of a hands-off policy.

"We've had to learn that winegrowing is really the thing whereas I think twenty years ago we were fascinated with the technology of winemaking." —Tony Soter, California winemaker and consultant

CANOPY MANAGEMENT

ONE OF THE NEW BREED OF "VINE SCIENTISTS," THE FLYING VITICULTURIST DR. RICHARD SMART IS THE WORLD'S FOREMOST EXPERT ON THE MODERN SCIENCE OF CANOPY MANAGEMENT, WHICH INVOLVES TRIMMING THE VINES' SHOOTS, REMOVING THEIR LEAVES AND USING DIFFERENT TYPES OF TRELLISING SYSTEMS TO OPEN THEM UP TO MORE SUNLIGHT. DR. SMART IS A NATIVE OF AUSTRALIA WHO STUDIED AT CORNELL UNIVERSITY UNDER NELSON SHAULIS, THE INVENTOR OF CANOPY MANAGEMENT. DR. SMART DID EXTENSIVE RESEARCH FOR THE GOVERNMENT OF NEW ZEALAND IN THE 1980S AND WROTE A FAMOUS PROFESSIONAL MANUAL CALLED *SUNLIGHT INTO WINE*. IN HIS EARLY STUDIES HE WAS ABLE TO PROVE THAT VINES WHOSE GRAPES AND LEAVES GET MORE SUNLIGHT PRODUCE RIPER FRUIT, MORE CONCENTRATED FLAVORS AND THUS BETTER WINES. HE FOUND THAT OFTEN EXCESS IRRIGATION CAUSED TOO MUCH LEAF GROWTH AND OVERLY SHADED FRUIT. A CONSULTANT SINCE 1990, DR. SMART HAS MANY CLIENTS WORLDWIDE AND ADVISES THEM ON ALL ASPECTS OF VITICULTURE, PARTICULARLY CANOPY MANAGEMENT.

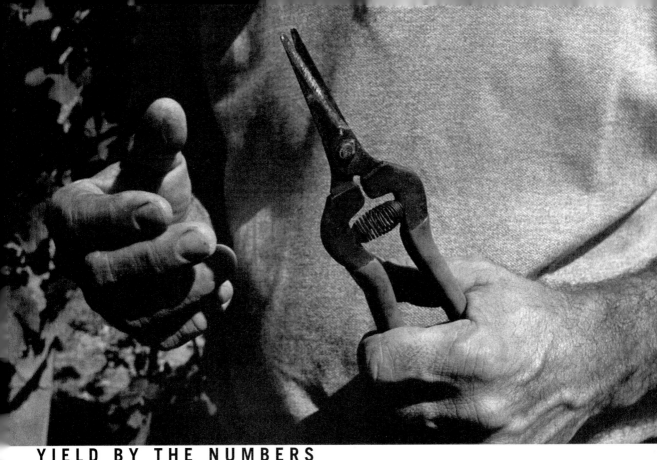

YIELD BY THE NUMBERS

EUROPEAN PREMIUM GROWERS USUALLY HAVE A SPECIFIC GOAL IN TERMS OF YIELD, WHICH CAN BE EXPRESSED IN TERMS OF HECTOLITERS OF WINE PER HECTARE OR KILOS OF GRAPES PER VINE. (A HECTOLITER IS 100 LITERS, WHICH IS EQUAL TO 26.418 GALLONS; A KILO IS 2.2 POUNDS.) A TYPICAL RANGE IS 20 TO 50 HECTOLITERS PER HECTARE, OR 1 TO 2 KILOS PER VINE. USING THIS FORMULA, A QUALITY VINEYARD WITH A PLANTING DENSITY OF 7,000 VINES PER HECTARE AND A YIELD OF 1.5 KILOS PER VINE WOULD PRODUCE ABOUT 4.7 TONS PER ACRE. DELIA VIADER'S CABERNET VINEYARDS, A SUPERIOR SITE ON HOWELL MOUNTAIN IN NAPA, YIELD ABOUT 2 TONS PER ACRE. LOWER-QUALITY, HIGHER-YIELD VINEYARDS CAN PRODUCE UP TO 11 TONS AN ACRE.

The Growing Cycle

The key stages in the vine's growing cycle are: dormancy in winter; budding in early spring, after which shoots and leaves begin to emerge; flowering in the late spring, after which the berries—the term is used interchangeably with fruit and grapes—begin to develop; lignification in early to midsummer, which is when the flexible green shoots turn to hard brown wood and the vine begins to concentrate less on producing vegetation and more on ripening its fruit; veraison, the point when the berries start to turn color and soften up; and ripening, when the acid in the berries gradually turns to sugar.

At Moraga Vineyards in Bel Air, California, buds appear from about March 1 to March 15, at which point the pruning takes place. In early March, there is often the threat of frost damage due to the cool microclimate in the canyon. Flowering or bud burst occurs around May 15, and harvest is between September 15 and October 15. The overall climate there is quite consistent and predictable. If you're a natural-born gambler, this takes some of the fun out of winegrowing; if not, you sleep better at night.

In Italy's Barolo Country, a typical vine's growth cycle is about 115 days, from flowering in late May to harvest in September or October. The biggest meteorological threat is from the huge thunderheads that build up over the Alps and can spit devastating hail on the vines in August, destroying an entire crop.

Irrigation, Fertilization and Spraying

Irrigation is often unnecessary in those winegrowing regions where rain is plentiful. In fact, sometimes it rains too much. In drier climates, such as California, water—or the lack of it—is the defining factor in the very existence of a civilization, let alone a wine industry. There, top producers use "drip irrigation"—systems of hoses or pipes that snake in and out, around and under the rows of vines to dole out exact measures of water.

Good premium winegrowers shy away from invasive practices in all stages of their craft. Their philosophy is to be "as organic as possible." Traditional modern farming methods, which rely heavily on pesticides, fungicides and fertilizers to prevent mildew, pests or disease and to supplement soil nutrients, give way to what Ted Lemon calls "modified modern farming."

One example of this is integrated pest management, a sensible, nonaggressive approach that allows for the use of inorganic materials only when absolutely necessary. In integrated pest management, the winegrower counts the number of mites per leaf, for example, then decides whether it's appropriate to spray. The problem with many pesticides is that they kill beneficial insects—the bugs who prey on the ones who might harm the vines—as well as the pests.

At Moraga, Tom Jones and his staff farm with minimal interference. Every year they do a soil analysis to monitor nutrients as well as take leaf samples to determine what the vines are ingesting. Then, if necessary, they add "micronutrients," small quantities of magnesium, potassium or possibly boron. Nitrogen, which can easily promote overgrowth, is avoided, though an individual vine that is struggling might receive half a cup of ammonium nitrate to boost its vigor.

It's crucial to keep the vines healthy, but not too fat and happy. Roberto Quintana, Moraga's vineyard foreman, likens the vines to children: "Every morning they wake up and tell you what they want. Then you give them what they need."

VITICULTURE

Of his irrigation philosophy at Peter Michael Winery, Mark Aubert explains: "Up here in the mountains, the soil is so rocky the vines can get drought stress pretty quickly because the water disappears. So we give them little drinks. One of the easiest things to dial in is an irrigation schedule. You give them a drink, let them get a little thirsty, give them another drink.... I'm up here every day, all summer long keeping an eye on the vines because each one of our different clones and rootstocks has a different thirst level."

Even more purist than the minimal interference approach is the totally organic one. Eschewing the use of chemical fertilizers and inorganic sprays altogether is very difficult in wet or humid climates, one reason why premium viticulture is so difficult on the east coast of the United States.

"I don't believe that being organic makes sense just to say you're organic," says Ted Lemon. "But I do believe that we should tolerate as high pest levels as possible and basically not spray. We're trying to produce fine wine grapes here. We're not growing rosebushes. We can tolerate a certain amount of mite damage."

A more exotic philosophy yet is biodynamism, which is practiced by some distinguished French winegrowers, among them Lalou Leroy-Bize and Didier Dagueneau. They treat their vines with homeopathic remedies and consult the phases of the moon to make important decisions. Where does it cross the line from science into hocus-pocus? To say, for example, that racking—moving the wine from one barrel to another during aging—should only be done when the moon is full may seem like an old wives' tale, but it may have some scientific basis. A full moon is likely to indicate high atmospheric pressure and low humidity, which is when the wine is less active in the barrel and less likely to be damaged by exposure to oxygen.

Vine Maintenance: The Bonsai Approach to Farming

In training the vines, the goal, as in anything connected with winegrowing, is to achieve balance—not too many leaves, not too many shoots or canes, not too many grapes. Many different types of maintenance are practiced on the vines: pruning, irrigation, fertilization, crop-thinning, leaf-pulling.

Premium winegrowers care for their vines as if they were bonsais, carefully shaping them with their clippers. Pruning in late winter or early spring ensures the correct number and spacing of buds on the vine and thus, eventually, the appropriate amount of vegetation and proper sun exposure for the grapes. The practiced viticulturist counts the number of leaves per shoot and, with a few strategic snips or plucks, puts the vine in perfect balance. The ideal is twelve to twenty leaves per shoot, one or two grape clusters per shoot and seven or eight clusters per vine. Later in the season, it's often necessary to pull some leaves to give clusters better exposure to sunlight.

With a vertical trellis system, the vine becomes bushy on top and needs hedging, which is like giving it a haircut to encourage lignification.

Another labor-intensive, hands-on operation is crop-thinning, also known as "the green harvest." It's usually done at 80 percent veraison, which means 80 percent of a grape cluster is showing color. Wielding his clippers with precision, the winegrower clips off a whole cluster here, part of one there. An experienced eye recognizes immediately how much to trim.

The decision to pull leaves and trim bunches relates to what viticulturists call "cluster morphology," referring to the shape and density of the bunches. Tightly packed clusters need more sun and air to prevent bunch rot, another word for *Botrytis cinerea*, the mold that's only desirable if you're going to produce sweet, concentrated wines. If *B. cinerea* occurs at the wrong time it can ruin a crop.

When to Replant

Unless there's misplanting, a pest disaster such as phylloxera or mismatched clones and rootstocks, American winegrowers generally pull and replace their vines when they are between twenty-five and fifty years of age. Many European wines boast of coming from old vines, some approaching one hundred years in age. Healthy vines do continue to produce excellent grapes into old age, but their yields decrease. More important, styles change, especially in the New World, and at some point market forces dictate a replanting.

In more established growing regions, the approach is more conservative. Once you've got a superior gene pool in your vineyard, you'd better hold on to it. Replanting at superior sites is often done by grafting from the vineyard itself rather than purchasing from a nursery. The vintners select individual vines that exhibit good shape, well-balanced growth, even distribution of grape bunches, low yields and so forth and propagate cuttings from them. Replanting is done at a slow, steady rate, say two or three acres per year, keeping the average age of vines high. In many superior vineyards, there is no regular replanting schedule; vines are simply replaced individually as they die.

The Harvest: What Is Ripeness?

Possibly the most crucial of all winegrowing decisions,

after matching site with variety of grape, is the determination of ripeness. The fundamental fact is that as the grapes ripen their sugar content increases and their acidity decreases.

Winegrowers measure sugars out in the vineyard with a tool called a refractometer. A small amount of grape juice is squeezed into it, then examined through an optical device that indicates the percentage of sugar by refraction, which is the degree to which a liquid distorts the angle of light showing through it. Knowing the amount of sugar in the grapes enables the winegrower to predict the "potential alcohol" in the wine, since it is the sugars that are transformed into alcohol during fermentation. The juice is also analyzed in labs to measure its total acid content. There are also tests to gauge chemical compounds called anthocyanins, polyphenols and phenolics. These include color, aroma, flavor and preservative components, particularly the tannins, which are found almost exclusively in the grape's stems, seeds and skins.

Premium winegrowers are generally most concerned about harvesting the grapes when the tannins are ripe—that is, as sweet and mellow as possible. Tannins can be harsh and unpleasantly bitter-tasting, especially if they are "green" or unripe. Winegrowers analyze the grapes scientifically; they also taste them, and break them open and examine them. Judging the ripeness of grapes is an art and a science, an empirical measurement and a gut decision. One top winegrower swore to me that the best test of a grape's ripeness is whether it can be plucked off the vine with no resistance.

In reality, there are many telltale signs. Are the grapes starting to shrivel? Are the seeds mature—that is, are

> **"There is no very good winemaker. There are only good grapes. When you have good grapes it's easy to make good wines."**
>
> —Michel Rolland, international consulting enologist

they turning brown or are they still green? Do the skins reveal sweet, ripe tannins? Do the numbers for sugar, acid and other compounds look about right? What is the weather forecast? Rain can dilute your precious crop; a heat wave can send the sugar content soaring too high.

Much rides on this assessment, since a serious mistake in judging the ripeness of grapes is virtually impossible to correct. If the grapes are picked underripe, there isn't much a grower can do except perhaps sell them to make Champagne. Smaller variations can be corrected by blending slightly riper lots with less ripe ones, but there's only so much leeway. At some point, the decision may have to be made to sell them off as "bulk wine."

Because there is incredible pressure to get the grapes off the vine, the winemaker must often put his or her foot down. "Sometimes you're the only person there to say, 'They're not getting worse, they're getting better,'" says Mia Klein. It takes patience and nerves of steel.

The harvest is a very hectic time in places like Napa Valley, where there's such a concentration of premium producers, many of them buying from the same grape growers and/or using the same wineries for processing grapes. On small estates, where they do all their own picking with a regular, reliable workforce, it's not quite as complicated as when winemakers like Tony Soter or Mia Klein are doing "custom crush." They have to coordinate their growers, their pickers and their wineries. The grapes don't wait. When they're ripe, they've got to be picked. Once they're picked, they've got to be processed. With numerous winemakers sharing a winery like Rombauer or Pepi or Napa Wine Company,

there's very little margin for error. Independent winemakers have to keep to their word and deliver the goods on time. Otherwise, they lose credibility.

Picking and Sorting

Large commercial vineyards often rely on automated picking machinery, but to make a premium wine, hand picking and hand sorting are really the only way to go. Picking machines literally shake the grapes off their stems, risking possible damage to the vine and ruling out whole-cluster pressing, which is a key to certain premium winemaking styles, particularly with Chardonnay and Pinot Noir grapes.

Machine harvesting has a few advantages for larger-scale winemaking: It can be performed around the clock and it allows the grapes to go directly into a refrigerated tank for transportation to the winery. In warm weather, picking often has to be done at night or early in the morning to ensure that the grapes arrive at the winery cool and without being crushed under their own weight in huge bins. Too much heat can jump-start fermentation, and there are certain processes that need to occur beforehand.

Sorting is another absolutely crucial procedure for quality wine production and another one where the French term *triage* is frequently used. (You also hear the term *selection*, both in reference to the grapes at harvest time and to lots or batches of wine later on.) Sorting can be done either in the vineyard as the grapes are picked or in the winery before they are crushed. In either case, it requires an experienced eye and it's a position of huge responsibility, which is why premium winegrowers don't trust just anyone with the job.

ATTENTION TO DETAIL

FOR YEARS, TOM JONES OF MORAGA VINEYARDS USED TO RUN NORTHRUP, THE HUGE DEFENSE CONTRACTOR THAT CREATED THE STEALTH BOMBER, SO HE KNOWS HOW IMPORTANT IT IS TO TAKE CARE OF EVERY LITTLE DETAIL.

Tom buys special Red Wing lumberjack shoes with stiff sides at $195 a pair for his workers because the vineyard is so steep in places that they are forced to walk on edge like skiers. If you take good care of your employees, you're also taking good care of your vines. When the grapes achieve a certain ripeness, the birds that nest in nearby chaparrals start to test them. Soon it's time to put up the nets, which Moraga has been deploying since the early 1980s. It takes about five days to net the entire property in half-acre swatches. The nets are unrolled by hand, six men holding them overhead.

Tony Soter makes the wine up in Napa Valley. Typically, when the grapes begin to ripen, the Moraga crew will pick small samples from around the vineyard, judge them by taste and then send the samples to Tony in a cooler via overnight express for independent judgment. Only when all are in agreement are the grapes harvested.

After harvest, Moraga's grapes take a seven-hour trip in a special refrigerated van—the red ones at 85 degrees F. and the white Sauvignon Blanc ones chilled to about 50—up to Napa for vinification. They make the trip in shallow plastic boxes specially designed by Moët & Chandon. Turned one way they can be stacked or "nested" into each other for easy storage; turned the other way they lock to protect the grapes from being crushed and give them adequate ventilation. In many vineyards, grapes are tossed into gondolas or large vats and end up damaged. What arrives at the winery is a mix of grapes, many with broken skins, leaves, juice and sometimes even dirt clods, which is taking the concept of *terroir* a little too far.

MAKING THE WINE: VINIFICATION

RED WINES

Destemming and Crushing

After harvest, most grapes, with the exception of certain red wine grapes such as Pinot Noir and perhaps Grenache or Cabernet Franc, go through a destemming machine before they are crushed. Certain high-quality wine producers believe in whole-berry or whole-cluster fermentation, where the grapes are placed in a fermentation vat without being crushed, sometimes with a portion of the stem left on. Generally, this adds an extra dimension or heft to wines made from the subtler grape varieties by retaining more tannins.

In some instances, a portion of the grapes will be destemmed and crushed while the rest are whole-cluster fermented. Like all key decisions, this one reflects the winemaker's judgment of the balance of sugar, acid, fruity components and tannins present in the harvested grapes. I liken these choices to television reception. First, you've got to tune in and receive some kind of clear picture. Then you can start fiddling with the dials—fine-tuning the color, contrast, sharpness and so forth—until you have "perfect reception."

Crushed or not, the grapes go into a fermenter, usually a large stainless-steel tank with an opening on top. Tanks or vats can also be made of concrete, ceramic or wood. Stainless steel offers the best hygiene and temperature control, but many fine operations are returning to the traditional wooden vats because they render more complex, more "authentic" or more "oaky" flavors.

Maceration and Pressing

Maceration is defined as the soaking of the grapes' solids—the stems, seeds and skins—in their juices. It marks the beginning of what is known in winespeak as extraction, meaning the processes by which the flavor, color and aroma compounds are taken from the grapes and put into the wine.

The remnants of the crushed grapes—juice and solids—are known as the must. During maceration, the juice can be pumped up over the "cap" of the must, which floats on top of the fermenter exposed to the air. The cap can also be punched down, either by hand, which is extremely hard work, or with hydraulic or compressed-air devices. The more the must is soaked, pumped over, crushed, punched down, pressed or spun around, and the higher the temperature, the more the flavor, color and aroma compounds are extracted from the grapes and end up in the wine.

Once the grapes have been processed and placed in a vat, they are subject to another major stylistic decision: What is the length of maceration and how and when will it occur vis-à-vis fermentation? Maceration can last anywhere from a couple of days to three weeks. Its length and timing depend on the grape variety and the vintage. In a hot, sunny year, where the grape skins have become relatively thick, the winemaker might decide to shorten maceration because the grapes and their juice are naturally potent and concentrated. A cooler, rainier year, where the skins are thinner and the juice possibly more diluted, would probably call for longer maceration than usual. The same type of judgment applies to other extractive processes such as punch down, pump over and pressing. The "weaker" the juice, the more punch down and/or pump over is done and the higher the percentage of pressed wine (see below) included in the mix. Grape varieties with heavier color and tannins, such as Cabernet Sauvignon, are more likely to be pumped over than

Clean winemaking is essential: a spotless steel fermentation tank in Barolo Country.

punched down. Some winemakers pump over or punch down once or twice a day, others do it only a few times during the entire maceration and fermentation process, just to make sure the cap doesn't get moldy.

It's important to note that maceration, which simply refers to the grapes' solids soaking in their liquids, and fermentation, which is the conversion of sugars to alcohol, are separate but overlapping processes; both must be carefully scripted and coordinated by the winemaker.

Another crucial decision involves the pressing of the grapes, particularly its timing. Red wine grapes can be pressed *before* the end of fermentation, which yields lots of color and fruitiness. Fermentation is then com-

pleted in barrel (the method most common in Australia). In another scenario, the grapes are pressed to coincide closely with the end of fermentation in order to maximize extraction while avoiding a "weedy" character that can result from maceration. A third scenario involves longer maceration, where the wine is kept on its solids well beyond the end of fermentation.

Whether or not the grapes are pressed—and if they are, what percentage of pressed wine is included in the final mix—again depends on vintage and variety. Pressing is a highly extractive process, so it's more likely to be used with a grape variety that has more delicate tannins such as Pinot Noir than one with heavier tannins such as Cabernet Sauvignon.

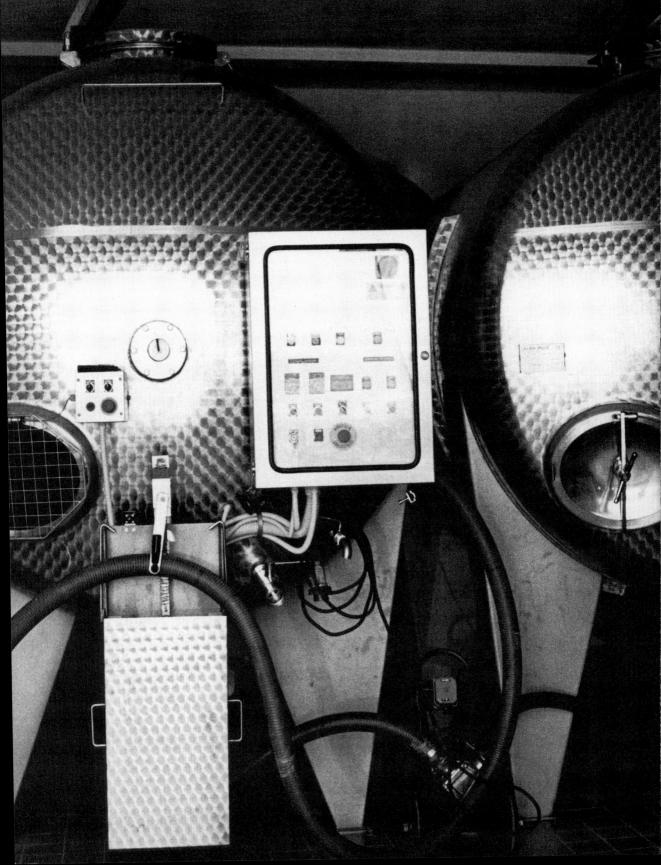

"You can't just go back to the old system. Today we are using certain traditional equipment but with much more sophisticated know-how, not only controlling temperature, but also controlling the microbiology." —Marchese Piero Antinori

In order to protect the must, sulfur dioxide (SO_2)—a natural preservative used in winemaking since ancient times—is added. When you see wine labels that say "Contains sulfites" that's what it's referring to. It's possible to vinify without preservatives, but there is a risk that bacteria will contaminate the wine and promote the development of acetic acid, which starts to oxidize the wine and eventually turn it to vinegar. Even high-quality premium winegrowers use SO_2.

Fermentation

Fermentation can only occur when the temperature of the grapes and juice is high enough to activate the yeasts. At about 65 degrees F. and up, they begin to work their magic, converting the sugars in the grape juice into alcohol.

While all three steps—crushing, maceration and fermentation—must occur to convert the raw grapes into fine red wines, winemakers choose their strategies depending on the situation. For Pinot Noir, Ted Lemon would destem only a portion of the grapes and leave them all uncrushed to capture as much of the "whole-berry fruit quality" as possible. Then he would choose cold maceration, on the theory that it extracts more stable color components from the grapes. The must is chilled to between 50 and 55 degrees F., then the refrigeration unit is turned off, allowing the temperature to rise very gradually in the insulated tanks over the course of five days to a point at which the yeasts can become active. The must is periodically punched down, breaking up the whole-grape clusters and releasing juice. The remainder of the stems soak in the juice, where it is believed they release potassium, bringing the pH up and the acid down.

Gary Galleron, a winemaker from Rutherford, Napa Valley, creates a different scenario, using a heat exchanger to bring the temperature of his red wine musts up to about 88 degrees F. shortly after crushing. Then he simply adds yeasts and the fermentation begins almost immediately. It's simply a different way of achieving the same results—good extraction of color and tannins to go hand in hand with fermentation.

Like Gary Galleron, many makers of high-quality wines "inoculate" the must—that is, they introduce cultured yeasts into the vat to kick off the fermentation process. Others insist on using only native yeasts, allowing the process of fermentation to occur naturally. Still others will only use cultured yeasts in those rare cases when the fermentation doesn't take off on its own. Cultured yeasts can either be purchased from outside sources or grown in the winery from the ones that already live there.

There is some debate as to whether native yeasts come in with the grapes from the vineyard or live in and around the winery. If you've ever examined wine grapes as they grow in the vineyard, you've noticed they have a whitish substance on them called the bloom. Those who believe in vineyard yeasts will tell you that's what they live on.

Fermentation continues until the yeast can't function anymore because of the level of alcohol—they become "drunk"—or all the sugar in the juice has been converted. The process can be halted early by adding extra alcohol. This is how fortified wines like Port are made and it explains why they're sweet—the yeasts aren't given the chance to convert all the sugars.

Generally, fermentation lasts six to eight days, during which time the must heats up to nearly 90 degrees F. and gives off a lot of carbon dioxide. Most wines are fermented to what is called "dryness," which in winespeak is the opposite of sweet. Technically, this means there is no residual sugar from the grapes; it has all been converted to alcohol. A number of fine wines, however, complete their fermentation with some residual sugar. This is particularly true of German white wines, which are higher in acid and thus need to retain more sugar for balance. Other notable exceptions are late-harvest dessert wines, which have quite a lot of residual sugar. A rule of thumb: Wines from cooler, more northerly climates tend to have higher acidity and lower alcohol content because the grapes don't ripen as thoroughly, and therefore don't develop as much natural sugar. By the same token, wines from warmer climates have lower acidity and higher alcohol content.

As an aside, some late-harvest wines, notably Sauternes, are made with grapes affected by "noble rot," the fungus called *Botrytis cinerea*. In certain years, when vineyard conditions are right, *B. cinerea* shrivels the grapes just so, dehydrating them and thus concentrating their flavors right so they can be made into these delicious wines. Certain special wines—like the Italian Reciotos of Valpolicella—are made with air-dried or "raisined" grapes that produce similar sweet and/or concentrated flavors.

Malolactic Fermentation

In conventional types of red winemaking, there is a secondary fermentation process called "malolactic fermentation," which happens after "primary" or "alcoholic" fermentation. In malolactic fermentation, the sharper malic acid in the grapes is converted into lactic acid, a mellower-tasting acid present in milk. This step is crucial in developing the subtlety, suppleness, complexity and all sorts of other qualities of a fine wine. Malolactic fermentation takes place either in vats or aging barrels, often helped along by inoculation with "lactic" bacteria.

BLEEDING

THE WINE'S FLAVOR AND ALCOHOLIC CONTENT MAY BE ELEVATED BY REMOVING SOME OF ITS WATER, A TECHNIQUE KNOWN AS *SAIGNER* ("BLEEDING") IN FRENCH. IT ORIGINATED IN BURGUNDY AND HAS BECOME QUITE PREVALENT IN BORDEAUX IN RELATIVELY RECENT TIMES. IT IS ACHIEVED BY RUNNING SOME OF THE LIGHTER JUICE OFF AFTER CRUSHING OR BY USING A MUST-CONCENTRATING MACHINE, WHICH BOILS THE JUICE AT ROOM TEMPERATURE IN A VACUUM. PURISTS DISDAIN THIS PROCESS, MAINTAINING THAT CONCENTRATION SHOULD BE ACHIEVED THROUGH PROPER VITICULTURAL TECHNIQUES— THAT IS, IN THE VINEYARD, NOT IN THE WINERY. ANOTHER ARGUMENT AGAINST BLEEDING IS THAT IF THE GRAPES ARE LESS THAN PERFECT, IT CAN ACCENTUATE FAULTS; IF THEY AREN'T TOTALLY RIPENED, FOR EXAMPLE, THE WINE MAY END UP WITH TOO MUCH ACIDITY.

WHITE WINES

The fundamental difference in white winemaking is that the juice is crushed and/or pressed out of the grapes and separated *before* fermentation. There is no maceration because if the juice is left in contact with the skins for any significant period of time, the wine begins to take on color and tannins. The juice from all wine grapes is clear or grayish. In fact, not all white-wine grapes have light-colored skins; skin contact is what imparts color.

In general, the white winemaking process emphasizes the fruitiness, sweetness and crisp acidity of the grapes while avoiding the tannins and other products of extraction that are so important to red wines. Since heat speeds up all chemical reactions, including extraction, white wines are made at lower temperatures than reds.

Like the grapes that make red wines, those used to make whites are destemmed and crushed, resulting in so-called free-run juice. The grapes are then pressed and the juice goes into a fermentation vat, usually stainless steel. In some cases, white wine is made strictly from free-run juice without pressing. In others, it is pressed from whole clusters.

After fermentation, most white wines are allowed to settle. The dead yeast cells, called the "lees," drop to the bottom of the tank along with any other sediment. The wine is then placed in another tank to age. Sometimes this process is enhanced by what is called fining, whereby an inert material is added to precipitate solids out of the solution. Most white wines are made in all stainless steel. A few, notably those made from the Chardonnay grape, are transferred to oak barrels with their lees and allowed to undergo malolactic fermentation and aging. Thus the term "aged on its lees" (*sur lis* in French). Sometimes the lees are even stirred, which adds further flavor and complexity to the wines.

Oak

Premium winemaking very often involves aging in oak barrels (*barriques* in French), which hold 225 liters or the equivalent of about twenty-five cases of wine each, for a period of ten to thirty months, sometimes even longer. (The top Barolo producers in Italy's province of Piedmont age their reserve wines a *minimum* of three years.) This holds true for nearly all red wines and for some whites, notably Chardonnay.

Oak lends its own flavors and tannins, which you might hear described as "oaky," "smoky," "toasty," "vanilla" and so forth, to the wine. For the winemaker, oak is a flavor enhancer, analogous to a chef's use of spices. The key is to achieve balance and integration of the various tastes and sensations contributed by oak and other components—"fruity" grape sugars, "tart" grape acids, "astringent" tannins, the heat and weight of the alcohol on the palate—so that the whole is a harmonious symphony whose sum is greater than its parts.

How much oak finds its way into the wine depends on such variables as the percentage of new barrels used, the size of the barrel (the smaller the barrel, the more wine is in contact with the oak), the length of time in barrel, the provenance of the wood and even how it was cured

"**Wood is something indispensable, but it can be abused. It's really just an instrument or a tool, like a pump.**" —Marc de Grazia

and/or "toasted" as the staves were bent into barrel shape over a fire. Conventional wisdom says that the best barrels for premium wines are made from French oak, which, at about $700 a barrel in the United States, is the most expensive option. Use of American and Slovenian oak is also fairly widespread. Most top winegrowers use oak from three to five different cooperages to ensure that no single influence dominates.

How long wines are aged in the barrel and what percentage of the barrels is new is determined by how much tannin a given wine is judged to contain. New oak has a more powerful influence; after a year or two, as it becomes permeated with wine, it tightens up and mellows so its effect isn't as strong.

"You learn from your grape sources how much new oak they can tolerate," says Ted Lemon. "The more complexity and concentration you're getting out of a site, generally speaking, the more new oak it will tolerate. But every site is different. There are some very delicate wines that can support 100 percent new oak, and there are some very powerful wines that actually don't do well with 100 percent new oak."

Since wood is porous, it allows for the long-term seepage of oxygen into the wine, rather than shocking it with a sudden dosage. Of the different types of wood, oak works best because it's relatively inert, allowing for subtler flavors than, say, pine, which would definitely overwhelm the wine with its distinctive aroma and tarry taste.

The older, more slow-growing and thus tight-grained the oak, the lighter and sweeter its flavor. French oak is often divided into three categories: Limousin, from the western part of the country, the most coarse-grained,

harshest-tasting, used for Cognac or other spirits rather than fine wines; Allier, Nevers and Troncais, from the central forests, tight-grained, subtler flavors, best for premium wines; Bourgogne, Champagne and Vosges, from the eastern part of the country, medium flavors. Ironically, the best French oak usually doesn't come from winegrowing regions, although the Nevers forest is very close to Sancerre.

American oak is tight-grained but has its own strong, distinct flavors, often equated with vanilla, and is used most in Spain and Australia, where the wines are big enough to stand up to it. Slovenian oak is excellent and is often used by the best Italian producers.

Oak is one of those road signs that tells you you're in the neighborhood of fine wines. If you see the catchwords "barrel aged, X percentage of new oak" on the label either it's likely to be good wine or the producer is telling the right lie.

Racking

Racking is the winemaker's term for moving the wine from one container to another during the aging process. It has two purposes: to separate the wine from any unwanted sediment, and to expose it to minimal amounts of oxygen. A certain amount of oxygenation is part of the wine's subtle aging process, but as with every other step in winegrowing, it has to be carefully monitored and controlled. Too much or too little air can tip the balance. At every racking, there's also a risk of possible exposure to contaminating bacteria.

It is the winemaker's task to determine exactly how much racking a given wine needs. More tannic wines, from the Cabernet family for example, call for more frequent racking; delicate wines such as Pinot Noir need less. At Château Latour, the wines, which are primarily Cabernet Sauvignon and Merlot, are aged in barrel for approximately eighteen to twenty-two months and racked every three months. By contrast, Ted Lemon usually doesn't rack his barrel-aged Littorai Chardonnays and Pinot Noirs at all.

Further Refinements

Fining, filtering, stabilizing and clarifying are all refining procedures that are more likely to be necessary in larger-scale operations where there is less close attention paid to the progress of each barrel of wine.

Fining is a way of precipitating out any solids or extracts —microscopic or otherwise—that might remain in the wine after it's been fermented and/or aged. Traditional fining is done with egg whites, which are put into the vat or barrel, allowed to settle to the bottom with whatever particles they pick up and left in the container when the wine is moved on its way toward bottling.

Wine can also be pumped through filters of varying sizes, either before or after barrel aging, to remove particles even as small as bacteria. Stabilizing or clarifying the wine involves chilling it and allowing it to settle in order to remove crystallized deposits of tartrate (tartaric acid), for example, which are harmless but unattractive and suspicious to consumers.

Some premium producers consider these practices indicative of careless winemaking. Most of them will tell you the less intervention the better. The belief is that if wines are manufactured and aged with proper attention and care, they won't need to be fined to remove tannins or filtered to eliminate bacteria or stabilized because the aging cellar wasn't cold enough to get rid of tartrates.

Top producers do "separate vinification"—that is, they keep lots of wine from different vineyards or different parcels separate throughout the winemaking process. When it comes time to bottle, they either carefully blend these lots with balance in mind or do single vineyard-designated wines. This final stage before bottling is also the last chance for selection, the weeding out of lower-grade wines.

The Final Step: Bottle Aging

After aging for about eight months to three years in barrels or vats, most fine wines are bottled and allowed to rest for up to another year. All this aging means premium red wines and some whites don't reach the marketplace for two to four years after the date of harvest.

Bottling marks the beginning of an exciting period of anticipation and speculation. Winegrowers are ebullient if vintage conditions have been declared favorable, nervous if they're in doubt or just plain depressed if it's been judged an off year. Plenty of work remains to be done in the meantime—marketing the vintage, bringing subsequent ones into the winery—and it all culminates in the wine's release date, when cases are shipped out worldwide. As they arrive and are cracked open, all the expert forecasts and whispers of inside information are exposed to the light of day. The people who really count—our customers, the wine drinkers— finally have a chance to validate the painstaking process of winegrowing by doing what they do best: tasting and judging the wines for themselves.

A recent Château Margaux vintage aging in oak. Those barrels contain more than $20 million worth of wine.

BUBBLY

THE MAKING OF THE BUBBLY: HOW CHAMPAGNE IS BORN

CHAMPAGNE, OF COURSE, REFERS TO THE REGION OF NORTHERN FRANCE, ABOUT NINETY MILES EAST OF PARIS, WHERE THIS MOST FAMOUS OF ALL SPARKLING WINES ORIGINATES. AUTHENTIC CHAMPAGNE IS MADE BY A PROCESS KNOWN AS THE *METHODE TRADITIONNELLE* (OFTEN REFERRED TO AS *METHODE CHAMPENOISE*) AND COMES ONLY FROM THIS REGION. MANY SPARKLING WINES ARE MADE THE SAME WAY BUT CAN'T LEGITIMATELY CLAIM THE NAME.

The base wine is made by pressing and vinifying numerous grape lots just as for white wines—without maceration or skin contact. Traditionally, the grapes are either Chardonnay, Pinot Meunier or Pinot Noir. After the still base wines are fermented, they are carefully combined to make a *cuvée* (blend), keeping in mind that they need to be relatively mild, smooth and neutral but with a certain potential, because of what comes next.

The next step is to bottle the *cuvée* in the typical thick green bottles, sealing them with a crown cap like the ones used on traditional beer or soda bottles. Before the bottles are sealed, a small amount of sugar and yeast is added to cause a second fermentation, which raises the Champagne's alcohol level to about 12% and creates the millions of tiny bubbles of carbon dioxide that give it its irresistible effervescence.

The wine is then aged on its lees, resting horizontally in a cool, dark cellar (*cave*), allowing it to develop gradually all the characteristic flavors and aromas of true Champagne. After up to eighteen months of aging—sometimes even more—the bottles are turned upside down and carefully shaken once so the sediment falls to the neck, then the necks are submerged in very cold salt water to avoid breakage but to freeze the precious bubbly inside. The crown caps are removed and the bottles turned right-side up, causing the frozen plug of sediment to pop out. The bottles are then topped off with a small amount of the original *cuvée* and a pinch of sugar, known as the *dosage,* which balances the wine, counteracting its naturally high acidity. Finally, they are resealed with the distinctive extra-wide corks that won't pop off until they are gingerly twisted and pulled by their end-user.

Vintages are only declared for Champagnes in definitive years; otherwise, they're called simply Brut, Sec or Demi-Sec, in descending order of dryness.

Chapter Three

ON TASTE AND TASTING

FROM THE RAINBOW TO DAYGLO

BECOMING A CONNOISSEUR

YEARS AGO, TALK-SHOW HOST DAVID FROST AUTHORED A POCKET VOLUME CALLED *THE BLUFFER'S GUIDE TO WINE.* I ALWAYS APPRECIATED THAT APPROACH, AND I OFTEN THINK OF THE WINE-TASTING COURSES I TEACH AND, BY EXTENSION, THIS BOOK AS A KIND OF BLUFFER'S GUIDE. THE VERY LEAST A READER SHOULD GET OUT OF IT, EVEN IF HE OR SHE MERELY SKIMS, IS ENOUGH BASIC KNOWLEDGE TO HOLD AN INTERESTING CONVERSATION—AND TO ASK THE RIGHT QUESTIONS. I DON'T EXPECT ANYBODY TO BECOME AN EXPERT OVERNIGHT, BUT YOU SHOULD BE ABLE TO GLEAN FROM THIS BOOK AN ENTHU-SIASM AND AN APPRECIATION FOR THE LIFESTYLE. IN THIS CHAPTER, I OFFER A CLEAR PICTURE OF HOW WINE IS ANALYZED AND DESCRIBED. I HOPE YOU WILL PUT IT TO USE IN MAKING WINE A PART OF YOUR LIFE.

A *connoisseur* is one with knowledge of a particular subject, from the French verb *connaître* ("to know"). How much do you need to know about wine? Only whether you like what's in your glass or not. Beyond that, the question becomes how much do you *want* to know. There's a lot to learn and in my opinion it's all valid. The more profound your knowledge of wine, the more profound your enjoyment of it. As the true experts say, the more they learn about wine, the more they realize how little they know. It's a delicious, delightful, never-ending quest.

Those "in the know"—the experienced professionals, the sophisticated connoisseurs—all possess good humor, a lot of humility and a respect for the art and science of wine. Wine is a moving target. Just when you think you know everything there is to know about your favorite, every vintage down through the years, it changes.

You can follow the recommendations of the so-called experts and have an enjoyable experience. You might even be able to fool somebody who doesn't know much —at least for a while. But the real long-term rewards of connoisseurship are in accumulating your *own* wealth of wine experiences and sharing them with your friends.

If you make a habit of spending $30, $40 or $50 for a bottle of wine, your friends are going to start putting you on a pedestal. They'll hand you a glass at dinner parties and ask you to make a pronouncement. If you can't tell the difference between Château Petrus and plonk, you're going to embarrass yourself.

People shouldn't have to rely totally on a Robert Parker or a Dennis Overstreet; they should possess the confidence to make their own judgments and choices. By the same token, as wine merchants, we need to show people exactly how to distinguish what's special. We can't glorify just anything. It's what I call the White Zinfandel syndrome (see sidebar, opposite). There are some experts who say, "If you like, it's good." In the real world, there is a better and a worse. I can't tell you what to like, but I can give you some

tools to recognize what's good. Then you'll never have a problem sorting out the Petrus from the plonk.

It's rather intimidating—and also amazing—to see a panel of experts blind-tasting and identifying wines by region, producer and even vintage. But consider the analogy of art connoisseurship: The first time you see a painting by Rembrandt you probably know you're in the presence of great art. Look at those lines and how they portray the emotions of their subjects. Look at the depth and complexity of the artist's skills. Once you've looked at enough Rembrandts you'll be able to recognize one right away, to tell it apart from any other artist, a Rubens, say. If you look at a piece that doesn't distinguish itself from others, then you can probably rule it out of the category of great works of art. Once you've learned to identify Rembrandt, you can move on to other great artists—Botticelli, Van Gogh, say, or even Manet and Monet (similar names, similar dates, different styles).

Take your time and get to know each artist's unique attributes, all the while making comparisons. Look at new artists all the time and compare them to the greats you've come to know. Pretty soon, you're on your way to becoming an art connoisseur. Always remember, even a great connoisseur can sometimes be fooled—by one artist imitating another, by a good forgery or by a great artist having an off day. If it happened all the time, though, connoisseurship would become meaningless.

The debate on what makes great art is unending. You might define it as work that depicts and/or provokes some kind of strong emotion. Some would maintain that great art can revolt or disgust or shock us. (Have you ever seen Sir Francis Bacon's paintings? Most experts consider them great modern art; they are also fairly repulsive to look at.) With wine, it's much easier because great wines should never do that. First and foremost, they should taste good. In great wine as in great art, what you notice first is there's so much variation and so much individual character. As you taste wines, you'll begin to recognize these attributes.

WHITE ZINFANDEL

I SUPPOSE ONE COULD BE ACCUSED OF SNOBBERY IN LOOKING DOWN ONE'S NOSE AT WHITE ZINFANDEL. IT WAS CREATED IN THE EARLY 1970S BY SUTTER HOME WINERY IN CALIFORNIA AS A BY-PRODUCT OF REGULAR RED ZINFANDEL PRODUCTION. THE WINEMAKERS LEFT SOME OF THE SUGAR IN, NOT ALLOWING IT TO FERMENT TO COMPLETE DRYNESS, BOTTLED IT AND SOLD IT BY THE TRUCKLOAD. IT HELPED POPULARIZE THE NOTION OF WINE-DRINKING WITH A WIDE SEGMENT OF THE U.S. POPULATION THAT MIGHT OTHERWISE NEVER HAVE EVEN CONSIDERED POPPING A CORK. BUT MOST SERIOUS CONNOISSEURS AND SOPHISTICATED WINE DRINKERS LOOK UPON IT AS A SYMBOL FOR ANYTHING TACKY FOISTED OFF ON A BLISSFULLY IGNORANT PUBLIC. WHITE ZINFANDEL CERTAINLY SERVES ITS PURPOSE, BUT YOU WON'T FIND IT FOR SALE AT THE WINE MERCHANT, BEVERLY HILLS.

Decide how much of a wine connoisseur you want to be. There is a happy medium somewhere between "Whatever tastes good to you is good" and following the authoritative pronouncements of some dinosaur critic who ranks among the world's best wines Bordeaux, Bordeaux and Bordeaux. Only you can decide your own level of satisfaction and comfort.

All it takes to become a wine connoisseur is the enthusiasm and the commitment. It does not take large sums of money or the amassing of a large collection of "name" wines. Maybe the bottle I recommend to you this week will tweak your curiosity enough that next week you'll decide to come back and buy several different bottles—or better yet, a mixed case—and start making comparisons.

Becoming a connoisseur is about making wine part of your lifestyle and taking the time to understand and appreciate it. If you don't have the time to do all the investigating yourself, you can do well by consulting with your trusted wine merchant. You might have to make a few compromises, but don't worry because there is always a level of sophistication available to anyone who wants it. Wine is one of the great fruits of the earth. It's still a miracle, but because of science and because of the new openness among wine insiders it need no longer be a mystery.

The first step toward becoming a wine connoisseur—Overstreet's Rule No. 1 of connoisseurship—is to slow down. Don't rush! Fine wine is a subtle pleasure of the palate. It takes time to grow the grapes. It takes time to ferment the juice and to age it. It takes time to taste and understand and appreciate. It's time well spent, but it does take time. We need to learn to take the time to savor what's in our glass. It's probably the most important principle to remember if you want to enjoy your wine. I'm not trying to be anybody's life guru, but I can be your wine guru, and if there was one mantra this would be it. Things are happening too fast in the world today, there's much information, too many people who never slow down.

In California, where I live and run my business, there's a healthy openness, a willingness to experiment that can be both an asset and a liability vis-à-vis wine. There's also an infatuation with the Flavor of the Month. Remember, new does not always equal good, especially with wine. As mentioned earlier, the New Wine Revolution is a synthesis. We should be adventurous and unpretentious, but we should also be wary of falling prey to the latest fad.

When evaluating new wines, I always like to keep in mind the image of a figure eight—learn from the past, project into the future. The figure eight always loops back to the old before it leaps ahead to the new.

¡POP!

The delicious moment of anticipation: opening a special bottle of wine.

THERE'S NO SUBSTITUTE FOR POPPING CORKS

Samuel Clemens, aka Mark Twain, is probably my favorite author. To paraphrase, he liked to say if you want to find out all about a riverboat you can spend a day interviewing its architect and its captain *or* you can just take a walk around and talk to all the deckhands and know just as much if not more about that particular boat. That's the way I feel about this wine adventure we're on. I hope to encourage people to experience wine to its fullest: Take a visit to wine country and walk the land, taste a wide variety of wines, take some time to pore over mailings from wineries and merchants. But much more important than heeding any critics or marketers is to try the wines.

You can subscribe to magazines, read books, take courses and follow recommendations. Absorb all the information and advice there is, but more important, go to your local merchant, buy a bottle, take it home and pop the cork. Alexis Lichine, probably the most famous ex-patriate American in the French wine business, was fond of saying that before you start consulting vintage charts or wine encyclopedias, invest in a corkscrew. If you've got a bottle or two you'd like to try right now, skip down to "The Tasting Sequence" below and enjoy.

I endorse the theory that the public will always find the best. I am convinced that if you chose four hundred people at random and, regardless of their experience, gave them a blind taste test, the vast majority would recognize the better wines. I call it the "Hedonistic Taste Test." Try it sometime at home with your dinner guests: a blind tasting of several wines—no notes, no comments, just see which bottles wind up the emptiest. It's the truest test of all. People know what tastes good to them; it's not something that can be taught—or should be. As a wine expert,

I can't dictate taste. All I can do is help my customers hone their perceptions, give them a nudge in the direction of self-confidence and let them do the rest.

There are two aspects of wine appreciation: the hedonistic (pure pleasure) and the intellectual (analysis). The minute you start popping corks and tasting a few good wines, you develop a hedonistic appreciation. Then, if you like, you can add the intellectual side.

Whether or not they know it, everyone practices a little bit of both. Connoisseurs follow the tasting sequence from visual examination to sniffing to tasting to waiting for the "finish." They break the wine down into component aromas and flavors, most of which are described by analogies with familiar smells, including everything from flowers and fruits to leather and kerosene. After this, they move on to the subjective, overall impressions and judgments, with adjectives and qualitative descriptors such as balance and finesse.

The analytical stage is a learned skill whereas the hedonistic pleasure scale is mostly a matter of preference and opinion. People who are totally uninitiated into wine can be every bit as astute as the most experienced connoisseur. They just can't describe what they're tasting as well.

AN EDUCATED PALATE BEGINS WITH YOUR NOSE

For everybody in the wine world—from grape growers and winemakers to sommeliers, connoisseurs and garden variety wine lovers—the main tool for appreciating and enjoying wine is an educated palate. Not to worry, there's no great secret to it. It's merely a matter of awakening hidden potential. Learning to distinguish fine wines is like learning to look at fine art, only you're using a much less practiced sense (smell) as opposed to one you use almost continuously (sight).

The tasting apparatus on the tongue is relatively simple and straightforward. It consists of taste buds that can detect sweet, sour, bitter and salty. (Only the first three are relevant to wine.) The sense of smell, on the other hand, is incredibly complex; it can detect over ten thousand different odors. It is believed there are between seven and eight hundred compounds present in wine that, in various permutations and combinations, can be perceived as a vast number of aromas.

Here we have this amazing sensory tool and yet we don't take advantage of it. We know what smells good and what smells bad, but we never really focus our sense of smell on the thousands of different odors available to it. In fact, we're brought up, especially in America, to *avoid* most smells. Millions if not billions of consumer dollars are spent every year on products designed to mask natural odors. This cultural aversion to smell is one of the biggest hurdles to overcome in enhancing your appreciation of fine wines.

Children are brought up to describe what they see and what they hear. As far as I can remember from my childhood and from bringing up my kids, the only smell we're educated about is "stinky," decidedly a negative. My young son, Patrick, is just learning about these things. I've often imagined what it would be like if children his age were trained to recognize smells the way they are trained to recognize visual cues such as colors or numbers or letters of the alphabet. We'd be a nation of wine-tasters.

Smelling and tasting are about nurture not nature. Award-winning master sommelier Larry Stone, who was a

tasting prodigy, is a case in point. He grew up in a food-oriented family. His father worked at the Pike Place Market in Seattle and as a boy he used to pass the time wandering around tasting sausages and fish and numerous products of the earth. He started tasting wines when he was about seven years old; by the time he was ten, he was doing blind tastings with his family.

Larry had a head start in two important areas: sensitivity and practice. His mind was opened early to the possibilities of taste, and he had lots of exposure. These are the two keys to developing one's palate: (1) paying attention (sensitivity, focus, concentration) and (2) familiarizing yourself with tastes and aromas (practice, experience). You need to be alert, listen to your nose and try to relate the wine you are tasting to those you've had in the past.

Professor Ann C. Noble of UC-Davis, creator of the aroma wheel, uses the analogy of a policeman at the scene of a traffic accident. He arrives on the scene and, trained to observe details, he can reconstruct what happened. Meanwhile, naive bystanders who witnessed the accident can hardly agree on the color of the car and whether it hit a tricycle, a bicycle or a motorcycle. Again, the crucial elements are observation, concentration and practice.

One way to demonstrate your untapped potential to appreciate aromas is to play a simple guess-the-smell game as suggested by many experts, including Leslie Brenner in her fine introductory manual *Fear of Wine*. It works well with kids or adults and it can be pretty hilarious. Have the "victims" close their eyes, then put a piece of cut fruit, say a strawberry, under their noses. What do they smell? Next, try it with a pair of similar fruits or vegetables, say,

On a wine-tasting tour of Italy, Dave and I demonstrate how to get your nose into the glass.

orange and grapefruit or raspberry and blueberry or carrots and fennel. It's really amazing to see how quickly people catch on and grasp the nuances of aromas, and to witness their sense of delight. It's as if they're discovering a talent they never knew they had. All they're really doing is listening to their noses.

WHERE DO ALL THOSE FLAVORS COME FROM?

Wine consists of a number of solids present in a solution. Among them, the volatile compounds, meaning those that mix with air, are the ones that create aroma. The amounts are minuscule, measured in particles per million, but our olfactory organs are sensitive enough to pick them up.

When we talk about a superior wine like Château Margaux having a hint of berries, there is some basis in fact. It may seem far-fetched at first, but wines do contain complex compounds that are shared with many fruits, vegetables and other organic products. If you smell strawberries in a wine, it's likely that particular wine shares certain chemicals with that berry.

If you pursue the education of your palate, some day you may be able to pinpoint the citrusy aroma of the compound known as linalool, which is present in orange blossoms, orange juice, litchi nuts, Handy Wipes and Fruit Loops (seriously). It's an aroma often found in wines made from the Gewürztraminer grape.

AT UC-DAVIS, PROFESSOR ANN C. NOBLE AND HER COLLEAGUES ARE
ATTEMPTING TO IDENTIFY THE CHEMICAL COMPOUNDS RESPONSIBLE FOR
THE AROMAS WE PERCEIVE. SHE CONDUCTS WINE RESEARCH IN TWO
AREAS: SENSORY AND FLAVOR CHEMISTRY.

THE AROMA WHEEL

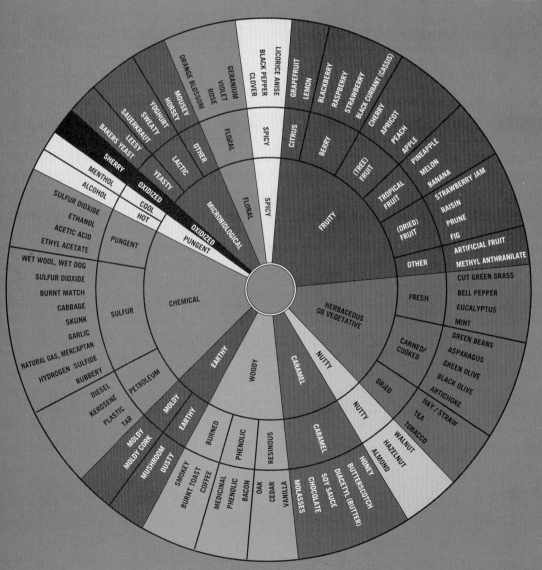

Flavor chemistry is the study of the structure of the volatile compounds that make up flavors and aromas while sensory studies explore the way we perceive those flavors and aromas.

In one experiment, she established a link between grapes that were shaded by leaves on the vine and a chemical called "bell pepper pyrazine." Technically called 2-methoxy 3-isobutyl pyrazine, it gives peppers their characteristic aroma and is often found in the Cabernet family of grapes, including Cabernet Sauvignon, Merlot and Sauvignon Blanc. Light meters were positioned in the vines to measure exposure. Grapes with low exposure were found to have a strong pyrazine flavor and aroma, with up to four times the amount of the compound present.

Crucial to this type of research is a standard descriptive language for the aromas and flavors of wines, along with trained judges who can reliably detect them. This is why Professor Noble and her colleagues developed the aroma wheel, a categorized, graphic representation of the smells detected in wines.

The wheel was developed by first collecting a huge number of wine aroma references from books and other publications. Then there was a survey of wine industry professionals as well as perusal of years of UC-Davis tasting notes with the goal of eliminating all judgmental terms such as "complex," "elegant" and so forth. First published in 1984, the wheel is edited periodically and is a great practical tool.

One important offshoot of the wheel is that it provides recipes for creating standards. Most of them can be prepared easily from items available in the grocery store. For example, if you want to demonstrate the bell pepper aroma, soak a 12-by-10-millimeter slice of green pepper in 25 milliliters of neutral wine for thirty minutes. (A neutral wine is defined as one that is "free of defects and has low-intensity aromas.")

A few of the aromas on the outside of the wheel are denoted by names of compounds. Methyl anthranilate, for example, is the one responsible for the aroma of Labrusca grapes or Welch's grape juice. Some of the aromas are associated with specific chemical compounds. As mentioned, "bell pepper" is attributable to pyrazine and comes from the "unripe" or "vegetal" characteristics of some grapes; "buttery" is attributable to diacetyl, a product of malolactic fermentation, and "vanilla" to vanillin, which often comes from the oak barrels. With regard to a fruity aroma such as blackberry, however, scientists don't have much of a clue.

Some of the aromas around the outside of the wheel are pretty bizarre, but they have all been detected at some point. "Wet dog," for example, can come from photo oxidation of Sauvignon Blanc, a danger as long as wineries persist in bottling these wines in clear glass. When they're exposed to light for any significant time, they become "sunstruck" and can develop aromas of ethyl mercaptan, which is similar to natural gas or skunk, or possibly "wet dog." How does this happen? One theory is it may be a similar reaction to what takes place when you get your hair permed or when your dog comes in the house wet. The proteins in the hair contain sulfide bonds, which give off that characteristic aroma when exposed to heat. Sometimes, wonder of wonders, you'll encounter a wine with a pronounced animal odor that ends up tasting great. It's something like the stinky cheese phenomenon: The stinkier it is, the better it tastes.

Where to draw the line drawn between a sign of character and a defect? First, it's a question of balance and then of personal preference. Most of us would object to "horsey" or "wet dog" unless they were just momentary hints that we could call "interesting." We probably wouldn't object to honey or apricot or mint, but we might pull back if there was too much of any one of them.

(Colored plastic versions of the wheel may be obtained for a nominal fee by writing Professor Noble at the Department of Viticulture and Enology, University of California, One Shields Avenue, Davis, CA 95616. She can also be reached by fax at 530-752-0382 or by e-mail at acnoble@ucdavis.edu. All proceeds support wine sensory research at UC-Davis.)

"Wine is the perfect blend of intellectual pursuits and sheer hedonism."
—Michael Bonaccorsi, Master Sommelier

WINE EDUCATION COURSES

Once you wake up to the possibilities of aroma, you can go on to educate your palate. Although it's by no means mandatory to take a course, it can help. You'd be surprised how quickly you develop some basic analytical tools. I'd recommend it if only because you'll meet other wine lovers. It's always fascinating to observe individual perceptions and preferences.

When I teach my tasting courses, I like to do it in an extremely informal, conversational way. I don't stand up and lecture. Basically, we just sit around a dinner table and pop some corks. I try to steer the discussion with as gentle a hand as possible. It's a hedonistic-Socratic approach: taste the wines, enjoy them, let me challenge you with a few questions that will awaken your mind to what your senses perceive.

The key to a good wine education course is a teacher who can take the hocus-pocus out of it. Wine is enough of a mystery to challenge the greatest intellects this planet has produced without cooking up some phony mystique or intimidating people with "wine snobbery." If you don't feel relaxed in the first few minutes and confident after the first session, the course is probably not worth pursuing.

Most serious wine education programs rely on some method of breaking a wine down into basic blocks of flavor and aroma, and then using those blocks to build an understanding of the concepts of structure and character. They usually employ "component tasting"—that is, using the standards created by combining neutral wines with everyday items to teach people to recognize different flavors and aromas. Then they move on to sniffing and tasting the wines.

In addition to her flavor research, Ann Noble teaches fledgling wine professionals. Among her courses at UC-Davis is the Basic Principles of Sensory Evaluation of Wine. She uses the aroma wheel and its accompanying standards to help students develop the tools of analysis. She calls it "aroma kindergarten" and likens it to giving young children crayons to learn the colors. It is truly amazing how quickly even the most inexperienced palates begin to pick up the flavors and aromas in wine after they're given some standards. In the case of white wine, students might practice with whiffs of pineapple, citrus, vanilla, clove, butter and bell pepper, then apply this experience to some wines, all the while concentrating and taking notes. Once they are practiced at detecting the taste components in wines, they can begin to discuss more inclusive concepts, such as balance and structure, moving on to increasingly qualitative judgments.

One of the best wine educators for my money is John Thoreen, wine director at Meadowood Resort in St. Helena, where he selects the wine list and teaches courses, many of them for corporate retreats or sales conferences. He has a delightful ability to make wine knowledge fun and accessible, and he's been at it for more than twenty-five years.

"My job is to help people relax about wine and develop a measure of confidence about their own palates," he says. "It's not my job to tell them what they should or shouldn't like. It *is* my job to get them to tell me what they see in a wine." John employs the Socratic method, which I also try to use in my courses, gently challenging students' perceptions, coaching them a bit if they're hesitant. He demonstrates the protocols of wine tasting, poking a little fun at them. He plays what he calls "wine games," for example serving two Chardonnays, brown-bagged, both good wines, one three times the retail price of the other. "Without the label, people are not so sure," he says. "They almost consistently go for the inexpensive wines. Now I choose pretty good inexpensive wines, but I also choose very good expensive wines."

John's introductory seminar is based on the principles of the great consultant, educator and author Emile Peynaud from the University of Bordeaux. It examines a wine's individual style by breaking it down into two important elements: structure and character. The equation is: Style in Wine = Structure + Character. John's basic worksheet begins:

"Style" in this context is a neutral term, not "stylish." All wines, like all people, have a style of one sort or another—assertive, quiet, dull, vivacious, generous, etc. Learning to understand wines is like learning to understand personalities and is equally subject to rash judgments.

Structure, according to the Thoreen-Peynaud approach, consists of three aspects: body (*gout sucre,* or "sweetness taste"), which is measured on a scale from watery through firm and generous to fat and heavy; acidity (*gout acide,* or "acid taste"), measured on a scale from flat through crisp and tart to green and shrill; and astringency (*gout amer,* or "bitterness"), measured from smooth through drying to bitter.

Character, according to this approach, is composed of color, aroma, bouquet and flavor. The aspects of character are:

Grape variety: Each variety has its own characteristics (John uses the analogy of different styles of dribbling a basketball).

Region ("Cabernet is not just Cabernet"): *Cabernet grown in the Pauillac commune of Bordeaux is distinct from the same grape grown on the Howell Mountain in Napa.*

Cooperage: Stainless-steel vats versus oak barrels.

Aging, winemaking techniques and character flaws

An example of a character description would be "Ripe strawberry, plum, black pepper and vanilla," while a structure description would be "Dry, full-bodied, smooth finish." Put the two together and you have a full profile of a wine's individual style. On the one hand, a wine can be elegant, restrained and refined; on the other, it can be rich and powerful.

The gist of this approach is that as a wine moves across our palate, it reveals a unique shape and texture. "The vocabulary of palatability is not mysterious," John says. "It's not cassis and a bit of rubber and a hint of vanilla. It's either full or astringent or sharp or soft. These are not mysterious words. I think that as much as people might say they love a certain wine and want to experience some more of its flavors, half of its taste is in fact that liquid structure. Flavors are important, but it's that feeling that you want to repeat."

"There can be a visceral enjoyment, an immediate satisfaction with wine. Everyone's on their own learning curve, essentially. As with any other sensory experience, the more that you fill in your background, the more gratification you can get from wine."—Scott Carney, Master Sommelier

TASTING WINES

If you lack confidence in your ability to taste wines, try this: Take a glass of good wine, something recommended by a trusted sommelier or wine merchant, and swirl it a bit. Then close your eyes and take a good whiff. (That's right, close your eyes. It's not an affectation but a way to focus and shut out distractions. Concentrating on what's in the glass is half the battle.) Ask yourself what you smell. If you can't articulate any aromas at first, don't worry. There's nothing wrong with you. It's just that you haven't yet established a solid link between the olfactory and the verbal centers of your brain. Think of it as blazing new trails in those synapses. These things take time.

Whether or not you have a specific answer to the question "What do you smell?" you are having a unique sensory experience. Close your eyes again, take another good whiff and concentrate, meditatively, on the aroma. Does it remind you of anything? It could be something as vague as "flowers" or "plants." Focus. Try to narrow it down. If it's flowers, can you say what kind? Is it roses? Great! You've just identified your first aroma in a wine and you're on your way to becoming a connoisseur.

THE TASTING SEQUENCE

Wine connoisseurs at all levels follow a basic tasting sequence that becomes second nature, like an airplane pilot's checklist before takeoff. Everyone should know the ritual. It can be executed with pomp and ceremony or discreetly, with quiet concentration. In any case, there's no need to be ostentatious about it. The goal is to get the most out of what's in your glass.

The sequence goes something like this: look, swirl, sniff,

taste, wait. Then do it again, with the same wine or, better yet, with another, side by side. There's nothing like a comparison to highlight the different qualities of two wines. At first, it's best to choose wines with a lot of contrast: for reds, that might mean a more powerful, spicy Syrah- or Zinfandel-based wine versus a lighter, fruitier Sangiovese or a Gamay-based one, or a Cabernet versus a Pinot Noir; for whites, it might be a smooth, luscious Chardonnay versus a light "vegetal" Sauvignon Blanc or a Riesling with some crisp acidity.

Given a glass of fine wine to describe, an inexperienced palate will very likely come up with something like, "That's very nice, I like it." With a second glass for comparison, you'll start hearing, "I like the first one because it's sweeter and it doesn't have such a strong aftertaste." Before long, they'll be smelling different berries or citrus fruits, even wet dog or sweaty old gym socks.

As with food, each wine tends to have a dominant characteristic, along with a number of other compatible but different ones. Seafood is salty, fruit is sweet, nuts are crunchy. The first step is to pick out that dominant trait. Is the wine sweet or acidic? Does it smell fruity or earthy? Is it light or heavy? Then we move on to other less obvious ones, some of them no more than momentary hints, to create an overall impression.

With experience, through trying many different new wines alone or in tandem, over a period of weeks, months, years, this process of tasting and assessing becomes automatic, as natural as reading the newspaper or getting dressed in the morning. The component tastes become familiar themes—like whistling your favorite tunes—easily recognizable across the tremendous range of vintages and varieties of wine.

Master Sommelier Larry Stone assesses a fine wine, which is showing off its "legs."

Visual Examination ("Look")

A wine's appearance can tell you a lot. First on the checklist is color. The best way to examine a wine is to hold the glass up against a white, well-lit background and tilt it carefully so the liquid is almost up to the rim. That way, you can see into and through it. In general, the darker the color, the riper and more concentrated the grapes, the heavier and more intense the wine's flavor.

Examine a glass of good Sangiovese and it looks ... well, red. Put the Sangiovese next to a Syrah and you've got a contrast that tells you much more. The Sangiovese looks *red* while the Syrah looks *purple*. An expert with an extensive mental catalog of wines can often guess the grape variety from color alone. An opaque, purplish color might indicate a full, ripe Zinfandel or Syrah-based wine while a bright, reddish ruby, more translucent color would indicate a young fruity wine such as Beaujolais.

A wine's color also mellows with age. Red turns to brick or reddish brown while greenish yellow changes to a deeper yellowish-gold. In a visual comparison you can usually tell right away which is the older vintage.

You can also check a wine's clarity. If there are any particles floating in the solution or if it's somewhat opaque, it probably just means it's unfiltered and unfined, which can be a plus in terms of added flavors or aromas.

Once you've tilted the glass once or twice and taken note of the color, bring it back to an upright position and take a good look at how the wine drips down the side of the glass in "tears" or "legs." This is a good indicator of the wine's viscosity. The bigger and slower the tears, the thicker and sweeter the wine. With fast tears or none at all—possibly just a smooth, thin coating on the inside of the glass—you can expect a lighter, fresher, drier wine.

COLOR TRICKS

ONE OF THE FIRST THINGS WE TALK ABOUT IN MY WINE-TASTING CLASSES IS COLOR. IF YOU WANT TO BLUFF YOUR WAY THROUGH A BLIND TASTING, ONE OF THE EASIEST TRICKS IS TO JUDGE A WINE'S AGE BY ITS COLOR. IF IT'S PURPLE, YOU CAN BE SURE IT'S LESS THAN THREE YEARS OLD. IF IT'S GARNET, IT'S THREE TO SIX YEARS OLD. ONCE IT TURNS TO RUBY AND THEN EVOLVES TOWARD MAHOGANY, IT'S SIX TO TEN OR MORE YEARS OLD. ANOTHER FOOLPROOF TRICK FOR JUDGING A WINE'S AGE IS TO COVER THE TOP OF YOUR GLASS WITH YOUR HAND, SHAKE VIGOROUSLY AND CHECK THE FOAM. IF IT'S WHITE, TOTALLY LACKING IN PIGMENT, THEN THE WINE IS OVER TEN YEARS OLD. IF IT HAS ANY PIGMENT, IT'S UNDER TEN. YOU CAN WAGER IMMENSE AMOUNTS OF MONEY ON THIS AND USE YOUR WINNINGS TO START ACQUIRING A WINE COLLECTION.

Aroma ("Swirl and Sniff")

As Jim Morrison said, this is the best part of the trip.

In preparation for taking that first delicious whiff, swirl the wine in the glass. The best way is to hold the stem or base of the glass and carefully rotate it so as not to spill any of the precious liquid. It's easiest to perform this trick on a table or other smooth flat surface but it's also possible to do it in midair. Once you get the hang of it, you can do it pretty fast and furiously. Most experienced wine lovers do it unconsciously. If you see somebody sitting in a cafe swirling their glass of lemonade as they stare off into space, it's a good bet you could strike up a conversation with them about wine.

Swirling agitates the wine, bringing much more of its volatile, smellable components into contact with the air. Ann Noble compares it to turning up the volume on the TV. She "cheats" all the time by clamping disposable plastic petrie dish lids on top of wineglasses and shaking them, which generates even more aroma. Then she can close the lids down to trap the aromas while she takes notes, lectures or does comparison tastings. Some people use their hands for this, but this is very risky since any traces of soap or other materials left on your palm can foul up the wine.

Once you've swirled, close your eyes and take a good breathful of the wine. Some tasters like to sniff delicately at first, then take in progressively larger whiffs. Everyone develops their own technique, but the main thing is to get at least one good whiff. Don't be bashful, stick your nose right in that glass. Take as much time as you need to meditate on the aroma. Go back to it as many times as necessary. Remember, fine wines change in the glass, over a period of seconds, minutes and sometimes even hours. The best ones open up in the glass like a peacock opening up his feathers, and you don't ever want to miss the show.

In wine circles, you may hear discussions about aroma versus bouquet. Wine experts generally say that aroma comes from the grapes but can also be attributable to winemaking techniques whereas bouquet comes from bottle age. I've heard bouquet defined simply as aromas that come with aging. It's a rather precious distinction, though, one that doesn't really apply to everyday discussions of wine. I like Ann Noble's attitude: "Telling the consumer 'You've got to be concerned about aroma versus bouquet' is baloney. Smell the berry, smell the oak, just get used to smelling it. Once you have those

building blocks then go back and look at the pattern, which is that most of the fruity aromas come from the grape and the oak characteristics—clove, vanilla, smokiness—come from the barrel. The soy, tobacco and so forth is what comes from aging. If you want to call that bouquet, fine."

Tasting the Wine ("Taste")

Now it's time to put it in your mouth. Take a decent size sip or small gulp, once again taking your time. Professional tasters slosh the wine around in their mouths or "chew" it, the exaggerated version of which causes all kinds of funny jaw palpitations and pinched facial expressions. Another fairly bizarre technique they use to make sure they're not missing anything is to hold the wine in their mouth, open their lips slightly and suck in some air. This often causes a series of slurping sounds, the kind your mother used to scold you about when you were trying to suck up those last few drops of your milk shake. (Recommendation: If you've never done it, practice first with water to avoid staining your clothes.)

Though it might seem comical, all this sloshing and slurping has a purpose. First, sucking in air has the same effect as swirling the glass. It aerates the wine, allowing you to pick up more of its aromas "retronasally"—that is, through the nasal passage at the back of your throat. Our relatively limited sense of taste relies heavily on our far more sophisticated sense of smell. If you've ever had to dine out at a fine restaurant when you had a head cold, you discovered very quickly how important the sense of smell is to taste. While everyone is raving about their dishes, all you can detect is a blob of texture in your mouth. Depending on which expert you consult, aroma accounts for between 60 and 80 percent of our sensory appreciation of wine.

Italian winemaker Silvio Jermann delivers a fascinating
discourse as we prepare to taste one of his many wines.

Sloshing or "chewing" the wine also spreads it all over your palate so you get the full taste experience. The taste buds that primarily detect bitterness are on top in the back of the tongue, the ones for sourness are on the sides and the ones for sweetness are on the tip. You can't actually smell sweetness, but you can taste it right away. Try creating a standard by dissolving half a teaspoon of sugar in a glass of water. There's no smell, but there is a distinct taste. It's just as easy to taste acidity.

Sweetness in wine reflects the amount of alcohol and/or residual sugar left over from the ripened grapes. Sourness stems from their natural acidity. Tannins are perceived as slightly bitter tasting. If you've ever experienced that dryish aftertaste on drinking a good strong cup of tea, that's another manifestation of tannins. The traditional view is that the astringent, somewhat bitter tannins are necessary in wine. They act as preservatives and slowly develop softer, more complex and interesting flavors and sensations with bottle age. In the New Wine Revolution, the view is that sweet, ripe tannins can be present in a wine from the beginning, avoiding that harshness while still guaranteeing aging potential. I like that. Why not have it both ways?

Because of the aforementioned complex of sensations, many flavor scientists use the term "flavor by mouth" rather than "taste." Taste is limited to what we can perceive on our tongues whereas "flavor by mouth" encompasses the whole range of perceptions in and around our mouths, including taste, retronasal aroma and "mouth feel." Different wines offer different degrees of sensations. Some have it all: loads of aroma, tremendous flavor by mouth, a persistent taste and a lingering mouth feel.

Mouth feel involves perceptions of the wine's texture and weight. Holding the wine in your mouth allows you to experience the full range of these sensations. First, you might feel the wine's thickness or viscosity, its syrupy weight or body, which indicates both the intensity of flavor and the level of alcohol. Alcohol can also bring a hot or burning sensation to the palate. Another aspect of mouth feel is the pleasant prickly sensation from bubbles of carbon dioxide, which is obvious in sparkling wines but is also present, quite subtly, in many other wines, particularly whites. Farther along that spectrum is a puckering sensation of acidity. Finally, there's astringency, that drying sensation from the tannins.

TO SPIT OR NOT TO SPIT

THE DECISION ABOUT THIS IMPORTANT ISSUE IS LARGELY A QUESTION OF PERSONAL PREFERENCE WITH AN ELEMENT OF COMMON SENSE. ANY ORGANIZED OR PROFESSIONAL TASTING WILL PROVIDE RECEPTACLES AND IT'S NEVER CONSIDERED RUDE IN THIS CONTEXT. I'D RATHER AVOID IT BECAUSE I LIKE TO DRINK THE WINE. BUT IF YOU'RE PLANNING ON TASTING FIFTY WINES AND YOU'VE GOT TO DRIVE HOME, YOU SHOULD DEFINITELY SPIT.

> **"I find that more often people are looking for an intensity of flavor. How it hits you. I look for the balance. It doesn't have to be that intense. It has to have acidity in the fruit and it has to have tannins. They all have to be very balanced . . . The other thing that's extremely important is the finish. Of course, it has to be a pleasant finish, but also a very long finish. The wine doesn't want to quit your mouth and is continuously saying goodbye to you. Those aftertastes to me are some of the greatest experiences in wine because they can be so lingering."** —Bipin Desai, theoretical physicist and wine collector

John Thoreen likes to use kitchen images to explain the concepts of taste and mouth feel. For body, he uses the analogy of butterfat in milk. Anyone who's a milk drinker understands immediately. Most people have a strong preference between skim milk and whole milk. "If they like the thin, blue, watery, anemic stuff, they gag on whole milk and vice versa," John says. "In wine, the body comes from the alcohol. Alcohol is the sort of butter fat of wine."

Once you've had a good taste of the wine in your mouth, it's time to spit or swallow. Then you wait to see if it has a "finish." In plain English, this is the aftertaste. There are two important questions about the finish: How long does it linger? What sort of different sensations does it deliver? Don't think that just because the wine is no longer in contact with your taste buds it can't continue to amuse and beguile you. Keep paying attention; great wines will linger anywhere from twenty seconds to two or three minutes and their tastes may continue to evolve all the while.

BALANCE, COMPLEXITY AND STRUCTURE

As in any sensual equation, a balance of contrasting elements is the key to perfection. Once that balance is achieved, much of a wine's distinct character is determined by how those scales are tipped ever so slightly.

Balance is a matter of judgment that always borders on opinion. If one side of the seesaw's on the ground, that's easy to judge. As it approaches the middle, it becomes more subjective. If a wine were purely sweet, you'd have a gloppy, syrupy mess. If it were totally acid you'd have . . . vinegar! With finer wines, there's more opinion involved because they don't tip the scales very far in either direction.

Sweeter wines should have a balance of acid. Acidic wines need a balance of sweetness; tannic ones, too, need a balance of sweetness. Anytime one particular element becomes too prominent, the wine can be said to be out of balance. Yet there's always the element of personal preference. My taste in lemonade might run to two lemons squeezed per glass with a pinch of sugar, while you might want half a lemon and two heaping tablespoons of sugar. And both of us would be right.

One very important point to bear in mind: Among the world's finest wines, even the sweet ones (Sauternes, the German Trockenbeerenauslese, Hungarian Tokay) are very well balanced; they might have much more sugar than other wines, but they also have a strong component of fruity tartness or acidity to balance all that sweetness.

Once you have a firm grasp of the building blocks of analysis—an ability to pick out and discern flavors and aromas—you can put them all together and determine whether the wine has complexity (a lot of blocks) and structure (a discernible pattern of blocks). Complexity is a matter of finding—or the wine delivering—many different aromas, tastes and sensations. Discussions of

structure involve opinion and personal preference, and lead to related concepts such as balance and harmony. Do you like the way the blocks are stacked? Do you find the pattern pleasing?

THE LANGUAGE OF WINE

The language of wine—some prefer to use the Orwellian term *winespeak*—runs the gamut from the serious to the sublime, from the humble to the absurd, from the flower garden to the barnyard. Since there is no unique wine vocabulary, no words that actually describe the smell of wine, we can only describe it by analogy: It smells like something else.

When the novice takes that first sniff from the glass and says, "It smells like wine," he's right. The aroma of wine is complex and unlike any other. Each of the world's great wines has a unique signature. Château Margaux smells like Château Margaux, Grace Family like Grace Family and so on. Experts can identify the famous ones instantaneously just by taking a whiff as surely as a sports car buff can recognize the whiny roar of a Porsche engine without turning his head. They can also pick out many separate components and, if they so choose, pontificate endlessly.

It's easy to ridicule pompous, overblown wine descriptions; some of them make me want to collapse in peals of laughter, others to ball the paper up and toss it in the garbage. I read an article in the excellent British magazine *Decanter* a few years ago in which one of its distinguished columnists defended, tongue-in-cheek, the use of the descriptor "hamster cages" for a certain immature Hermitage. Winespeak *can* easily go over the top, but even then it can still be fun.

Ultimately, the point is that all this verbiage can be useful and informative, but also that it shouldn't be taken too seriously.

It's important to be able to separate the two main categories of wine description: objective (quantitative or analytical) and subjective (qualitative or interpretive). When a wine is described as smelling like a fruit, a vegetable, a solvent or even a barnyard odor, that perception is based on objective analysis. When it's described as complex, balanced and harmonious, that's an interpretation.

Part of the wine writer's stock-in-trade is to be highly subjective and opinionated. Their challenge is to sell themselves and to hold their readers' interest. Among the pitfalls of wine description is the tendency to compile long, monotonous grocery lists of fruits, vegetables and other items off the shelf.

I thoroughly endorse any moves toward putting winespeak description in plain English. When you read a phrase like "layers and layers of complexity" you might wonder where those layers are—inside the writer's head? That particular phrase probably translates into "every time he smelled the wine it was different." Professor Noble, who likes to debunk any sort of pretentiousness, recalls once coming across the phrase "prismatic luminescence" to describe a wine. She points out that "Pours well" probably means the same thing, it's just a lot less poetic. I don't believe we should rule out poetry, but I do want to avoid obfuscation. The best poetry has an elegance of expression that makes it easy to enjoy, if not simple to understand. The same should be true of wine description.

WINESPEAK IN PLAIN ENGLISH

ATTACK
The first flavor that hits you when you put that wine in your mouth.

BALANCE
A main attribute of structure, but very subjective.

BODY
The weight of the alcohol on the palate and also the amount of flavor the wine delivers.

COMPLEXITY
When there are a lot of flavors and aromas in a wine; you often hear the phrase "there's a lot going on in there" as the taster's eyes light up or he gazes admiringly into the glass of wine.

ELEGANCE
Like "refinement," a term denoting subtlety and restraint.

EVOLUTION
How the wine's flavor changes in the glass or in your mouth.

EXTRACT
To say a wine has "a lot of extract" means that it contains a good measure of the solids from the grape; an analogy would be to squeeze a tea bag to inject more flavor into the liquid.

HARMONY
All the different components are well integrated.

REFINEMENT
Subtlety of aromas and flavors; the wine doesn't hit you over the head or shout at you.

RICHNESS
Like body, a judgment of the weight and/or volume of aromas and flavors.

STRUCTURE
How a wine is put together. Does it have a number of components and are they in balance?

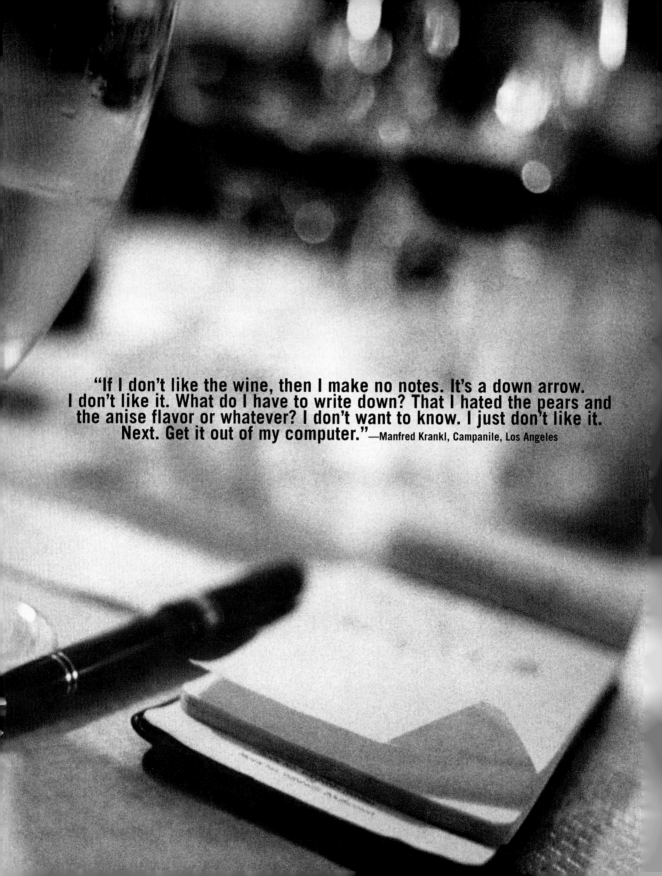

"If I don't like the wine, then I make no notes. It's a down arrow. I don't like it. What do I have to write down? That I hated the pears and the anise flavor or whatever? I don't want to know. I just don't like it. Next. Get it out of my computer."—Manfred Krankl, Campanile, Los Angeles

WINE AND MEMORY: TO SCRIBBLE OR NOT TO SCRIBBLE

Once you've mastered the basic tasting sequence, there are times when you may want to record your impressions. If you want to develop your palate by comparing the wine you're currently tasting to those you've tasted in the past, then you have either got to remember past tastings or have written them down.

With notes, as with anything else in wine, there is a broad range of practices. Some people take copious notes and put a lot of time and effort into their filing systems. Some just jot down a few quick impressions, maybe one or two descriptors after each stage of the tasting sequence. Others use shorthand, musical notes, even coded symbols or hieroglyphics of their own devising. I hardly ever take notes anymore, although I used to. I found that a life with wine and my enduring love for the world's finest beverage has been enough incentive to remember all the wines I *need* to remember. If you love something, you remember it. A particular time, a particular place, a particular glass or bottle of wine constitutes a memory. I decided that if I couldn't remember a wine, then it probably wasn't worth remembering.

Tasting a wine often triggers a Proustian moment. All of the sights and sounds and tastes and feelings of a lost moment in time come flooding back from the recesses of your memory. This is yet another reason to take your time and savor that glass of wine before you start scribbling. Who knows what poignant memories it might trigger? Why risk missing out on such a moment by jumping right into an analysis? Let the aroma and taste of the wine wash over your soul first, let it talk to you and take your mind where it will go. And only then take notes if you like.

Wine-tasting notes, in my estimation, should be like a Woody Allen movie. They should give you a feeling of spontaneity as if you're eavesdropping on someone else's conversation. They aren't a graph or a matrix; they don't need to be structured like some company report or investment prospectus. Like a snippet of that conversation from the next table, the notes should sum up the occasion, the food and the enjoyment of the wine.

It's important to remember who the audience for a given set of notes will be. If you're just jotting down reminders for yourself, you can probably get away with shorthand. Anyone who's in the business—importers, distributors, merchants—has to toe a fine line between selling their wines, making their product stand out from the pack and blatant hyperbole. Robert Parker's notes shout. Some might argue that his volume is monotonously high. But who can argue with his enthusiasm or his remarkably sharp perceptions? Some wine description is pure shill, carnival barking. That's fine, too, as long as its audience can see through all the hype.

In your tasting notes, even if you're a beginner, it helps to think first of what you actually perceive in the wine and second what you think of it. Separate the subjective from the objective. Be as outrageously opinionated as you like, have *fun* with it. But let's not deny that there are certain standards and parameters.

I like my friend Al Stewart's approach to notes. His are short, subjective, emotive; they give his opinion of the moment and are set up for historical reference. In other words, he can go back to them years later and compare how a wine tastes *now* to how it tasted *then*.

Here's a tasting note from the first time Al ever had 1982 Château Cheval-Blanc, March 5, 1985: "Huge, thick, very dark, fragrant, amazingly drinkable, monumental wine, will be very great indeed." He was right. It's now a wine most collectors would kill for, very rare, one of the all-time greats.

Here's a note on a 1982 Haut-Brion Blanc from 1985: "Fifty percent Sémillon gives a creamy edge to the Sauvignon Blanc. A very fine wine and after six tastings a favorite. Great nose, restrained power and very accessible now."

Contrast Al's terse, personal notes, intended for his own reference with the Château Cheval-Blanc's notes on its 1990 wine and on Petit Cheval (its second-tier wine):

Petit Cheval: Very deep, intense, attractive red color. Compact, concentrated nose that is already opening up, with hints of candied fruit and prunes. Just the right amount of oak and toastiness. An altogether exotic bouquet.

Overripe fruit, cherry and cocoa on the palate. Considerable richness and concentration with lots of tannin. Fine, long, aromatic aftertaste.

Cheval-Blanc: Deep, dark, intense color showing a touch of age.

The bouquet is remarkably concentrated and complex. There are hints of overripeness (candied fruit) and roasted almond and cocoa. There is a creamy quality, with a touch of caramel and vanilla, as well as a spicy side, with black pepper. Manages to be both powerful and elegant.

On the palate, 1990 Cheval-Blanc is beautifully rich, with round, velvety tannin. It is quite flavorsome: toast, coffee and caramel and a pinch of liquorice at

the end. The aftertaste is warm and exceptionally long. Still young, but already irresistible. An unqualified success.

There is some hype here. Of course, the château isn't going to say anything bad about its own wines. The 1990 vintage, however, is considered one of this century's best, so a certain amount of hype is appropriate. It's interesting to note how these more comprehensive notes separate the "nose," or "bouquet" (aroma), from the "palate" (flavor by mouth). Is it possible that so many flavors could be detected in a single wine? If you keep in mind that Cheval-Blanc is a complex wine that's been studied carefully over the years by many critics and admirers, and that the château relies on a number of tasters to detect all these components, it's not as far-fetched as it may seem.

Still another approach is reflected in winemaker Bo Barrett's tasting notes on his 1994 Château Montelena Zinfandel, written on release in 1997, after a year of oak aging and a year of bottle aging:

Our 1994 Zin has a nice dark-garnet color and is bright all the way to the edge of the glass. The nose is nice, ripe Zinfandel berry fruit with a smoky-briary spice. On the palate it has a nice open entry of bright fruit that follows the nose. Fat and spicy Zin flavors dominate a round mid-palate which has a moderate weight. By "moderate weight" I mean that it has good red wine "grip"—lots of juicy bold flavors but not too tannic. It's naturally somewhat youthful now and would like to see a couple more years of bottle aging for all the complexity to develop. To summarize, it is a tasty, medium-weight red wine with big, deep flavors, but not massive. We enjoy the Zin with a wide range of foods, from grilled fish to spicy BBQ and everything in between.

Note the informal (California), optimistic (selling) tone to these notes. Also note they follow the basic tasting sequence. They don't mention finish but they do take into account Peynaud's criteria of attack and weight on the palate.

I belong to a Friday tasting group, the local chapter of Les Sauvages du Vin. We've had a lot of fun over the years, with tastings every two to four weeks that start over lunch at an area restaurant or in the private dining room at The Wine Merchant and often last well into the afternoon. It's a great group with a fun, lively spirit that tastes a lot of serious wines but doesn't take anything too seriously. Our notes are generally concise and informal, a consensus of comments from around the table. A few examples:

From September 27, 1996, the 1989 Château Haut-Brion: "This wine won the day! Complex—smoky, cassis, tobacco and minerally. Tremendous depth. Incredible."

From May 30, 1997, the 1993 Castello di Ama, Chianti Classico DOCG, Vigneto San Lorenzo: "This wine exhibited greater fruit than the first bottle [a Brunello di Montalcino]. It was rich and plummy and very, very drinkable. It had a silky quality."

From June 20, 1997, the 1990 Guigal Hermitage AC: "Here was a powerful, full-bodied wine with peppery crushed fruits, concentrated, with firm tannins that gave it a velvety quality."

From August 29, 1997, the 1987 Geyser Peak Reserve Alexandre (Meritage), Alexander Valley AVA: "This was a giant, round very smooth cuvée with ripe black currant in the nose and deep flavor. It was well structured and intense."

Generally, we try to taste good wines, but there is the occasional disappointment, in which case we don't pull any punches. A few examples:

From June 5, 1998, the 1984 Jordan Cabernet Sauvignon, Alexander Valley AVA: "This old bottle was DOA. The color alone signaled 'bad taste.' I've enjoyed young Jordan but don't hold it if you have it."

From the same tasting, the 1984 Bellerose Cuvée (Cabernet Sauvignon, Merlot, Cabernet Franc), Sonoma: "Fruit was long gone and only a mouthful of astringent liquid remained. Pucker up baby, where's the wine? I've had this Bordeaux style when it was much better."

And finally, again from that June afternoon, the 1984 Diamond Creek Volcanic Hill Cabernet Sauvignon, Napa Valley AVA: "A disappointing bottle. Lots of astringency but little fruit. This was apparently a highly respected wine which defined California Cabernets in the seventies and early eighties."

"Every wine, like every person, has a style that is describable."
—John Thoreen, The Wine Tutor and Wine Director, Meadowood Resort, St. Helena, Calif.

WINE

GROUP PSYCHOLOGY

Wine demands a witness. It is meant to be shared. Sipping a glass of fine wine and conversing with friends is one of life's great pleasures. What would be the point of drinking a bottle of '47 Cheval-Blanc alone? You would be robbing not only yourself but also those with whom you would drink it of a real treasure. So, whenever possible, conduct your tastings with some friends.

Getting together for a wine tasting, no matter what the degree of formality, is a special treat for wine lovers and connoisseurs alike. Not only is it the perfect occasion to socialize with like-minded people, but it's a chance to exchange wine knowledge, to share experiences. Even after years in the business, I approach every wine-related event knowing there's a good chance it will be an eye-opener.

There is, however, a danger connected with group tastings that can easily be avoided with a little common sense and etiquette. The people with the loudest voices, the strongest opinions, the most perceived expertise can drown out the others. It's why I *never* give my opinion first in a wine-tasting, particularly at a class. The participants should always be given time to scribble their notes, or at least to formulate their impressions and opinions, before anyone blurts theirs out. Even a few "oohs" and "aahs," as well meaning as they may be, can influence someone's opinion or cause them to stifle an interesting comment. Be aware that you can affect other people's perceptions just as they can affect yours. Activate your poker face. A good rule of thumb is don't volunteer an opinion, not even so much as a raised eyebrow, until someone has asked you what you think. And always defer to your host or the organizer of the tasting. It's simply proper etiquette.

(Of course, there are exceptions to every rule. On some occasions, it is perfectly all right to utter a yelp of surprise or to jump with joy. Obviously, the less formal the occasion, the closer the friends, the more people there are, the less attention everyone's paying, the more demonstrative the responses can be. Sheer, unbridled enthusiasm has its time and place.)

If one's impressions or opinions are well considered and genuine, they are hardly ever wrong. If someone doesn't like one of my favorites, a wine I *know* is great, such as Ausone or Cheval-Blanc, I disagree but am still curious to hear their reasons.

The psychological factor is extremely important in tastings of all kinds. There's a famous question you'll hear repeated in enological circles: Why do wines always seem to taste better in their place of origin? Due to innovations such as refrigerated containers and careful shipping and warehousing practices, we've all but eliminated damage in transit. So why do Aunt Irma and Uncle Harry come back from their Italian holiday, try the same wines at your table and invariably say, "The wine tasted better over there"? As my friend Manfred Krankl, proprietor of Campanile restaurant in Los Angeles, told me, "If I were sitting outside on the porch in La Morra with Elio Altare and his *mamma* eating prosciutto, they could serve me warm dishwater and it would taste great!" Ambience. Occasion. Company. Who can account for the sum total of their effects?

By the same token, I would hate to admit that my mood, my feelings toward certain individuals, or even what I ate for lunch, can affect my judgment of the wines I select for my customers. But at times it's true, and it's one reason experience is so crucial, why we need to keep tasting

"I think there is a generation of people coming into the business that's interested in sharing what they know. There is a sense of the communal in and around wine. There's a saying that you never meet stingy wine collectors because wine collecting is really about sharing with people and getting jazzed by what you're tasting. I've found a great amount of generosity in the people that I've met in the business." —Scott Carney, Master Sommelier

the same wines over and over again. The scientist who takes one measurement and is satisfied isn't much of a scientist. Likewise, how closely should we rely on numerical ratings that are based on one tasting of a given vintage of a certain wine?

The particle physicist and great wine connoisseur Bipin Desai points out that in blind comparisons it's simply human nature to look for differences rather than similarities. Could two glasses of wine ever be identical? Bipin recalls blind tastings where he's poured the same wine at the beginning and at the end. Invariably, the glass of Wine A served in the last flight always beats out Wine A served in the first flight, as people naturally assume that the best wines are being saved for last.

Wine professionals get together for tastings all the time. They can be lavish promotional events put on by trade organizations or distributors trying to sell their portfolios of wines. They can be tastings for journalists to showcase the wines of a country or region. They may be held in connection with an auction or they can be casual groups of winemakers trying each other's wines or wines of other producers and regions. One of the most compelling things about wine is that it highlights the significance of individual preference while at the same time providing a lot of common ground for shared enjoyment. People who taste together on a regular basis get to know each other's palates.

There are all kinds of opportunities and excuses for getting together with friends or colleagues to taste wines. There are a lot of wonderful clubs, public wine tastings, conventions and festivals (the Oregon Pinot Noir Festival is an excellent example). But the ones I like best are "civilian" tastings over a meal with friends. That way you can focus on enjoying several wines with food, which is how they're meant to be enjoyed, and not become overwhelmed by the huge number of wines usually presented at large-scale commercial events. I've been to plenty of tastings where more than a hundred wines

have been poured. Usually I'll go home with just four or five impressions and the rest is a blur. There may have been forty or fifty great wines, but I missed out on most of them, which is a shame. It's more important to have a depth of feeling, to experience, say, five or ten wines at a tasting—or two or three at a dinner party—than a dizzying kaleidoscope of fifty to one hundred.

Quick comparative tastings can be very deceptive. The flashier wines will overpower the more subtle ones. A big Zinfandel will easily outwrestle nine other less muscular but equally delicious wines at a tasting, but when you take it home and try to finish a bottle over dinner, you'll find it's just too much. Then, a quieter, more moderate taste is what's called for.

The bottom line regarding tasting is to share the wine experience—the stimulation, the conversation, the excitement—respect your own impressions and those of others and have fun. (For some thoughts on how to organize a tasting, please refer to Chapter 6.)

THE PROBLEM WITH NUMBERS: RATINGS AND VINTAGE CHARTS

People are looking for something to hang their hat on, to banish their insecurities, to save them some time and effort. Unfortunately, this means they're also avoiding the challenge and the adventure of making their own choices. Naturally, with our busy workloads and the general information overload in modern society, it's easier to follow numerical ratings or vintage charts.

The fact is that the determination of a wine's quality is largely subjective. It goes back to the distinction between *testing* and *tasting*. To imply that wines can be scientifically tested for quality is misleading. Wines are lab-tested during production for levels of alcohol, phenolics and other extracted compounds, but the amounts and combinations that indicate superior quality defy measurement or prediction. Wine ratings—numerical or otherwise—are based on the opinions of professional

> *"I trust my own palate now more than ever before. Because once you've had a rainbow of tastes and exposure to wine, you really develop a sense of what you like. There were wines I thought I must like and I didn't like. It just happened. Some wines I had to work so damn hard that they tired me out."* —Wolfgang Grunwald, collector

tasters. Granted, they have highly developed palates and vast experience, but the bottom line is that wine is not a quantifiable product. Their ratings will always reflect *their* palates, not yours.

I have nothing against Robert Parker or *The Wine Spectator,* Hugh Johnson or Stephen Tanzer. Parker is tireless, an excellent writer with a superb palate, deserving every bit of his hard-earned success. The Johnsons, the *Wine Spectator,* the Tanzers deserve equal kudos. It's hard work trying all those wines and coming up with something interesting to say about every single one.

If you care enough about wines to spend the time and learn something about them, ratings and charts are a crutch you don't really need. You need to rely on your own unique sense of taste, form your own opinions and develop your palate. If we blindly follow the numbers or buy only those wines we've seen recommended in the press, we're robbing ourselves of the opportunity for so many delicious surprises. If you take some chances, you are going to make mistakes. But the thrill of the big hits will far outweigh the disappointment of the misses.

This is not to say you should disregard the opinions of experts altogether. But they shouldn't be your only guidepost. Develop a variety of information sources on new and interesting wines: work with your merchant, stay in touch with fellow wine enthusiasts, surf the web, put your name on mailing lists. Make your choices, taste the wines, take notes. Then and only then compare your opinions to the expert ratings. Compare your preferences to Parker's; if they're the same nine out of ten times, then you happen to have a similar palate to one of the world's greatest wine experts and promoters. If your preferences are different, then *vive la différence.* You may find, for example, that you can follow a Parker recommendation for a Bordeaux or a California Cab, but that he gives much lower ratings to wines from another region, say, Provence or the Languedoc in France, wines that you find absolutely delicious. Everyone has their biases—in grape varieties, in growing regions, in winemaking styles.

The biggest danger is when wines start to be made to score points, when the journalistic powers-that-be start to dictate taste. Certain wines are made to please the critics (*Wine Spectator, Wine Enthusiast,* etc.); they consistently score around 90-plus points and that becomes the producer's biggest marketing tool. The unfortunate result: homogenization. If you took twenty of Robert Parker's top-rated wines—all in the 94 to 98 range—and did a blind taste test with some of the world's top wine experts, even they would be hard put to tell those twenty wines apart.

Vintage charts can be as problematic as numerical ratings. I go back to the experience I had with Ted Lemon's 1993 Littorai One Acre Pinot Noir. Had we been following someone else's vintage chart, that's a wine we probably would have ignored. Instead, we had a blow-your-socks-off experience.

It's tempting to dismiss certain vintages categorically. The word goes out: 1993 was a bad year for California wines. Yet it's really not possible to generalize about a vintage across the different grape varieties and microclimates of a given winegrowing region. It's when we fall into that trap that we miss out on some really special, and often very reasonably priced, wines. Again, the solution is to take a little more time, do a little more research, ask a few more questions. Ultimately, that's how you become a connoisseur: by increasing your knowledge.

Chapter Four

BUYING WITH CONFIDENCE

AT THE WINE MERCHANT, BEVERLY HILLS, OUR GOAL IS TO HELP PEOPLE COMPLETELY INTEGRATE THE SOPHISTICATION AND PLEASURE OF FINE WINES INTO THEIR EVERYDAY LIVES. WE ARE SELLING WINES BUT WE ARE ALSO SELLING A LIFESTYLE.

In this chapter I present some guidelines and standards to boost your confidence in the all-important step of acquisition. Among other topics, I'll discuss what to expect from a merchant and from a restaurant, how to read a label, how to deal with high prices and shortages, when to send a wine back. Once you put this together with the tasting skills from the previous chapter and accumulate some experience, you'll have earned the right to call yourself a true connoisseur.

First, a few words about the total wine experience and how we try to provide it at The Wine Merchant, Beverly Hills.

As The Wine Merchant, I see myself as a facilitator. I help people learn about wine. I help them procure the wines they want and introduce them to the wine lifestyle. It's not enough simply to be a wine purveyor. Wine shouldn't stand alone. It should be part and parcel of a lifestyle. When customers come into my store, I want them to walk out with a great bottle of wine but also with a wine experience. I want to expose them to all the lore, the anecdotes, the richness and variety of the wine world.

The moment a potential customer walks into the shop, I want him to be totally attuned to his senses, ready to enjoy wine fully. That's why we place so much emphasis on "atmosphere." It's that extra attention to detail that makes the difference.

Although I don't claim to be a big innovator, I'd like to think I've been able to survive for over a quarter of a century because I've stayed on the cutting edge. Like any merchant, I'm in business to make money. At the same time, I believe there are no bargains in life. My philosophy is that you must always raise the standards. This requires serious investments of time and money.

I'm constantly looking for vintners, winemakers and restaurateurs who share this view because they are the ones who deliver quality.

As merchants, we realized a number of years ago that we had to choose one of two routes. Either stack the cases high in a warehouse-type environment and beat the competition on price alone, or take the Hollywood approach. The latter was really the only one that made sense in Beverly Hills. So we built our own little motion picture set at 9701 South Santa Monica Boulevard. It's a fantasy oasis, a Disneyland for wine lovers. The goal is to evoke what many winemakers call "the wow response." We want first-timers to walk into the shop and pause for a moment with the idea that they could have some serious fun here—taste some *serious* wines and have some real *fun* with it.

We designed the interior of the shop to look like an exclusive London men's club, circa 1925. We added a wine and cigar bar, then a rustic "male clubhouse" called The Lodge that has bear rugs and big-game trophies mounted on the walls, where patrons can enjoy a drink and watch sporting events via satellite on large-screen televisions. For more intimate gatherings, there are several private party rooms including one I call the Havana Room, which captures the aura of Cuba's capital, circa 1957. Above the wine bar are balcony lounges where private parties can tuck themselves away while still gazing down at the action below. Hidden away in the basement, near the climate-controlled storage lockers, is the Proprietor's Room for VIP parties.

At six o'clock in the evening, the curtains come down in the windows and the shop transforms itself into a nightclub. We have a piano bar and jazz singers. I want our patrons to feel as if Sydney Greenstreet could stroll into the joint at any moment.

BUYING WINE IN A STORE

There are plenty of people in Hollywood who are relative wine novices. There are also plenty of longtime residents who are pretty jaded; they've had more than their share of the great 1945 or 1961 first growths. No matter who they are, we want our customers to enjoy the total experience. Part of that is showmanship, a little P. T. Barnum if you will.

I like to share wines. Period. I get a lot of vicarious pleasure out of turning customers on to a few good, even great, bottles of wine. I'm simply sharing with them something I love and I'm excited about. If you give them a taste of the wine experience, make it special, they will come back. Wine is meant to be shared and enjoyed. It is not simply a commodity to be traded for the purpose of making money.

Whether it's the first time they are walking into the store or they're a longtime "regular," the first thing we try to do at The Wine Merchant is get a customer excited about wine. To begin with, we have to select the finest wines; then we have to help our customers focus. Once they're concentrating on the wine, we can start a conversation.

It doesn't matter if it's Keanu Reeves just off the set of his latest film or Joe Smith from Podunk, Iowa, the first thing I tell my customer is to relax. Forget about the frantic pace, the distractions, the 8 A.M. client meeting, lunch with your agent, dinner with your producer, picking the kids up at soccer practice. Once you are relaxed and focused, my job becomes easy: I don't have to seduce anybody with scintillating conversation or clever anecdotes. I've got one of the best products in the world, so I let it do the talking. The substance of our conversation is right there in that glass. I might open with the question "What do you like?" If the answer is something refreshingly cool and fizzy, then I'll reach for a bottle of my favorite bubbly, say a nice chilled Brut Champagne from a reliable producer such as Taittinger. If the answer is something rich and full of ripe fruit, then maybe I'll go for a bottle of Bordeaux from St.-Emilion, with its velvety soft component of Merlot.

If the customer's a complete novice or simply can't put their preference into words, then we can really have some fun. I can pull a bottle of one of my personal favorites off the shelf. We start there. If he or she likes that one, then we move on to comparisons with similar wines; if not, we try something different. We've established a benchmark, the basis for a conversation that might last for weeks, months or even years.

My feeling is that the wine shop of the future is a full-service establishment, something like what we're trying to achieve at The Wine Merchant. It's a concept embodied by the Italian *enoteca,* which is a highly civilized institution that is a combination merchant and wine bar that dates back to Renaissance Florence. I believe customers should have the opportunity to taste wines before they buy them. I remember not so long ago when music stores introduced the little kiosks with headphones where customers could sample recordings before buying them. It's one of those ideas that makes you wonder why somebody didn't think of it years ago. I'd like to see the same thing in wine shops. The best shops will extend their hours of business, open wine bars, offer classes in wine appreciation. To me, this "total experience" is the present and future of the wine shop.

THE WINE SHOP OF THE FUTURE

JOSH WESSON IS ONE OF THE BEST WINE EDUCATORS IN AMERICA. HE'S YOUNG, DYNAMIC AND HUMOROUS; THERE'S A SPRINKLING OF BORSCHT BELT COMEDY IN HIS PRESENTATIONS. HE LIKES TO JOKE THAT HIS FIRST PAIRING WAS GEFILTE FISH AND MANISCHEWITZ: THE SWEETNESS OF THE WINE WAS A PERFECT FOIL FOR THE SALTINESS OF THE FISH. JOSH HAD A FIFTEEN-YEAR CAREER IN RESTAURANTS BEFORE JOINING FORCES WITH PARTNER RICHARD MARMET TO LAUNCH THE BEST CELLARS WINE SHOP ON LEXINGTON AVENUE NEAR 87TH STREET IN MANHATTAN.

If you're in Manhattan and you want to take a look at the future of retail, go to Best Cellars. The store's clean, modern design and total accessibility reflect the owner's philosophy of taking the snobbery and intimidation out of finding fine wines and putting the fun back into it. Not that you wouldn't want to converse with the informed, helpful staff, but the place is virtually self-service, like a wine automat. It offers about a hundred wines, all neatly arranged in easy-to-read vertical displays and all priced under $10.

At Best Cellars wines are divided into eight basic categories by taste and style rather than region or grape variety: Fizzy (sparkling wines); Fresh (light-bodied white wines); Soft (medium-bodied white wines); Luscious (full-bodied white wines); Juicy (light-bodied red wines); Smooth (medium-bodied red wines); Big (full-bodied red wines); Sweet (dessert wines). At Best Cellars, the goal is to provide customers with the information they need to make quick, easy and delicious selections.

The concept is brilliant; the store is a triumph.

WHAT TO EXPECT FROM A WINE MERCHANT

Part of receiving top service from your wine merchant is becoming a good customer—not necessarily one who spends a lot but one who knows enough to get the most out of the staff and their stock. It's always a good idea to patronize one store regularly and become known to the staff. Choose the establishment carefully, though, before rewarding it with your loyalty.

Three main criteria for a wine merchant are selection, service and research:

Selection: What about the scope and variety of the shop's inventory? Does it offer a wide or representative selection? Are the prices within range of those in comparable shops? Are the staff's recommendations good? Do they follow a dynamic strategy, acquiring new and different wines as the months or years go by?

Service: Is the service smooth, easy and convenient? The proprietor and/or one of the employees should be attentive, patient and helpful. You should be able to carry on a conversation about wines without feeling rushed or pressured to buy. Information is a valuable commodity in the wine business. Your merchant should be willing to provide that free of charge, as part of cultivating a relationship. If the wines you want aren't in stock, your merchant should be willing and able to order them for you. If that's not possible, he or she should have a viable explanation—for example, the allocation of a certain wine is sold out and it won't be available until the next vintage—and should be able to offer you an equally delicious alternative.

Research: How does the merchant select wines? Any business is only as good as its research and development department. Fine merchants spend countless hours seeking the best for their customers. We learn about wines through scouting trips, tastings, word of mouth and visits from salespeople representing wineries or distributors. We do a lot of reading and research. We travel a lot. A scouting trip to France or Italy might last two weeks, with about fifty winery visits and over three thousand miles on the rental car. It sounds crazy, but it's fairly typical. All the good ones do it.

Like everything else in wine, it comes down to popping corks. If I'm doing my job as The Wine Merchant, I'm trying at least twenty and frequently as many as a hundred or more wines each week, constantly making mental notes of the ones I want to order for the shop. Does a particular wine fill a niche, do I know certain customers or groups of customers it might please? Is it something new and different that's just too good to resist? Can I pour it at the wine bar? Will people stand up and salute or is it just a passing fancy?

Just as you should have expectations of a good wine merchant, I look for certain qualities in a customer. I value customers who are excited about wines and open to new flavors and suggestions. Someone who takes a hedonistic approach, not a competitive, acquisitive, snobbish or secretive one. Someone who doesn't have "attitude" but merely thirsts for the answer to the all-important question: What's good and how can I put some of it in my glass? It's someone who knows how to ask questions and listen to the answers. I have many longtime customers who are great connoisseurs and collectors yet who continue to approach wines with a refreshing curiosity, a genuine enthusiasm, the desire to learn and to experience new flavors and aromas. My customers should be able to challenge me, I should be able to challenge them and together we should be able to have some great wine experiences.

At The Wine Merchant, Beverly Hills, we've worked hard to create an elegant enclave.

WHAT'S MY WINE?

WHEN I'M SITTING IN MY SECOND-FLOOR OFFICE ABOVE THE SHOP, THE PHONE OFTEN RINGS AND I GET THE WORD: "SO-AND-SO JUST WALKED IN THE STORE." AS I AMBLE DOWNSTAIRS, I'VE GOT A FEW MOMENTS TO SIZE UP THE PERSONALITY AND IMAGINE WHICH WINES I OUGHT TO RECOMMEND. WHEN TED TURNER FIRST WALKED INTO THE SHOP, I CONJURED A NO-NONSENSE SELECTION FOR HIM. THE FIRST THING HE SAID TO ME WAS, "I WANT *YOUR* WINE DESCRIPTIONS, *YOUR* RECOMMENDATIONS, NOT SOMETHING YOU CRIBBED FROM SOME WRITER OR MAGAZINE." I GUESSED RIGHT ABOUT MR. CNN; HE WAS ALL BUSINESS.

REGARDLESS OF WHO THE CUSTOMER IS, YOU WANT TO FLATTER HIM WITH AN APPROPRIATE CHOICE AND YOU WANT HIM TO ENJOY THE WINES. IT'S THE SAME THING WHEN YOU INVITE GUESTS TO DINNER. THINK ABOUT THEIR PERSONALITIES AND WHICH WINES FROM YOUR CELLAR YOU THINK WOULD DELIGHT THEM. I TREAT MY BEST CUSTOMERS LIKE ROYALTY AND I'M SURE YOU'LL WANT TO DO THE SAME FOR YOUR FRIENDS. SO LET'S PLAY A LITTLE GAME OF WHAT'S MY WINE. I'LL PRETEND A FEW OF THESE LUMINARIES WALKED THROUGH THE DOOR OF THE WINE MERCHANT AND I'LL MATCH THEIR SHAPES TO SOME GRAPES.

JENNIFER LOPEZ

Jennifer's a knockout so I'd bring her a big, heavy Syrah that emanates luscious dark fruit and a sensuous texture that is simply overwhelming.

LEONARDO DI CAPRIO

I suspect Leonardo doesn't like anything too heavy, so I'd suggest a Grand Cru Chablis from either the Les Clos or Vaudésir vineyard, a beautiful wine but not too serious, a bit whimsical. He'd also be intrigued by the gunshot flintiness of this wine that reflects the chalky character of the soil. For a Chardonnay, it's has the dryness of Sauvignon Blanc, but it's also very rich.

TED TURNER

With Ted, let's get right to the point. He'd like a big, stern, austere Bordeaux, a wine built to last. I'd recommend Château Latour, with its lead-pencil graphite character. He could take it up to his ranch in Big Sky Country and drink it alongside some seared buffalo steaks.

BILL GATES

It sounds corny, but I'd treat Bill to some Domaines Ott, a Pinot Gris blush (rose) wine from the south of France (Provence). I'd suggest he have it for lunch out on the deck at his fabulous new home. Bill needs to lighten up a bit, especially after his run-ins with the antitrust lawyers at the Justice Department, and this is a really fun wine—like a White Zinfandel with pedigree.

CAMERON DIAZ

I'd automatically reach for a succulent, spicy Gewürztraminer from Alsace. This reflects her personality and goes well with Asian spices and all kinds of other interesting foods.

MICHAEL JORDAN

For America's greatest athlete, I'd choose a powerful, unctuous blow-your-socks-off white Burgundy from an outstanding year, say 1996. The Bâtard-Montrachet is the one. He could build a relationship with this wine, taste some now and put some away to enjoy during his retirement years. It will also appeal to his instincts as a businessman: For a white wine, it's an excellent investment. Michael might get a chuckle out of the story behind this vineyard: In the Middle Ages, two brothers whose family owned it rode off to fight in the Crusades. One of them got waylaid in Italy and came back with several illegitimate children, thus the name Bâtard for his portion of the vineyard. The other brother fought the Infidels, came back missing an arm and a leg, and was knighted. So they called his section Chevalier, which is French for knight.

SHARON STONE

Sharon personifies the glamour and class of modern Hollywood. For her, nothing but the best: an awesome Burgundy, either the Romanée-St.-Vivant or the Richebourg from Leroy. (Madame Lalou Leroy-Bize, one of the world's greatest winemakers, is the proprietress; I wonder if she and Sharon have met . . .). When these wines are young, they are quite tight and firm; as they age, they loosen up a bit and become even more magnificent.

ISAAC MIZRAHI

Isaac seems to possess a brilliant, bubbly, larger-than-life personality. He must be a *Champoo* freak. I couldn't help but introduce him to Salon Champagne, an esoteric, cutting-edge Blancs de Blanc that was developed by a Parisian furrier years ago. It is fresh, dry, lively and exudes a zillion tiny bubbles. Just like Isaac.

RALPH LAUREN

For the fashion mogul who cultivates a staid, gentlemanly image, a copybook Claret, the cookie-cutter benchmark: Château Léoville-Las Cases. I'd order several cases of the superb 1996 vintage. You could serve this wine to the Queen Mother or anybody else who comes to dinner. Ralph Lauren doesn't need to show off by pouring Mouton or Lafite; the Léoville is a second growth

St.-Julien but the insiders rate it as high as all the first growths.

JAY MCINERNEY

For this modern-day Hemingway, I'd recommend one of the best wines coming out of Spain: Signor Perez's Clos Martinet, out of Priorato, a blend of Syrah, Grenache (Garnacha), Carignan, Cabernet Sauvignon and Merlot. This is Spain's answer to Italy's Supertuscans or to the superb Umbrian, Sagrantino di Montefalco. It is the wine for whom the bell tolls, for anyone who's still got the fire in their blood, who isn't burned out yet. The new frontier is the Old World and the true bohemian will appreciate this gem of a wine.

ANTHONY HOPKINS

I see him inconspicuously browsing the Bordeaux, then taking a quick glance at the California selections. I'd pull out a bottle of young vintage Port, say the 1994 Taylor, and tell him, "This stuff is fiery, youthful, out-of-control—something a mad Welshman would enjoy."

YO-YO MA

I've heard he goes up to the Peter Michael Winery in Knights Valley, sits down by the creek and plays his cello. What a perfect image. So we offer him one of Sir Peter's extraordinary Chardonnays. A no-brainer.

Silvio Jermann created this special label and packaging to mark the 110th anniversary of his family's winery.

THE ART OF LABEL-READING

Once you've found a wine merchant whose service is reputable and reliable, you're ready to start browsing in the shop. In order to do that, you'll need to know how to read a label. The more information the consumer can glean from the label, the better. If you're not sure what it all means, ask questions. Here is a checklist of elements to look for:

Origin: You should be able to identify the country, region, appellation, vineyard. Most wines have their country of origin printed on the label. Sometimes, the region and appellation overlap, sometimes it takes three or more lines of copy to pinpoint exactly where a wine is from. In the top winegrowing regions of France, certain vineyard sites have proven to be so superior that they merit their own appellation, which can sometimes be confusing if different producers own or lease part of that vineyard and each makes their own wines from it. In Burgundy, some of the most famous sites— Grands Echézeaux, for example, a superlative *grand cru* of less than thirty acres—are divided up among five or six producers. It's a similar situation in Barolo Country in Piedmont, where the names of certain hillside vineyard sites—Bussia, for example, or Cannubi—appear on the labels of a number of different producers.

Vintage: The year in which the grapes were harvested. The significance of this varies from site to site, from region to region and from year to year. The more consistent the climate, the less significant it is. California and Australia have less variation than, say, Oregon and France. In European regions, the weather can have a profound effect on the wine from one year to the next. By the same token, even vineyards a mile or two apart can receive very different amounts of rain. Don't fall into the trap of following generalizations. Take a chance and try some wines for yourself.

Is there a quality guarantee of some kind? Look for official stamps of approval and rankings. In Germany, for example, the main categories are *Tafelwein* (simple table wine), *Landwein* (a cut above), then *Qualitätswein* (quality wine) in two categories: *Qualitätswein bestimmer Anbaugebiete* (QbA), an intermediate rung, and *Qualitätswein mit Prädikat* (QmP), the good stuff. In Italy, there's *Vino da Tavola* (table wine), then DOC (*Denominazione di Origine Controllata,* meaning literally "controlled denomination of origin") and DOCG, the *Garantita* or guaranteed version of DOC. In France, it's *Vin de Table* (table wine), *Vin de Pays* ("country wine," or wine of a specified region), followed by the higher AOC or AC category. In Spain, the top ratings are DOC and DC, respectively.

Are there any special classifications or qualifications? Some wines are labeled reserve, for example, or special *cuvée,* which indicate higher levels of selection at the winemaking stage. German wines are classified into six categories by their level of sweetness, beginning with the driest, *Kabinett,* and followed by *Spatlese, Auslese, Beerenauslese, Eisewein* ("ice wine," where the grapes are left to freeze on the vines, concentrating their flavors) and *Trockenbeerenauslese.* Sometimes there is an additional indication of *trocken* or *halbtrocken,* meaning dry or half dry (medium dry), respectively. *Spatlese* is literally translated as "late harvest." *Trockenbeerenauslese* (TBA) is one of those daunting German conglomerate words that translates to "dry grapes that are late-harvested." The three "*ausleses*" are ascending categories of rare, expensive and sweet wines from increasingly late-harvested, highly selected grapes, sometimes naturally shriveled, often affected by *B. cinerea*.

Does the wine have a "nickname" or "made-up" name? Many wines made outside the regulations that govern appellations can only be called table wines. They often distinguish themselves with fantasy names that can come from the name of the estate, family member names or simply from somebody's imagination. The so-called Supertuscans—Tignanello, Sassicaia and so forth—are the most famous example of this. In the Friuli region of Italy, producer Silvio Jermann is equal parts inspiration and imagination; he called one of his wines Dreams. In Pouilly-Fume, another imaginative winemaker, Didier Dagueneau, named one of his wines Asteroid.

Who is the producer? Is it a *château,* denoting an estate in Bordeaux or another region that emulates Bordelais winegrowing? Is it a *domaine,* denoting a property or holding usually in Burgundy or some region that emulates it? In Italy, there are various words referring to an estate or producer including *tenuta* (a holding), *podere* (a farm), *fattoria* (literally a factory or an estate that produces agricultural products), *Azienda Agricola* (agricultural agency, an independent producer). Is the producer an individual or a company? Generally, it's best when the wine is bottled at the estate (*mis en bouteille au château* or *a la propriété*). This indicates most careful selection and most complete quality control. Often, wines are made and/or bottled by middlemen. These *negociants* were traditionally an important force in French wine markets, particularly in Burgundy and the Rhône. *Negociants* can either buy wine in bulk from top producers in an area and bottle it, or actually buy the grapes and make the wines themselves. This type of arrangement is not necessarily the best guarantee of quality; however, there have been and will continue to be some excellent wines made this way. There are also excellent wines made in some areas by co-ops, for example in certain areas of northern and central Italy where the small producers may not have the capital to build their own wineries and vinify their own wines. In general, look for estate-produced and -bottled wines, but be aware there are exceptions to the rule.

Grape variety In France, Italy and Spain, wines are generally named by region and not variety, so this can be difficult. You have to remember that in Burgundy they make their reds from Pinot Noir and their whites from Chardonnay; in Chianti, the red grape is Sangiovese; in the regions of Bordeaux it's different blends of Cabernet Sauvignon, Merlot and/or Cabernet Franc; in Spain's Rioja district it's Tempranillo. Tradition dictates that the front label of these wines will probably never announce their varieties, but I can see them moving toward a listing on the back label in the not-too-distant future. If you like Barbaresco wines, does it even matter that they're made from the Nebbiolo grape, the same one that makes Barolos? Probably not, but as different regions begin growing "non-native" grapes, it becomes interesting to compare. Over the coming decades, we will see many expressions of the Sangiovese grape from California, South America and wherever else enterprising producers decide to plant it. (See pages 122–125 for a listing of the principal red and white varieties.)

How much alcohol is there? Look for the percentage of alcohol by volume. This can vary from 7% for light, sparkling wines like a Moscato D'Asti to 14% for some of the more powerful red wines such as Barolos, Bordeaux or California Cabernets. Here on pages 117 to 120 are a few examples of labels, deciphered:

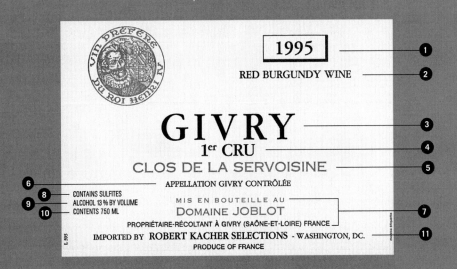

1 Generally not rated a stellar vintage in Burgundy but can be very good.

2 This helps you to figure out where the wine is from in a general sense, but it is also code for "made from the Pinot Noir grape," since this is true of all red Burgundies.

3 A village appellation in the Côte Chalonnaise area of Burgundy.

4 There are three general classifications in Burgundy: regular *cru,* from a village or commune, *premier cru* ("first growth") and *grand cru* ("great growth").

5 The vineyard designation; *clos* is an enclosure and many of the top vineyards in this region are referred to that way.

6 This wine is part of the official Givry AC.

7 Bottled at the *domaine* or property named Joblot. Jean-Marc Joblot is the winemaker. *Proprietaire-recoltant* essentially means they're winegrowers, that they own the company and make the wines.

8 The traditional preservative—SO^2.

9 A substantial wine; can age seven to twenty years.

10 The standard bottle size, about twenty-five ounces.

11 It often helps to note the middleman since he's usually making selections of wines to export, import or distribute. If you find you really like a wine from a particular importer, then expand your horizons by trying some of his others.

General comments: This is a pretty good, specific label. It does not state that the grape variety is Pinot Noir; this is the way it is with French wines. The fact that it's a *cru* Burgundy, bottled at the *domaine,* single vineyard–designated and selected by a reputable importer all point toward high quality. It's from Givry so the price is going to be more reasonable than, say, a similar wine from Gevrey-Chambertin or Chambolle-Musigny, two marquee names in the region.

WEINGUT

Dr·Bürklin-Wolf

1996

Wachenheimer Gerümpel

Riesling Spätlese

Alc.11,0%
by vol.   Pfalz   750ml

Qualitätswein mit Prädikat A.P.Nr.5 142 043 29 97
Produce of Germany D-67157 Wachenheim

Estate Bottled

1 This means winery.

2 Highly reputable: a top family estate in the Pfalz region.

3 A very fine year in Pfalz; not necessarily so in other winegrowing regions of Germany.

4 Wachenheim is the appellation, in the Pfalz region, and Gerumpel is one of the very top Riesling vineyards there.

5 The grape variety is Riesling. The sweetness category, Spatlese, is one notch above the driest, Kabinett, so it should have a pleasing amount of sugar.

6 Fairly substantial for a German white wine, but less alcohol than a California Chardonnay or a white Burgundy.

7 The large winegrowing region south of the Rhinehessen, north of Baden-Baden and not far from Alsace, with a relatively warm climate for ripening the grapes.

8 QmP, the highest level of quality guarantee.

General comment: This is your typical understated, informative, unprepossessing German label. What it doesn't tell you is what you'll taste when you pop the cork and try some of the wine: hints of apricots and peaches with a style that is delicious, charming and not too fruity. It is a light-bodied wine with sophistication and finesse.

1 An excellent vintage, worldwide.

2 The word means "art" in Italian and hints at high aspirations for the wine.

3 It's bottled at its origin by the producer Domenico Clerico (Italians sometimes list their last names first in more formal situations) in Monforte D'Alba, all good signs.

4 A substantial wine, slightly lighter than a pure Barolo.

5 This is key. The fact that it comes from a distinguished Barolo producer and commune but is only a "red table wine" is intriguing. It turns out to be a wine made outside of the Barolo DOCG regulations, like the Supertuscans, from a blend of mostly Nebbiolo and some Barbera grapes grown in the illustrious Ginestra and Bussia crus.

Elsewhere on this bottle you will note "A Marc De Grazia Selection Imported by Michael Skurnik Wines." These are two very highly regarded middlemen; try their wines when you have the chance.

General comment: This label is simple and understated. It represents by far one of the best wines in Italy. I'd like to see a little more information and maybe a flash or two of the brilliance that's inside the bottle. On the other hand, I kind of like the idea of a fairly bland exterior with a powerhouse inside.

97 Geyserville Vineyard, bottled January 99
Growers will remember this year fondly for its exceptionally abundant yields, following two very small vintages. Another characteristic of the 1997 harvest is that all the grapes seemed to ripen at the same moment. Because of the time required for picking, this resulted in very rich, full wines. We had dropped half the crop on the younger vines, and fifteen percent on the older vines, to ensure the intensity we seek. Structure is particularly solid; firm acidity adds elegance and definition to the ripe fruit. This Geyserville is a fine example from a great decade. It will be at its best over the next five to six years.   PD (11/98)

Since 1962, Ridge has championed single-vineyard winemaking, searching California for those rare vineyards where climate, soil, and varietal are ideally matched. Using traditional methods and minimal handling, we strive to produce exceptional wines from superior and distinctive fruit. For information on the wines, or visiting our Monte Bello and Sonoma County wineries, call (408) 867-3233.
                                        ® REGISTERED TRADEMARK

RIDGE 1997
CALIFORNIA
GEYSERVILLE®

GEYSERVILLE VINEYARD: 74% ZINFANDEL,
15% CARIGNANE, 10% PETITE SIRAH, 1% MATARO
SONOMA COUNTY   ALCOHOL 14.9% BY VOLUME
PRODUCED AND BOTTLED BY RIDGE VINEYARDS   BW 4488
17100 MONTE BELLO ROAD, BOX 1810, CUPERTINO, CA 95015

This is a clear, functional, information-packed label from a top California producer. No need for a cryptologist here.

With American wines, not surprisingly, there's a lot less guesswork involved in reading the labels. Sometimes they feature a lot of advertising copy or marketing hype; other times they sincerely reflect the philosophy of the winery. I like the succinct slogan on the back label of Peter Michael's wines: "Mountain vineyards, classical winemaking, limited production." The minute you try those wines, you know it's true.

Once you've sorted out the facts on the label, take a look at the whole package—front and back labels, graphic design, bottle shape—and ask yourself what it tells you symbolically about the philosophy of the winegrower. Is it functional or elegant, flashy or stolid? Is it masculine or feminine, soft or hard, light or heavy? Does it look old or new? Sometimes there are hidden messages, comparisons or analogies suggested. The "script" typeface, simple white label and the soft-shouldered bottle of Tony Soter's Etude Pinot Noir, for example, echo the packaging of the great Romanée-Conti wines from Burgundy.

The label on the Mulderbosch Sauvignon Blanc from South Africa looks like a green official government tape with a red wax seal on it, an eye-catching design that makes a claim for the quality and consistency of the wine.

A number of California producers, including two of my favorites, Harlan Estate and Viader, have gone back to the old-fashioned wide-shouldered bottles that were standard in the nineteenth and early twentieth centuries for the finest Bordeaux wines and have always been a hallmark of the great Château Haut-Brion's package. It's amazing how a slight variation in bottle shape can make a strong statement about the wines.

Some people like to soak the labels off their favorite bottles and save them in a scrapbook, which is either obsessive behavior or simply a conscientious effort to keep track—it depends on how you want to look at it. I prefer to keep a little pocket "wine notebook" and jot down key information from labels. There is nothing more frustrating than remembering you had a fabulous bottle of wine last week at such and such a restaurant but you can't remember the name.

Read the label, then examine the entire package: what does it tell you about the wine?

GRAPE VARIE

PRINCIPAL RED VARIETIES

BARBERA
A commonly grown grape in Italy's Piedmont region; lighter and more tart, not as "serious" as its neighbor Nebbiolo.

CABERNET FRANC
A lighter cousin of the noble Cabernet Sauvignon, sweeter and more "feminine." It tempers Cabernet Sauvignon in many Bordeaux and Bordeaux-type blends; it is also the principal grape in the smooth Loire Valley reds of Chinon, Saumur-Champigny and Bourgeuil.

CABERNET SAUVIGNON
The world's most famous noble red grape variety that is the basis for the top Bordeaux wines. It is full-flavored and tannic with great aging potential. Cabernets from California and Australia can also be superb. It is grown in South America and it provides a key blending element to many of Italy's Supertuscans.

CARIGNAN
An ancient grape planted abundantly all over southern France, mostly for table wine.

DOLCETTO
A sweeter, earlier-ripening Piedmontese variety as compared to Barbera and to the noble Nebbiolo.

GAMAY
Primarily used to make Beaujolais wines, which are refreshing, pleasantly acidic and not built to age.

GRENACHE, OR GARNACHA
French and Spanish names for the most widely planted red variety in southern France and Spain. An important component in the wines of France's southern Rhône region, including Châteauneuf-du-Pape and Côtes-du-Rhône. Also used as a blending component with Tempranillo to make Spain's great Rioja wines.

MALBEC, OR MALBECK
A very dark colored grape that is grown most successfully in Argentina's Mendoza region.

MERLOT
A key grape variety in Bordeaux for blending with Cabernet Sauvignon and Cabernet Franc, especially in Pomerol and St.-Emilion on the right bank of the Gironde. Also extremely popular in California as a varietal, although some of the best American Merlot is actually grown in Washington State. It is also successfully grown in South Africa, Australia, New Zealand and Italy. Merlot yields a smoother, "rounder" wine that is often referred to by experts as plummy, luscious, velvety.

MOURVÈDRE
A blending component in Châteauneuf-du-Pape along with Grenache and Syrah.

TIES
AND WHERE THEY ARE GROWN

NEBBIOLO

The main component in Barolo and Barbaresco wines, it produces concentrated, full-bodied wines with high tannins, acid and fruit that have tremendous aging potential. Along with Sangiovese, it is Italy's noblest grape.

PINOT NOIR

The red grape of Burgundy that some would argue is the noblest of all. Also grown with superior results in California and Oregon. It is known for its "transparency"—that is, it transmits the characteristics of *terroir* very well. It is thinner-skinned and more fragile than its Bordeaux counterpart, Cabernet Sauvignon, but it definitely yields among the world's best wines.

PINOTAGE

A South African red-wine grape that is a cross-breed between Pinot Noir and Cinsaut.

RHÔNE VARIETIES

Grape varieties grown in the Rhône Valley, including Syrah, Grenache, Mourvèdre, Viognier, Marsanne, Rousanne.

SANGIOVESE

A native Italian variety that is the major component in Chianti and Brunello wines as well as in most of the Supertuscan blends. Italy's most widely planted grape, it is king in Tuscany.

SYRAH (KNOWN AS SHIRAZ IN AUSTRALIA AND SOUTH AFRICA)

Produces very full-bodied, concentrated, flavorful wines, especially in France's northern Rhône (Côte-Rôtie and Hermitage). Known for its berry aromas, it is also grown with excellent results in Australia, South Africa and to some extent California.

TEMPRANILLO

A full-bodied grape blended with Garnacha to make Spain's Rioja wines; also the principle variety in Ribera del Duero wines.

ZINFANDEL

Grown only in America, it produces dark, purplish fruit and concentrated wines.

PRINCIPAL WHITE VARIETIES

ALBARIÑO
Makes the fresh, fragrant, pleasingly acidic wines of northwest Spain and northern Portugal, where it is called Alvarinho.

CHARDONNAY
One of the world's favorite varieties, it produces some of the greatest white wines, especially Burgundies (Côte D'Or and Chablis). It is also grown with great success in California, Australia, New Zealand, South Africa and northern Italy. Ripe and full-bodied in the New World, it can support malolactic fermentation and aging in oak. In the more austere Old World style it is a superior transmitter of *terroir*.

CHENIN BLANC
Most prominently grown in the Loire Valley for Vouvray wines, both sweet and dry. Also grown in California, South Africa and New Zealand. The grape has good acidity and loads of potential but suffers from a bad reputation due to some poor wines that have been made from it.

GEWÜRZTRAMINER
Principally grown in Alsace, Germany and Austria and also in some cooler New World regions. Features spicy, fruity aromas.

GRÜNER VELTLINER
Austria's specialty, it produces a light, dry, vivacious, food-friendly wine.

MALVASIA
Most commonly grown in the Italian province of Tuscany for blending with Sangiovese in old-style Chianti red wines, it is now more often made into a white table wine or blended with other white varieties.

MARSANNE
A traditional variety in France's Northern Rhône usually blended with Rousanne. Also grown in Australia and California.

MÜLLER-THURGAU
Grown primarily in Germany and Austria, it is used mostly as the main ingredient in down-market wines such as Liebfraumilch.

...AND WHITE

MUSCAT

An ancient variety used to make a number of prominent but very different wines, including Moscato D'Asti, the slightly sweet, sparkling wine from Piedmont; Muscat de Beaumes-de-Venise, a luscious sweet dessert wine from the Southern Rhône; and Muscat D'Alsace, a dry light wine.

PINOT BLANC

(known as Pinot bianco in Italy) Grown in Alsace, Germany, Austria and northern Italy, it is related to both Pinot Gris and Pinot Noir and is relatively full-bodied.

PINOT GRIS

(known as Pinot Grigio in Italy) Grown in Germany, northern Italy and Alsace, where it is made into some very fine wines with relatively low acid.

RIESLING

By far the dominant variety among Germany's premium producers, it is light in alcohol and high in both acid and fruit. It is also grown in Alsace.

ROUSANNE

Grown in the Northern Rhône region as well as other parts of southern France, where it is usually blended with Marsanne, and also, more recently, in California.

SAUVIGNON BLANC

(aka Fume Blanc) An extremely popular variety that produces many of the world's finest white wines, including Sancerre, Pouilly-Fume and white Bordeaux (Graves), where it is blended with Sémillon. New Zealand is also known for superlative Sauvignon wines and there are also some very good ones from California. The wines are often described as flinty or chalky tasting with herbal and/or citrus aromas.

SÉMILLON

Grown primarily in France but also California and other New World winegrowing regions, it is rich with a relatively deep yellow color and most often blended with Sauvignon Blanc. Due to its susceptibility to *B. cinerea*, it is often used for dessert wines.

VIOGNIER

Traditionally the principal grape in the Condrieu region of France's Northern Rhône, it is also grown in other parts of southern France and has recently caught on in California. Often termed fashionable or trendy, it is very aromatic, with flavors of citrus and a touch of the exotic.

"MICK WOULD LIKE TEN CASES OF..."

In the early eighties, Roederer's Cristal Champagne became all the rage. If you were truly au courant, you wouldn't think of ordering anything else. At a certain point the demand so outstripped the supply that the company began insisting that buyers purchase ten cases of their lower-echelon nonvintage Brut for every case of Cristal ordered. One fine summer day, I got a call from Bill Graham, who was promoting the Rolling Stones' tour. In his unmistakable voice, Bill announced that Mick Jagger wanted ten cases of Cristal for the backstage party after their upcoming concert at Anaheim Stadium.

When I explained Roederer's new policy, Bill assured me it was absolutely no problem. "This is the Champagne that Mick really likes and this is what he has to have at the backstage party." I called Bill back two days later, just before the Stones concert, and said, "I have your ten cases of Cristal. Where should we deliver it?" After he gave me the instructions I reminded him, "Let's not forget the hundred cases of Brut. Where do you want them shipped?" He said, "Dennis, do you have a very large trash can?"

(By the way, Cristal was selling for about $90 a bottle at that time; the bottom line for the Stones that night was $250 a bottle.)

FUTURES

In the commodities markets, investors and speculators buy contracts for delivery of specified amounts of a certain commodity at a later date. These contracts are called futures. With respect to wine, the practice of selling futures started in Bordeaux, with the classified-growth châteaus, and is pretty much confined to collectible Cabernet-based wines.

The grapes are harvested in the fall, and about six months later, in May or June, the châteaus offer the first *tranche* ("slice") of their wines to the trade (wholesale). The smaller châteaus set their prices first, then gradually the heavier hitters weigh in with their offers. In total, estates will sell anywhere from 10 percent to a third of their total harvest as futures. They are allocated, through the whole-salers, to major merchants around the world according to track record. Merchants must stick to their commitments through good vintages and bad; otherwise, they risk losing their allocations. Newcomers to the business are not always received enthusiastically. Money talks, however, and even in the ancient, venerable business of fine wines, greed has been known to make an inroad or two.

Six months after the first *tranche* and a year after harvest, the châteaus offer a second *tranche,* this time to the general public. In good vintages, the excitement is building considerably and prices are on the rise. This is the time to lock in your purchase of these wines—nowadays, you can either enlist the assistance of your trusted wine merchant or go straight to the Internet and buy through one of the many merchants operating on-line. (Visit our web site, if you like, at www.winemerchantbh.com or e-mail us at bhwm1@aol.com.)

The final release date (shipping date) of a wine varies from one winery to the next, but it is generally one and a half to two and a half years after harvest. If the demand is particularly strong, some châteaus will release their wines gradually, in 10 to 20 percent allotments over a period of several years as prices continue to rise. It is a fine calculus based on the perceived quality of the vintage and indications of market conditions worldwide, one ultimately determined by supply and demand.

Buying wine futures in a strong vintage is like betting the favorite in a horse race. It's hard to go wrong. These are agribusinesses that have built their reputations over a period of many decades, if not centuries. They set their prices carefully and work hard to uphold standards. The downside of buying wine futures is that in the United States, as opposed to other commodities, it is an unregulated market. Beware the Trojan horse! In other words, make sure you're buying from a reputable merchant who will be around in two years to take delivery of your wines.

SHORTAGES, HIGH PRICES AND PRICE PSYCHOLOGY: A Few Suggestions on How to Cope

It is true that many fine wines are very expensive. Increasing demand and short supply have sent prices of certain "names" skyrocketing. This is a grim reality for consumers in the premium wine market. How to deal with it?

First of all, it's very difficult for anyone, particularly for those of us born and bred in the United States, to rid ourselves of the notion that higher price means better quality. This is not to say that most Americans aren't looking for the best bargain. In the United States, wine is generally considered a discretionary purchase. (Not so in Europe, where it's much more of an everyday staple.) When we go shopping for luxury items, we *assume* that the most expensive ones are of the highest quality. A $9 Penfolds Shiraz from Australia may represent top quality, the equal of almost any wine in the premium category, but collectors who are paying many times that price per bottle for comparable wines will not be very inclined to agree with that assessment. For those of us who are on a budget, it's reassuring to know that quality is not always in direct proportion to price.

Find alternatives. If you can't get the Marcassin Chardonnay, maybe you can have Long Vineyards or Kistler. If you can't find that, there will be a good and satisfying bottle of wine for you. Great wines are being made by lesser-known producers in lesser-known appellations all over the world. The variety of wines available in the U.S. market is staggering, certainly the widest and deepest selection anywhere in the world. That's something to be excited about and it means that there are always going to be excellent wines available for reasonable prices.

There is more information being disseminated about how and where to find these hidden treasures than ever before. There are new ways and means to buy wines. Use all your resources: your local wine merchant; sommeliers at your favorite restaurants; friends (the best source in many ways); catalogs; mailings direct from the wineries (call or write and have yourself put on the mailing list or the waiting list for new vintages released); publications of all kinds; wine-buying clubs. Check the Internet; there is a ton of good information about fine wines in cyberspace.

Don't buy wines by the label. Although many individuals who come into my shop do it, the sensible approach is simply to concentrate on quality and avoid becoming obsessed with price and provenance. In famous regions, many growers are resting on their laurels, coasting on their names and reputations. This is a regrettable phenomenon. With today's better-educated, more discerning consumers, this practice is going to backfire. In a given region you can find a wine that is equal to, and in many cases better than, the big names for a fraction of the price.

It is also true that the top producers make very small quantities of highly sought after wines, wines that even the committed collector may have a hard time obtaining. These are the wines spearheading the revolution, and the trend is that they will continue to emerge. If you can't obtain a bottle of Grace Family or Harlan Estate, or if you don't want to spent $50 to $200 on one, there are excellent alternatives.

Bobby Kacher, who imports and distributes a stellar list of French producers, about half of which are in the premium price range, feels high prices are mostly a function of a wine's pedigree. The correct winegrowing techniques, when applied to lesser-known real estate, are

going to produce equally fabulous wines. Wines from his Burgundian producer Jean-Marc Joblot in the appellation of Givry sell for $20 to $25 a bottle. They are every bit the equals of their more expensive neighbors from Gevrey-Chambertin, which sell for $40 to $50 more, and a fraction of the cost of the Domaine de la Romanée-Conti wines, the Rolls-Royces of Burgundies.

Many wine lovers are dismayed by the behavior of aggressive international investors and collectors whose flamboyant spending habits send the prices of classified-growth Bordeaux and *grand cru* Burgundies sky high. These high-end buyers drive the market for certain wines, putting them out of reach of 99 percent of consumers. They do, however, serve a purpose: They stimulate growth in other segments of the market, causing overall expansion of the industry.

Still, the fact remains that while many of the best wines in the world cost from $30 to $200 per bottle and up, there are many more that are *less than $10 a bottle.* As the New Wine Revolution spreads to places like Austria and Spain, Portugal and Chile, where the ancient traditions of winemaking may just be reawakening, we will find more and more reasonably priced premium wines. So if you're turned off by the high prices and short supply of the "name" French and California wines, look elsewhere.

A final suggestion: **postpone gratification.** Half the fun is the hunt, tracking down that bottle of hard-to-find wine that you've been coveting ever since you read about it or heard about it or tasted a glass. Once you've got what you're looking for, don't drink it right away. Savor the satisfaction of having found it; save it for a special occasion.

129

HOW MUCH IS A WINE WORTH?

IF YOU TREAT WINE AS AN INVESTMENT, THEN IT'S WORTH WHAT OTHER PEOPLE ARE WILLING TO PAY FOR IT AT ANY GIVEN MOMENT. THIS IS WHAT I CALL "THE INVESTOR MENTALITY." ACTUALLY, I PREFER "THE COLLECTOR MENTALITY," WHICH DICTATES THAT A WINE IS SIMPLY WORTH WHAT YOU PAID FOR IT. THE TRUE WINE LOVER IS NOT CONCERNED WITH ANY POSSIBLE CONNECTION BETWEEN PRICE AND VALUE. IF YOU LOVE A WINE—OR ANYTHING ELSE, FOR THAT MATTER—WITH PASSION, IT BECOMES PRICELESS, IN WHICH CASE HOW MUCH IT COST YOU OR WHAT YOU COULD SELL IT FOR BECOMES IRRELEVANT. CONSIDER THIS: IF SOMEONE GAVE YOU A BOTTLE OF FINE WINE, IS IT WORTH NOTHING BECAUSE IT WAS FREE? OF COURSE NOT. IN SOME SENSE, IT'S WORTH MUCH MORE THAN ITS CURRENT MARKET PRICE BECAUSE IT REPRESENTS THE GENEROSITY OF A FRIEND.

In the late eighties, my friend Al Stewart, a collector and sincere wine lover, tracked down ten bottles of '82 Château Le Pin, the superlative Pomerol, in the Midwest for $190 each, a relatively steep price. Shortly thereafter, the wine was "discovered" by the international market and began to sell at auction for prices in the area of $4,000. Suddenly, it was one of the most expensive wines in the world. Meanwhile, Al tasted his and found it "an amazingly forward wine, very accessible, not very tannic, basically just a bowl of fruit." Concerned about its aging prognosis, not wanting to let it die in the cellar, he decided to drink it. About six months later, he had a dinner at home for his mother-in-law where they consumed three bottles of Le Pin. "The next day," he recalls, "I thought, well that was expensive, we just drank $600 worth of wine." Or was it really $12,000 worth? By the same token, if you bought the '86 Cheval-Blanc for $37.50 and it's now up to between $500 and $1,000, isn't it still a $37.50 bottle of wine to you? The bottom line is the true value in a wine is only realized when you drink it. (For more on collecting, see chapter 5.)

"In the past it was just price, price, price. Now it is quality. It is a revolution in the last ten years." —Marcel Guigal

Count Stephan von Neipperg of Château Canon-La-Gaffeliere and Château La Mondotte

THE WINE LIST, PLEASE

"I learned to drink wine by going out to dinner and ordering it in restaurants."
—Greg Gorman, photographer and collector

ORDERING WINE IN A RESTAURANT

Many people have their first encounter with fine wine in a restaurant, and if it's a good experience they become return customers. Part of what we try to do at Overstreet's Wine Bar is create a comfort level so that even a wine novice doesn't feel nervous or intimidated. Our No. 1 priority is to turn people on—not off—to the wine experience. Everything follows from there.

Most restaurants have some sort of wine program. Unfortunately, in many cases, it's a prepackaged one provided by a distributor ("a distributor list") that relieves the restaurant of any responsibility for choosing the wines it sells. Any list that isn't specific about a wine's origin, producer and vintage should be suspect. Likewise, a list that features only one producer per region or country is questionable. If you're concerned about the wine list, inquire as to who is responsible for buying the wine for the restaurant. If the answer is "We work with a distributor," that's a tip-off. In a fine restaurant, this should never be the case. There should be at least one staff member—whether it's the sommelier, the mâitre d' or the chef-owner—who's knowledgeable about wines and can provide a fully integrated food-and-wine experience.

The sommelier wears two hats. First, there is a fiscal duty to manage the purchase and sale of wines, turning a profit for the restaurant. Second, there is a responsibility to provide the customers with the best possible selection of wines and optimum service. Good wine service enhances the value of a meal and distinguishes a diner's experience in a restaurant.

Find a restaurant and/or sommelier you trust and establish a rapport. Remember, wine takes time; don't be impatient. Strike up a conversation with the sommelier and make some choices together. Let the sommelier challenge you and vice versa.

WORKING WITH THE SOMMELIER

Because of the mystique that has surrounded wine for so many years, many people are leery of, if not downright intimidated by, the sommelier. The encounter with the wine steward can be a tense moment in an otherwise enjoyable evening. Diners are often afraid to reveal a lack of knowledge or sophistication; all they want is to avoid embarrassment.

If the thought of talking to the sommelier makes you nervous, if you have visions of making a fool of yourself, try to relax and forget about that. Think about finding your comfort level. And always bear in mind that it is not meant to be an adversarial relationship. It should be a mutual sharing of information for your ultimate benefit.

Consider this: What is the point of buying wine in a restaurant if you could go down the street and pay half the price at a store? In the restaurant you're paying for ambience, good service and information. Forget about impressing your date! If you want to take full advantage of the wine experience at a fine restaurant, you need to engage in a conversation with the sommelier. You're paying for this service anyway, so why waste your money? Why not make use of it?

Earlier in this chapter, I mentioned a few characteristics the wine merchant looks for in a customer. Let's ask the same question with respect to the restaurant patron. First of all, nothing delights a sommelier more than to be asked for a recommendation. When the majority of diners call on the sommelier, they have already made a selection. It is sad to say, but much of the time this selection is a cop-out: a wine the diner has had many times before, a safe choice, one that may represent the latest buzzword on the airwaves but is totally mismatched with the food and/or the occasion. Don't be stubborn or lazy. Don't take the easy way out. Instead, acknowledge the sommelier's expertise. When a diner is dead set on a poor selection, the sommelier has a dilemma: How to steer that customer in the direction of the best possible choice without contradicting his wishes? The risk, from the sommelier's point of view, is that the customer will have a less-than-memorable wine experience in his establishment.

The keys to enjoying the restaurant wine experience to its fullest are getting over your fear of embarrassment, keeping an open mind. Don't be afraid to ask questions. A good sommelier will *never* make you feel stupid or inadequate. In wine, there is no such thing as a stupid question. If you don't ask questions, how are you ever going to learn?

What is the top-flight sommelier looking for in a customer? Someone who will ask for recommendations, who has an adventurous spirit, who will engage in a conversation and not be afraid to try something new and different. Someone who can ask questions and listen to the answers.

What kind of information do you need to give the sommelier to get the most out of your restaurant wine experience? You can start by trying to explain what kind of wines you like or you think you like. Be as specific as possible. If you can remember regions, producers, vintages, vineyards, let the wait staff know. If not, tell them what you like in general terms. If you're not sure what you like, just say so. It's nothing to be ashamed of. You are not

being tested or challenged. On the contrary, the sommelier's job is to please you, to help open up the wonderful world of wines to you.

Once you've found your comfort level and overcome any trepidation about talking to the sommelier or wait staff, it's time to consider the criteria for judging a restaurant food-wine experience. There are two main areas to judge: the wine list and the service. First, the list.

ASSESSING THE WINE LIST

Take some time to peruse the wine list. (This *will* impress your date.) Note what type of coverage and/or focus it has. Is there a range of selections, across the spectrum of regions, grape varieties and vintages? Is there a particular theme that is consistent with the type of food served in the restaurant? Here are some yardsticks by which to appraise a restaurant list:

● **How is the list structured?** Is it divided simply between reds, whites and sparkling wines? Is it by countries, which are in turn broken down into regions? Is it some combination thereof or does it use nonstandard categories?

● **Is the list selective or encyclopedic?** A modest list of twenty or thirty wines at a casual bistro may appear limited but may actually represent a very carefully considered selection. As restaurant patrons, we should appreciate that it's easier in many ways to be inclusive: It's far more difficult to satisfy criteria of excellence with a more limited selection of a hundred or fewer wines than with five hundred or even a thousand selections.

● **Is the list balanced?** Within each section are the wines evenly distributed across a range of appellations, producers, prices and vintages? In many cases, you'll

KEEPING AN OPEN MIND

PEOPLE TEND TO GET STUCK IN A RUT. IN WINE, THE REFLEXIVE ORDERS FOR MANY YEARS WERE, "I'LL HAVE A GLASS OF CHARDONNAY" AND "WE'LL HAVE A BOTTLE OF CABERNET WITH THE MAIN COURSE." TRANSLATION: "I'D LIKE A DECENT, MID-PRICED GLASS OF WHITE WINE BUT I CAN'T BE BOTHERED TO THINK ABOUT A CHOICE" OR "LET'S HAVE A BOTTLE OF GOOD RED WINE WITH OUR STEAK."

In reaction, there arose the famous acronym "ABC"— "Anything but Chardonnay" or "Anything but Cabernet."

For a while "Cabernet" meant "red wine." Then America discovered the other great Bordeaux variety, Merlot, and suddenly it became the rage. If you wanted to impress your date, you uttered the words, "I'll have a glass of Merlot."

Savvy restaurateurs and sommeliers can employ a few tricks to ease people out of the rut. They might offer Chardonnays, for example, but from a variety of regions: a white Burgundy, perhaps something from New Zealand or Italy, possibly Oregon.

Manfred Krankl has seen the Cabernet-Chardonnay craze and the backlash. In fact, he has often been closely identified with "the ABC thing." "I hate it when people try to use me as an example of that," he says. "They say, 'Manfred, you hate Chardonnay.' No! I don't hate Chardonnay. I just don't like *only* Chardonnay. There are some very good Chardonnays out there. God knows some of the greatest wines in the world are Chardonnay. To say, 'You're going to be super

uncool if you drink Chardonnay or Cabernet' or 'I only drink this' or 'I will never drink that' . . . It's stupid to get yourself boxed in."

Chris Meeske of Patina simply tries to give his clientele as many options as possible and help them make an informed choice. He will never try to talk them out of an order. He did decide to take a stand about the Merlot craze, though: "I stopped serving it by the glass. It got to the point where the quality of Merlot wasn't able to justify its price. People ask for Merlot and what they really mean is they want something with rich, deep black fruits, maybe spicy but soft, ripe tannins, something that's very accessible and easy to drink. I can provide that for them without giving them Merlot. For example, I have a Spanish wine from the producer Pesquera in Ribera del Duero; it's called Condado de Haza and it's made from the Tempranillo grape. It's just a beautiful, soft, rich round wine that is everything that people want when they ask for Merlot but they hardly ever get." Touché—or should I say Olé!?

TEN SMART QUESTIONS TO ASK THE SOMMELIER

1. Can you recommend something off the beaten track?
2. Is there a staff favorite?
3. Do you have a personal favorite?
4. Do you offer tasting flights?
5. Is there anything new on the list that you'd like to recommend?

6. Can you offer any wines that are *not* on the list?
7. Do you know any stories about this wine?
8. I recently had X wine; do you have anything similar?
9. What do you suggest to go with these two entrées?
10. I usually order Y; can you offer me something different?

open it up to the white wine category, for example, and, reading down the list, find thirty Chardonnays, a couple of Sauvignon Blancs, maybe one Riesling and one Gewürztraminer. This doesn't work. Why? Because everyone's going to order Chardonnay. As Manfred Krankl points out, "It's like going to a restaurant that has thirty fish dishes and one steak. I'm not ordering the steak. This is a fish place as far as I'm concerned." A good, modern selection of twenty to twenty-five whites should have, say, four or five wines in each of four or five varieties—Sauvignon Blanc, Chardonnay, Viognier, Riesling, Gewurztraminer, Pinot Blanc and so forth. It should also have a range of prices and vintages.

● **Does the list include some wines that are scarce or unavailable, that may have been snatched up by collectors and connoisseurs, for example some older Burgundies?** This is always a bonus, particularly if it's a special occasion and you're prepared to splurge.

● **How well does the list represent the best of each region?** Try mentioning one or two of your favorite wines and gauging the reaction. If those wines are not available, the sommelier or wait staff should be able to offer equivalents. Many fine restaurants like to feature smaller producers, which to me are always more interesting than their brand-name equivalents.

● **Does the establishment maintain an extensive cellar?** While some sommeliers deserve credit for their ingenuity in selecting smaller lists, others create impressively large lists and we should applaud that as well. A big list requires a huge investment; inventory is costly, space is at a premium, arranging for proper storage can be difficult.

● **Are there half bottles, magnums, by-the-glass selec-** tions or even smaller tasting portions (usually only found in wine bars) in addition to standard 750-milliliter bottle sizes?

● **Is the list dynamic?** Great wine lists are constantly changing. Sommeliers and buyers rotate their wines, offering new selections every year, every month, sometimes every week. At the same time, they offer a solid base of tried-and-true favorites. At Overstreet's, we like to revise our offerings seasonally. In November, the Beaujolais Nouveau arrives; in the spring, we feature young, fruity wines as well as the new releases of California Cabernets and Bordeaux; in summer, the emphasis would be on white wines.

Manfred Krankl ensures a cutting-edge wine experience at Campanile by careful maintenance of his wine list, which is computerized and updated every day. That way, no one will ever have the experience of ordering a wine and hearing, "Sorry, we're out of that one." With wines that are in dwindling supply, the number of bottles remaining is listed so that larger parties have the option of avoiding selections that may run out. Wines that sell out are more often than not replaced by different ones so that repeat customers at Campanile will always find something new. Manfred estimates that fully half of his wine list changes within any given one-year period.

Don't fall for "window dressing"—that is, a few rare old first growths at exorbitant prices, wines that sell once every couple of years. It's pretentious. Much more impressive is the sommelier who can offer wines from interesting regions—an Austrian Grüner Veltliner, for example—and/or small producers that the customer wouldn't normally encounter elsewhere. This actually takes more time and effort and represents an extra measure of service.

ALTERNATIVE CATEGORIES:
HOW THE LIST IS DIVIDED

SPAGO IS THE QUINTESSENTIAL L.A. SHOWCASE, THE PLACE DINERS GO TO SEE AND BE SEEN. WORLD-RENOWNED CHEF WOLFGANG PUCK'S BRILLIANTLY INVENTIVE CUISINE IS NO MERE ACCESSORY TO ALL THAT GLITZ. HE BECAME AMERICA'S FIRST GREAT CELEBRITY CHEF NEARLY TWO DECADES AGO, AND HE'S REMAINED AT THE FOREFRONT EVER SINCE. WITH MASTER SOMMELIER MICHAEL BONACCORSI IN CHARGE, THERE ARE SOME VERY EXCITING THINGS HAPPENING IN THE WINE DEPARTMENT AS WELL. SPAGO HAS A DYNAMIC AND EXCITING LIST THAT FEATURES "FREE-FORM" CATEGORIES—MUCH LESS RIGID AND FORMULAIC THAN THE NORM. MIKE USES HIS HEADINGS TO HIGHLIGHT CERTAIN GRAPES, PRODUCERS OR REGIONS. HERE IS HOW A RECENT LIST WAS BROKEN DOWN:

Champagne (with a subcategory for Rose Champagne)

California Sparkling Wine

Sauvignon Blanc

Other Interesting American White Wines (including Sémillon, Pinot Blanc, Gewürztraminer, Chenin Blanc and Viognier)

California Chardonnay

German White Wines

White Burgundy (with subcategories for four featured producers)

Other French White Wines (with subcategories for White Bordeaux, Loire Valley, Rhône and South of France, Alsace)

Austrian White Wines

Italian Whites

Red Bordeaux (Left Bank: St.-Estèphe, Pauillac, St.-Julien, Margaux, Graves; Right Bank: Pomerol, St.-Emilion)

Red Burgundy

California Cabernet Sauvignon

Merlot

Zinfandel

American Pinot Noir (with a separate category for Williams & Selyem)

Austrian Red Wines

Spanish Reds

Italian Reds

Interesting American Red Wines (including Barbera, Grenache, Syrah, Sangiovese, Mourvèdre and others)

French Red Wines (including mostly Rhône and southern France).

Another newer trend is to organize the list by grape variety; Danny Meyer of New York's superb Union Square Cafe is one proponent of this system. In general, look for a wine list that's organized in interesting, nonstandard categories and let those be your guide for new ways of approaching the wine adventure.

"Wine is one of the most compelling reasons to get together with people. It's one of the great facilitators of conversation. Wine helps break down the barriers."

—Greg Gorman

SERVICE CRITERIA

A well-put-together wine list is nice, but what good is it without appropriate service? The first thing you should expect with regard to service is to feel comfortable. Next, you should expect an informed staff that can offer help when you want it. Service should be mostly reactive, very occasionally proactive. The extent of the staff's meddling should be "Would you like to see the wine list?" and later on "Have you made a choice?"—*unless* you ask for help, in which case, the staff should be responsive, informative, amusing, entertaining, challenging—all to an appropriate degree. The staff's responsibility is to read the customer's needs and desires and cater to them.

Take note of how the sommelier or wait staff presents you with the wine list. Just this simple act, with its varying degrees of emphasis, can say a lot about how the restaurant views its wine program. Once you've ordered, the presentation of the wine itself should be smooth, precise, courteous, respectful and nonintrusive; not pretentious and overblown. When you order, you should be asked how and when you'd like the wine. When the wine arrives at the table, the person who ordered it should be asked who would like to try it.

Whether it's traditional, formal, hip, casual, flashy or low-key, a wine restaurant should be willing and able to accommodate a range of scenarios from serious, involved discussions and tastings to just a glass and a conversation with a friend.

INFORMATION

How well educated is the sommelier and/or wait staff about wines? If you seem to be interested, can they tell interesting anecdotes, give you cogent information about the region, producer, production methods, vintage, aromas and tastes of the wine(s)?

If you become passionate about wines, you'll want to test a restaurant by having a conversation with the resident expert(s) about the wine list. Every bottle of wine has a story to tell. All you need is a curiosity, a thirst for discovery. Ask a few questions, relax and enjoy. What better way to listen to a story about fine wine than over a glass of it?

Some of the best wine educators, sommeliers and connoisseurs would much rather tell a story about the wine than talk about whether you can smell apricots or lavender or whether it's got a hint of clove in the finish.

Says Debbie Zachareas, manager of EOS Restaurant and Wine Bar, "Sometimes I like a wine so much I don't want to pull it apart and analyze it the way the *Spectator* does or the way Parker does. I'd rather give people the story of the winemaker or some other particulars and do it with a real passion."

The best sommeliers exercise restraint. Once you engage them in conversation, though, they should be able to convey their knowledge with enthusiasm—and without becoming overbearing, aggressive or showoffish. They should be delighted that someone cares enough to ask questions and should be quick with a good anecdote to enhance your enjoyment of the wine.

Since wine is a moving target, a sommelier's education never ceases. A good one stays abreast of all current developments and trends—vintages and aging, new producers and wines that arise—in order to offer the best to his or her customers.

Many of my favorite restaurants devote significant time and effort to educating their wait staff about wines with activities such as tastings and field trips to wineries.

Some fine establishments don't have a wine steward or a sommelier, instead giving the responsibility to each and every waiter or waitress. "It's a great way to integrate wine with the whole meal experience rather than make it something mysterious, somehow apart," says Campanile's Manfred Krankl, who imbues his staff with his knowledge, passion and enthusiasm. "I view myself more as the coach." He does a lot of work before the game, but when it starts he just sits on the sidelines.

Chanterelle's Roger Dagorn operates in a discreet, reassuring manner with an anecdote here, a recommendation there. When he's out of town on business—almost always related to wine-tasting—the wait staff is ready to fill in with the same light touch.

When someone like Manfred or Roger educates his staff, he's doing the whole wine industry a service. Those waiters and waitresses are going to spread the gospel. Many of them will pursue careers as sommeliers, restaurateurs, chefs, wine buyers and sellers—or maybe just connoisseurs—and they will take their valuable expertise with them.

One way sommeliers can sharpen their skills is by entering competitions, which are essentially multi-tiered exams. There is a blind-tasting portion where contestants are required to identify a wine's grape variety, producer, vineyard and vintage if possible. There are tests of theoretical knowledge of viniculture and viticulture as well as practical knowledge of service, matching foods and wines, presentation, opening and decanting. I have always been amazed at the poise and depth of expertise exhibited by these competitors.

LARRY STONE

LARRY STONE, SOMMELIER AT RUBICON IN SAN FRANCISCO, IS ONE OF AMERICA'S TOP WINE EXPERTS. IN 1986, HE WON A COMPETITION SPONSORED BY FOODS AND WINES OF FRANCE, THE FRENCH GOVERNMENT PROMOTIONAL ORGANIZATION, AS BEST SOMMELIER IN AMERICA, AND THEN WENT ON TO BECOME THE FIRST AMERICAN TO WIN THE INTERNATIONAL COMPETITION IN PARIS.

He beat the French on their home court—not an easy task. "There was a lot of study involved," he says. "I was up all night memorizing soils, topographical maps, different sites." He also trained for the blind-tasting, working with a friend for two years, tackling flights of eight wines three times a week. By the end of this period, his identifications were about 90 percent accurate.

Larry's list at Rubicon highlights a wide range of wines, specializing in historical examples of California wines, especially Cabernets, Meritage and Chardonnay. He also sells quite a few older Rhône wines and Burgundies, which, along with the Cal Cabs, are compatible with the restaurant's modern French-influenced cuisine of the Alain Ducasse school.

THE MASTER SOMMELIERS

THE HIGHEST DEGREE OF WINE EDUCATION IS REPRESENTED BY THE MASTER SOMMELIER TITLE. THE COURSE OF STUDY ENCOMPASSES NOT ONLY BACK-GROUND KNOWLEDGE AND IDENTIFICATION BY BLIND-TASTING BUT INCLUDES THE PRACTICAL ASPECT OF SERVICE AS WELL. AS OF THIS WRITING THERE WERE THIRTY-SEVEN MASTER SOMMELIERS IN THE UNITED STATES:

Nunzio Alioto	Alioto's Restaurant, San Francisco, California
Robert Bath	Shafer Vineyards, Napa Valley, California
Wayne Belding	The Boulder Wine Merchant, Boulder, Colorado
Michael Bonaccorsi	Spago, Beverly Hills, California
Scott Carney	The Tonic Restaurant & Bar, New York, New York
Roger Dagorn	Chanterelle, New York, New York
Fred Dame	Seagram Chateau & Estate Wines Co., San Mateo, California
Richard Dean	The Mark Hotel, New York, New York
Catherine Fallis	Sheegar Productions, Novato, California
Jay Fletcher	Syzygy Restaurant, Aspen, Colorado
Doug Frost	Kansas City, Missouri
Chuck Furuya	Fine Wine Imports, Honolulu, Hawaii
Tim Gaiser	Virtual Vineyards, San Francisco, California
Steven Geddes	Southern Wine and Spirits, Las Vegas, Nevada
Evan Goldstein	School of Services & Hospitality, Rutherford, California
Peter Granoff	Virtual Vineyards, San Francisco, California
Ira Harmon	Western Distributing, Westminster, Colorado
Greg Harrington	Southern Wine & Spirits, Las Vegas, Nevada
Andrea Immer	Starwood Hotels and Resorts, White Plains, New York
Jay James	Bellagio, Las Vegas
Emmanuel Kemiji	The Ritz-Carlton, San Francisco, California
Fran Kysela	Kysela Imports, Winchester, Virginia
Michael McNeil	The Ryland Inn, Whitehouse, New Jersey
Sally Mohr	The Boulder Wine Merchant, Boulder, Colorado
Steve Morey	Seagram Chateau & Estate Wines Co., San Francisco, California
David O'Connor	Oakville Grocery, Menlo Park, California
Damon Ornowski	Carbondale, Colorado
Ed Osterland	San Diego, California
William Sherer	Moose's Restaurant, San Francisco, California
Cameron Sisk	WineBow Importers, Brooklyn, New York
Joseph Spellman	Sommelier Selections, Chicago, Illinois
Larry Stone	Rubicon, San Francisco, California
Angelo Tavernaro	Piazza D'Angelo, Henderson, Nevada
Madeline Triffon	Unique Restaurant Corp., Detroit, Michigan
Claudia Tyagi	Rio Suites Hotel & Casino, Las Vegas, Nevada
Barbara Werley	Caesars Palace, Las Vegas, Nevada
Ronn Wiegand	Restaurant Wine Magazine, Napa, California

CORKED?

EXAMINING THE CORK

LET'S NOT PERPETUATE THE MISCONCEPTION THAT A SOMMELIER HANDS A CUSTOMER THE CORK TO SMELL IT. THE ONLY THING YOU CAN TELL ABOUT A WINE FROM SNIFFING ITS CORK IS HOW THE CORK SMELLS. YOU CAN TELL A LOT ABOUT THE WINE, HOWEVER, BY EXAMINING THE CORK. TAKE A LOOK AT THE STAIN LEFT ON IT BY THE WINE. THE DARKER IT IS AND THE MORE WINE HAS PENETRATED INTO THE CORK, THE BIGGER THE WINE. IF THE STAIN IS LIGHT OR NOT PENETRATING, IT'S GOING TO BE A MUCH BRIGHTER, MORE UP-FRONT, LIGHTER WINE.

SENDING WINES BACK

WHEN A WINE IS "CORKED"—THAT IS, IT HAS GONE BAD IN THE BOTTLE DUE TO A ROTTEN, MOLDY CORK—YOU'LL SMELL A MUSTY ODOR. LIKE SOUR MILK, IT'S USUALLY OBVIOUS WITH ONE WHIFF. IF NOT, YOU'LL DEFINITELY TASTE A FLATNESS, A MUSTINESS WHEN YOU SIP IT. SIMILARLY, IF THE WINE IS OXIDIZED (AKA MADERIZED), YOU'LL NOTICE IT'S TURNING RUST COLORED AND TASTES WASHED-OUT AND ACIDIC. IT'S HALFWAY TO VINEGAR. IN EITHER CASE, THE WINE SHOULD BE SENT BACK.

Unless there's an obvious defect like the two mentioned above, a customer can't reasonably expect the restaurant to take a wine back. It's not really fair to challenge the staff to do that, especially if you do it aggressively and/or for no particular reason. But if it's within the context of an ongoing conversation with the sommelier, including a recommendation, fine restaurants and wine destinations must always do their best to please. The operative principle from the diner's perspective is to be open and honest but not snooty. When the sommelier asks if you like the selection, simply reply, "It's not at all what I expected" and, if possible, try to explain specifically what it is you don't like. Was the wine too sweet or too bitter? Did it feature an aroma of freshly cut grass, which you can't stand? "If it was a wine that I recommended and they didn't like it, I'd take it back and have them order something for themselves," says Scott Carney. He'll then either pour the rejected wine by the glass at the bar for somebody who will appreciate it or taste it later with his staff, turning it into an educational experience.

RECOMMENDATIONS

Is the sommelier or wait staff ready to make recommendations if called upon? Are their recommendations well explained? How good are the wines they recommend and how well do they match the foods you ordered?

Contrary to one popular belief, it is not at all tacky for the sommelier to ask how much you are willing to spend. In fact, good sommeliers *should* ask if you have a price range in mind. It's the ones who don't ask and then automatically recommend the most expensive wines on the list who are suspect. Another acceptable scenario is for the sommelier to offer recommendations in two or three different price ranges, say, lower, higher and/or mid-priced, but definitely not high, higher and highest! If you make it clear that this is a special occasion and you're prepared to splurge, then a high-priced recommendation is fine. If the price is in the stratosphere, though, the wine had better be good enough to send you into orbit.

The wait staff in a fine establishment should almost never make an unsolicited recommendation; they should, however, be delighted when customers do ask and are open to suggestions. The challenge from the sommelier's viewpoint is to help his customers relax and, ultimately, accept a recommendation without feeling humiliated. Scott Carney figures only about 25 to 30 percent of customers on average will ask for a recommendation; most people already have their finger on the bin number of the wine they want and the sommelier becomes simply an order-taker. As a customer, it's great to turn the choice over to an expert, but you should only do it if the trust is there.

At those restaurants where the staff actively suggests food-and-wine pairings, they have to toe a fine line between deference to the customer and the commitment to delivering a great wine experience. It takes subtlety and sometimes humor to pull it off.

BY-THE-GLASS AND TASTING FLIGHTS

All wine bars and many fine restaurants offer selections of wines by the glass. A standard by-the-glass pour is four to six ounces. A fine wine bar should also have tasting alternatives, smaller pours of between two and four ounces. These may be offered on an individual basis or in flights of two to six different but related wines.

A flight might consist of wines of one grape variety from four different regions—Riesling from Germany, Alsace, the United States and Switzerland, for example—or four different wines from one region—say, Alsatian Gewürztraminer, Pinot Blanc, Pinot Gris and Riesling. It might be a vertical tasting, say four consecutive vintages of a particular wine, or a horizontal tasting, four different Australian Cabernets from the same vintage. Both by-the-glass and tasting flights should have plenty of variation and should be rotated periodically.

EOS, an outstanding wine bar in San Francisco, offers an impressive list of between forty and fifty by-the-glass offerings that include a number of standards—a familiar brand of Merlot, say, or a smooth, buttery Chardonnay—alongside at least ten choices fit to stimulate any master sommelier or wine writer. The twenty to twenty-five red and twenty to twenty-five white by-the-glass selections always include Rieslings and Gewürztraminers, at least one wine from Austria, one from South Africa and perhaps some intriguing selections from Spain, and they change several times a week. (There are also twenty to twenty-five dessert wines available by the glass.) You can also order two-ounce pours of a flight of four wines. Now that's what I call a selection!

At Campanile, Manfred Krankl serves wines by the eight-ounce carafe, which is essentially a third of a bottle. They are generally selections that are not available in half bottles and are too unusual or too expensive to serve by the glass. He rotates them about once a week. The eight-ouncer works well if you don't want to invest in a full bottle—you can have a substantial taste of a $50 bottle for $16—or if only one diner drinks wine. "The by-the-glass program doesn't pay off immediately," Manfred says, "but I think it does in the long run. People buy more wine here than they used to in every respect: more quality, more variety, more expensive wines. It opens up the spectrum for everybody. People become more quality conscious and a little more adventuresome—the producers, the retailers and the salespeople as well as the consumers."

Some fine establishments offer special wine-tasting dinners or menus. Any good sommelier will be flattered if you ask him to organize one for you and your friends.

PRICING

Tasting flights and by-the-glass programs make a lot of sense on two fronts: first, you can try more wines than you could if you were ordering by the bottle, and second, very expensive wines become much more accessible.

The normal retail markup on a bottle of wine is double the wholesale price. Restaurants routinely charge double the retail price; that is a 100 percent markup over retail. If they're charging much more than that, they're gouging.

EOS is that rare bird: a full-fledged restaurant that is also a wine bar. There, Debbie Zachareas can serve premium wines and sell them on a volume basis. She practices the philosophy she learned at the Sterling School of Hospitality: "You take dollars to the bank, not margins." Her markup is only double the *wholesale* cost of the bottle, and it's the same for by-the-bottle or by-the-glass. If a bottle costs her $15, then at EOS it's $30 by the bottle or $7.50 by the glass (the bar pours about four glasses out of a bottle). Debbie's by-the-glass prices range from

$3.50 or $4.00 up to about $15.00. (In Beverly Hills, we're in a comparable but somewhat higher range. It's the price of real estate, baby!) At EOS, if someone wants to try a DRC (Domaine de la Romanée-Conti) wine but doesn't want to shell out $30 for a glass, they can try a two-ounce pour for $15. Let's face it, these wines are out of most people's price range. It's fabulous wine, though, and this is a great way to try some and decide whether you think it's worth the price.

Part of the sommelier's skill is to be ahead of the market, buying wines that become highly sought-after and selling them later at a decent profit. "You're not supposed to use the wine list to show what an interesting guy you are," says Scott Carney. "You're supposed to turn a good profit without offending the sensibilities of your clientele. It's sort of a fine calculus." When he was at the Gotham Bar & Grill, Scott had the foresight to buy "name-brand" Burgundies in the excellent '85, '88, '89 and '90 vintages. The restaurant invested in proper warehousing and it was eventually able to add more sheen to its fabulous reputation by offering these prestigious wines that had quickly become scarce out in the market.

Whether a wine lover is buying wines in a restaurant or at a wine shop, if the proprietor or sommelier has done anything to call attention to the price of the wine, even if it's unintentional, there is something wrong. The wine-buying experience should *only* call attention to what's in the bottle. Once again, that's where the focus belongs: on the wine itself and on all the glorious flavors, varieties and *terroirs* that are expressed in and through it. If you take an adventurous approach, keep an open mind and avail yourself of everything your wine merchant or sommelier has to offer, you will begin to enjoy the total wine experience. Your appreciation of and love for wine will grow by leaps and bounds, and you may very well be drawn to collecting.

LONDON UNDER GROUND

SOMETIMES, WHEN YOU'RE IN A PUBLIC ESTABLISHMENT, IT PAYS TO INQUIRE POLITELY ABOUT THE WINE CELLAR. UNLESS YOU KNOW THE RESTAURANT WELL, YOU MIGHT BE IN FOR A RUDE AWAKENING.

A few years ago, my wife, Chris, and I went to London and were invited out to the theater as the guests of a lyricist and composer. Afterward, we went to a well-known hotel restaurant along with a distinguished local wine writer. A bottle of fine red Bordeaux was ordered and it took a long time for it to be brought to the table. When it finally arrived, it was quite cold. I asked about that and the wine writer said it was because they had such wonderful old underground cellars in London. I suspected the wine was over the hill. Because it was so cold, though, it was hard to distinguish any specific faults. We asked the sommelier if we could see the cellar. He said he was terribly sorry, but that was against all the rules of the hotel and restaurant. No patrons were allowed to visit the cellar due to insurance restrictions and so forth.

Needless to say, we had a very enjoyable evening, but I left still wondering about the wine. I asked Chris if we could go back to the same restaurant on our own a couple of nights later. We did and the same sommelier came to the table. I made my selection—Champagne this time—and I asked him again if I could see the cellar. He reminded me that it was against the rules. I pressed him a bit, explaining that we had come all the way from California and were so very interested in the way they did things in Britain. Finally, he agreed to let us see the cellar. We went down through a huge kitchen that served not just the restaurant but the whole hotel. It was very warm in there. When we got to the back, there were boxes and bins of wines stacked right up against a wall, with hot water pipes and vents running all around. I asked him if they kept all their wines there. He said yes, they simply chilled them before they brought them to the table, which is why it took a little extra time on occasion. I can't fault the sommelier's honesty, but it just goes to show, you can't always tell by the temperature of the wine. (See Chapter 5 for guidelines on storage conditions.)

A FEW OF MY FAVORITE
WINE DESTINATIONS

RESTAURANTS WITH A DEEP, WIDE SELECTION, ARE RELATIVELY RARE. ONE OF MY FAVORITES IS VALENTINO, IN LOS ANGELES, WHICH AS FAR AS I'M CONCERNED IS THE BEST ITALIAN RESTAURANT IN THE UNITED STATES. (I'M FAR FROM BEING A RESTAURANT CRITIC, BUT THERE ARE MANY OF THAT ILK WHO AGREE.) IT HAS A SPECTACULAR WINE LIST THAT IS OVER A HUNDRED PAGES LONG AND IS THE ENVY OF MANY A SOMMELIER OR COLLECTOR. IT'S LIKE A ROLL CALL OF THE FINEST WINES IN THE WORLD. I LOVE VALENTINO NOT ONLY BECAUSE OF THE FOOD AND SERVICE BUT ALSO BECAUSE OF MY FRIEND PIERO SELVAGGIO, THE MANAGER-PROPRIETOR, WHO LENDS IT SO MUCH ADDED CHARM. HE ALSO WORKS VERY HARD TO MAINTAIN THAT LIST.

Another of my favorite restaurants that offers a superior list is chef Joachim Splichal's Patina, which is set in a spare, tastefully appointed house on Melrose Avenue in Los Angeles. Consistently rated at the top of its class since its founding in 1989, it is the flagship of a fabulous string of seven restaurants that includes Pinot Blanc in St. Helena, Napa Valley, as well as five other Pinot locations in the L.A. area. At Patina, they use Riedel Vinum series stemware (also for sale through the restaurant), just one of the 1,001 details that constitute a total wine experience. Patina has a wonderful tasting menu that changes every couple of weeks; Sommelier Chris Meeske pairs specific wines with each course. They also offer a variety of entertaining food-and-wine events.

Here are a few more of my top choices:

• Campanile, Los Angeles, founded in 1989 by Manfred Krankl, who early on developed a reputation for an eclectic and adventurous list.

• Chanterelle, a small gem of a French-style gourmet restaurant located in the Tribeca neighborhood of Manhattan, owned and operated by the husband-and-wife team of Karen and David Waltuck and renowned for its food, decor, service and aura of quiet elegance. Roger Dagorn, a master sommelier, current chairman and past president of the Sommelier Society of America (SSA), is the sommelier.

• EOS, a thriving, hip, modern wine destination in San Francisco where you can enjoy wine on just about any level you choose. It features a list of about five hundred by-the-bottle selections that rotates frequently and delivers flavor and personality to a diverse clientele in a casual, comfortable atmosphere.

• Barolo in Manhattan's Soho district, which has an inclusive list of Italian wines managed by sommelier Renzo Rapacioli.

• Hayes & Vine is a delightful wine bar, patterned on a European model but with a very American silhouette, located in the Convention Center area of San Francisco. It's a clean, modern, elegant, relaxed, hip, state-of-the-art establishment, a prototypical wine bar for the new millennium. It exudes an air of California casual chic and it offers a truly intriguing list of wines that changes frequently. Even for the most jaded connoisseur, this is the type of wine joint where every time you walk in you're likely to make an exciting new discovery.

• Michael's of Santa Monica is an L.A. institution, known for its elegant setting, superb California cuisine with the best fresh ingredients and a wine list that has had depth and quality from the early days. David Rosoff came on board at the beginning of 1996 and spiffed up the offerings, adding wines from South Africa and Australia, Oregon and Austria to a substantial base of French and California classics.

• Other recommendations: The Tonic Restaurant Bar, New York City, a classic wine destination, courtesy of Scott Carney, master sommelier, formerly of the Gotham Bar & Grill and Tavern on the Green; Rubicon, San Francisco, where Larry Stone is sommelier; Spago, Beverly Hills; Zuni Cafe, San Francisco, featuring Judy Rodgers's rustic Mediterranean cuisine and a casual-hip downtown atmosphere; Oliveto, Oakland, another top Italian restaurant (both the Zuni Cafe and Oliveto wine lists are managed by sommelier Steve Kopp); Rancho Caymus Inn, Rutherford, Napa Valley, from the folks at Flora Springs Wine Co.

• My favorite chef: Thomas Keller, The French Laundry, Yountville, California, who also has a bistro down the street called Bouchon.

Chapter Five

IN THE CELLAR

STORING AND COLLECTING WINES

THERE ARE THOSE WHO SAY A COLLECTOR IS ANYONE WHO BUYS MORE WINE THAN THEY CAN DRINK THAT EVENING. I LIKE SIMPLE DEFINITIONS, AND THIS ONE MAKES AS MUCH SENSE AS ANY OTHER. WHETHER YOU HAVE TWENTY OR TWO HUNDRED OR TWENTY THOUSAND BOTTLES OF WINE, YOU CAN PROBABLY CALL YOURSELF A COLLECTOR. FAR MORE IMPORTANT THAN WHAT YOU HAVE IS YOUR ATTITUDE.

Like any other hobby, collecting wine has a tendency to mushroom. Over the years, I've known many wine lovers who've become virtually obsessed and ended up with a lot more wine than they or their friends could ever possibly drink. I guess it's a modern-day manifestation of our hunter-gatherer instinct; we love the hunt. There's also a real satisfaction in knowing you've got a stash of some really good stuff put away for a special occasion, for a rainy day. True collectors are passionate and enthusiastic. They are also generous; they don't hoard. Let's always remember that fine wine demands a witness. It needs to be shared with someone for the experience. That's the whole fun of building a cellar, of acquiring some special wines.

Have you ever seen the bumper sticker that says "He who dies with the most toys wins"? Well, it doesn't apply to wine. He who dies with the biggest wine cellar is actually a loser because it means he never had the pleasure of drinking all those delicious wines. When I had my first real success at The Wine Merchant, I bought a house with a wonderful wine cellar that had been owned by Errol Flynn. The real estate agent recounted a famous statement that Flynn made.

He said anyone who dies with more than $10,000 in the bank or more than ten bottles left in his cellar was a fool and certainly had not lived his life correctly.

You can be a collector if you've got two cases of wine in your basement. If you followed Parker or *The Wine Spectator* and bought twenty-four bottles because they were rated 90 points or higher, you're not a collector, you're an investor. If you took some time to cultivate your interest, even if it was just a five-minute chat with your favorite wine merchant, if you bought those wines in search of new taste experiences, then you're a collector. If you have a thousand cases that you bought by the labels, then in my book you're not a true collector.

My definition of a true collector is someone who buys wines because he or she loves to drink them and share them with friends. They don't buy them for the prestige. Their collections are not trophies; neither are they investments.

In this chapter, we'll discuss some fundamentals and guidelines that will help you master the common-sense aspects of collecting.

Pablo Torres of the '21' Club, New York City, working in the restaurant's cellar.

GUIDELINES FOR STORAGE

Whatever your plans for a wine, whether it will be cellared for years or served within a month, proper storage is essential. There are many options for storing wine, from simple racks you can position in a corner of your living or dining room to temperature- and humidity-controlled cabinets, from large custom-built wine cellars to leasing space in a warehouse. As with any aspect of wine enjoyment, you have to decide which option is right for your budget and your time and space constraints. It's best to start small, with the simplest, most economical solution, and build as you accumulate wine knowledge and experience.

Your first priority should be to ensure proper storage conditions. Wines should be kept away from fluctuations in temperature and from light, heat and vibration, all of which can cause long-term damage. The bottles should lie on their sides so the corks stay in contact with the wine to ensure that ever-so-slight seepage of oxygen that's so important to the wine's subtle aging process.

Younger wines can be stored at room temperature (68 to 72 degrees F.) for months without fear of damage; just be sure the conditions are constant. Older, rarer, more fragile wines should probably be stored in cellar conditions —a bit cooler and more humid than modern temperature-controlled living environments.

If you are serious about collecting and storing wines, you should consider investing in a dedicated wine-storage unit for your home or leasing space in a wine-storage facility. As the number of sophisticated wine lovers and connoisseurs increases, I see these facilities becoming more common—in warehouses, at mini-storage locations, at clubs and restaurants. Home wine-storage units come in sizes ranging from a small mini-refrigerator-type appliance to deluxe units larger than any food fridge, capable of holding fifteen hundred bottles or more. One of the best places to find out about them is through mail-order ads in the wine magazines or newspaper food sections.

WINE STORAGE TEMPERATURES

OPTIMUM: 58 TO 65 DEGREES F. with no more than 2 degrees fluctuation in a twenty-four-hour period.

ACCEPTABLE: 65 TO 75 DEGREES F. with no more than 4 degrees fluctuation per day.

DANGER: 65 TO 75 DEGREES F. with 10 degrees or more fluctuation.

If you are buying a home storage unit or custom-building one, insulation should be a part of the package; it's more efficient, energy-wise and it's also extra insurance in case of an extended power failure.

HOW TO MAKE WINE VINEGAR

NOT SURPRISINGLY, WONDERFUL WINES MAKE WONDERFUL VINEGARS, AND BECAUSE THEY WILL KEEP INDEFINITELY, THEY ARE A SMART WAY TO SALVAGE LEFTOVER WINE THAT WOULD OTHERWISE BE THROWN OUT. HERE'S HOW TO DO IT:

Place three tablespoons of good vinegar (or a batch you've already made from premium wine) into a clean glass jar or wine bottle with the leftover wine. Cover the jar or bottle with gauze or cheesecloth, secure with a rubber band and stopper it with a removable top. Store the jar or bottle, stoppered, in stable conditions at 70 to 80 degrees F. Continue to add leftover portions of the same (or similar) wine until the container is full. (You can also add flavorings such as tarragon, rosemary, cloves or garlic for extra zing.) When the container is full, stopper it and age for as long as you wish.

In 1981, recognizing that few L.A. homes had basements, I started a storage business called The Wine Cellar at a warehouse facility in West Los Angeles. It consists of about 15,000 square feet of storage space kept at a constant 58 to 62 degrees F. with 75 percent humidity. I had large refrigeration and humidification units custom-designed to provide these ideal long-term storage conditions, which are what you would find in a fine European cellar. The storage units come in three sizes: cages that hold between 100 and 150 cases of wine; large lockers for 40 cases and smaller ones for 24 to 32 cases. We have 24-hour security, easy access and a private party room for tastings and dinners. I believe The Wine Cellar was the first facility of its kind in Los Angeles, and I feel flattered that others have followed our lead.

Here are a couple more important practical considerations having to do with storage and aging:

Ullage: This refers to the amount of space between the wine and the cork. In an upright bottle, it should be no more than half an inch. If it is more, it means that the wine is seeping and/or evaporating, that it has been improperly shipped or stored or simply that the cork is getting too old. The solution is simple: recork the bottle. If you're not confident doing it yourself, take it to your local merchant, who should be able to take care of the problem.

Leftover wine: You can recork and save an unfinished bottle of wine in the fridge overnight or for a couple of days. At our wine bar, we use a wine preservative, which is a spray can that injects a mixture of inert gases—argon, nitrogen and carbon dioxide—into the wine bottle, replacing the oxygen. You simply recork the bottle and store the wine until the next use with no fear of oxidation or spoilage. There are several of these products on the market now.

If there's too little wine to bother with or you're concerned that it may already have started to go bad, you can make vinegar (see sidebar). The better the wine, the better the vinegar.

AGING POTENTIAL: RULES OF THUMB

FOR RED WINES: The darker the pigment at the end of the cork, the more "ageable" or collectible the wine is.
FOR WHITE WINES: The higher the alcohol content, the longer it can age—examples: big white Burgundies like Meursault and Montrachet; Sauternes like Château d'Yquem.

WINE AND TIME

Wine's aging process is a mystery and a miracle that is not fully understood by science. What we do know is that with age, the family of compounds known as phenolics, which includes tannins and anthocyans (color compounds), gradually combine, intermingle and form complex interconnections, giving wine a smoother, subtler, more integrated matrix of flavors and aromas. This is mostly true of red wines, since they contain more of these compounds. There are some white wines that possess enough acid (which along with tannin is believed to act as a preservative as well as a balance of sweetness and fruit) that they can improve with age.

Is there such a thing as a wine that's too old? Absolutely. Technically, what happens is molecules of the larger compounds begin to drop out of the solution as sediment, draining away color and flavor, and the wine gradually begins to oxidize.

I recently experienced a 1982 Vosne-Romanée, which is a wine with a deservedly huge reputation, from the village that is arguably the pinnacle of Burgundy's *grand crus*. Unfortunately, this one was a disappointment. It was on its way out if not dead already. Like dried flowers, its once-luscious flavors and aromas were but a hint of their former glory. It was like listening to the last words of a prophet; you had to lean very close and listen hard and even then you couldn't be sure what he was saying.

Are there wines that will *always* improve with age? Nothing lasts forever, but there are some very old ones that can still deliver an amazing experience. Some collectors I know are drinking wines from 1921 and they swear they're still great. Hugh Johnson, in his pocket encyclopedia, has said that the great St.-Emilion Château Figeac, for example, can age "indefinitely."

Are there wines that absolutely shouldn't be drunk until they've attained a certain age? More and more this is a thing of the past. It used to be that an early tasting of a wine that was "meant for aging" was a fairly difficult experience. Like listening to a piece of dissonant modern classical music, we knew we were supposed to like it but it took more intellectual effort than we were willing to give. (Just give me Mozart!) No more. Today, fine wines that are built to age can also taste good right out of the chute. They can be full-bodied and tannic yet well balanced with plenty of ripe fruit.

Wines that improve with age are still the backbone of any serious collection, but the priority has shifted to drinkability. It may be that certain "ageable" wines in certain vintages are actually better when consumed young. They are fruity, round and delicious; some of them may never be that spectacular again. This is why it's always a good idea, if you're collecting, to sample a bottle or two of a wine immediately and track it as it ages, gradually drinking down the rest of your supply. The point is to drink a wine at its peak and if that peak is within a few years of bottling, why risk missing it? As any collector will tell you, the worst sin is to let a wine die in your cellar. It's like investing in the stock market. Everyone always wants to know the best time to sell, but there is never a formula and always a certain amount of risk. If you cash in some stocks to buy yourself a nice house, try to forget about any regrets that you didn't sell at the top of the market. Just enjoy the house.

GUIDELINES FOR BUILDING A COLLECTION

Who really needs a wine cellar? The minute you see more than eight bottles accumulating on top of your refrigerator, in your hall closet or somewhere else around the house, whether you think you need a cellar or not, you have just acquired one. From this point, there are only two ways to proceed.

The first plan, which I don't care to cover in much detail, is for an *investment cellar*—that is, putting together a collection strictly for financial gain. It's a very simple formula. All it takes is seed money. You don't even need to build a cellar at home. Store the wines at a temperature-controlled facility so that when you want to sell them in the future at auction this can be listed as a credential, absolutely guaranteeing their provenance. Your collection will consist of trophy wines from the classified-growth châteaus of Bordeaux, a few prestigious *negociants* in Burgundy and a handful of small California premium producers. I don't see a whole lot of pleasure in this approach. The wines aren't much more than museum pieces about which you can say "I have it and you don't and I don't really plan on sharing it with anyone unless there's some sort of financial gain involved." Enough of that. I think by now my position on trophy collecting or the investment approach is quite clear.

The other type of cellar is what I call a *working cellar.* You started by acquiring eight or nine bottles and now you're taking it seriously because you've found that wine is a lot of fun, that it's a lot more fun when you share it with someone and it's even more fun to tell stories about it after you've consumed it. Two or three months, even two or three years, after you've consumed a really fine bottle, the grandeur of the occasion seems to continue growing and the tasting of a wine becomes a legendary experience in the retelling. This is what I mean when I talk about collecting.

The first step in building a collection is to decide what you like. The traditional collection has always been built on a foundation of red Bordeaux. Nowadays, though, collectors are just as likely to balance their acquisitions between New and Old World, Italian and French, Californian and Australian, with whatever focus or emphasis suits their fancy.

When you're acquiring a wine cellar for enjoyment, there is no hard-and-fast formula. So many merchants and wine writers talk about what kind of collection you should put together for $500, for $10,000 and so forth. I don't believe in giving prescriptions: "Buy X amount of this and Y amount of that." I prefer to offer guidelines and encourage the fledgling collector to develop his or her own preferences. In keeping with this philosophy, here are a few thoughts to consider when starting to build a collection:

1. Remember that 85 percent of all wine is consumed within the first year after it's produced.
2. Never put a sign on a case of wine or above your cellar door that says: "Do not open until the year 2010."

As in all matters wine-related, balance and variety are crucial in building a collection. Don't miss the rainbow! Don't limit yourself to one type of wine, to one variety or region. To achieve balance in your collection, apply some of the same criteria listed in the previous chapter for judging restaurant wine lists: scope and variety, personal preference, building a base, finding a theme. Emulate a distinguished restaurant list or follow the blueprint on page 161.

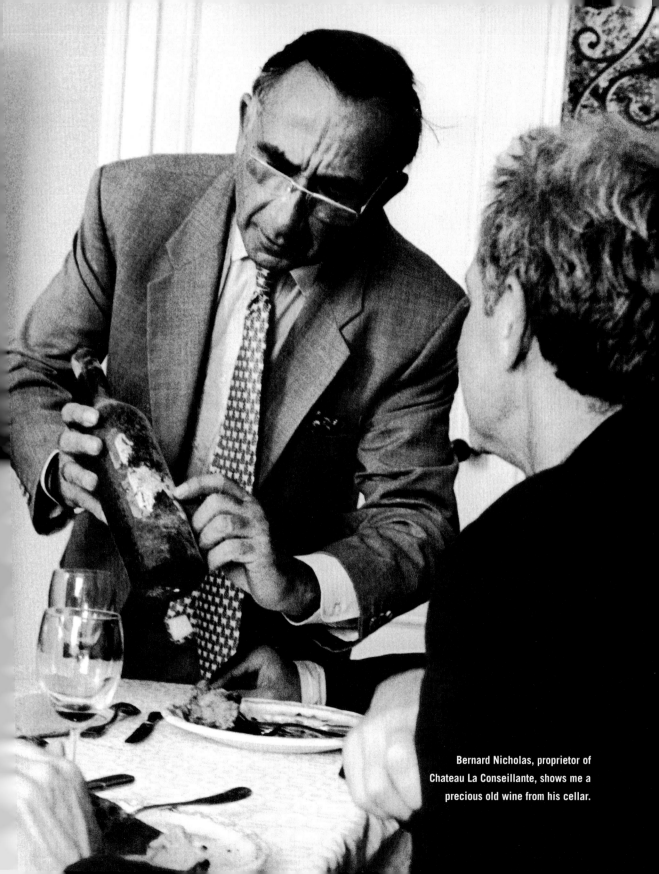

Bernard Nicholas, proprietor of Chateau La Conseillante, shows me a precious old wine from his cellar.

When you're buying wine, you need to develop a plan. First, just don't run out and look at those racks of wine on the shelf and start buying. Take your time. Put some thought into your purchase. How much are you going to spend? With whom are you going to enjoy these wines?

Decide if you want your collection to be vertical or horizontal or a little bit of both. It's your choice! Some collectors concentrate on buying each and every vintage of a handful of favorite producers—a vertical approach. Others may pursue a wider variety of producers with more emphasis on certain highly rated vintages—a more horizontal approach. You might, for example, collect a case each of ten consecutive vintages of your four favorite Burgundy producers *or* you might decide to buy a case from each of ten producers but only in the four best vintages of the decade.

Collectors often have a preponderance of the classic Bordeaux and Burgundies, then they add a couple of interesting sidelights, for example, verticals of a couple of top Australian producers such as Penfolds or Lindemans. You can take an eclectic approach, buying your favorite flavor of the moment and amassing a wide variety of wines. You might start out with a Latin theme, building a collection of Barolos and Supertuscans from Italy along with Riojas from Spain. Then you might go Germanic with some late-harvest gems from up north or maybe branch out into some California collectible instead. A working cellar is always in a certain state of flux as you drink from it and continue to pursue new avenues to replenish it. It reflects the changing tastes and focus of its collector. If you want to organize more formal tastings, which can be a lot of fun, following a more structured or logical acquisition strategy will make more sense.

Seasoned collectors will agree that the only foolproof way to buy wines is through a reliable merchant and/or shipper who will guarantee optimum shipping conditions and replace wines that have gone bad. It's risky to buy from other collectors or at auctions because even if you're dealing with the most reputable houses—Sotheby's, Christie's and so forth—you're still not absolutely sure whether the wines were stored properly or if they had been damaged at some point. This is especially true with older wines. In the United States, for example, even as recently as the mid-1980s, many collectors stored rare and valuable wines in less-than-ideal conditions.

Which red wines should you collect? Bordeaux is the first one that comes to mind. Others recommended for collecting are: California Cabernets; Barolo, Brunello, Barbaresco and Taurasi from Italy; Hermitage and Côte-Rôtie from the Rhône Valley; red Burgundy; Spain's Rioja.

Which white wines? Because of their lack of tannins and their fresh, fruity style, most white wines are meant to be drunk in the first few years after their release. Some age well for five to ten years, but obviously if you're starting a collection, it's going to be skewed much more toward red. White Burgundies; white Bordeaux; some Rieslings; Sauternes; late-harvest German, Alsatian and Loire Valley wines, and fine vintage Champagne often possess sufficient body and structure to suggest aging potential, which means they are all potentially collectible.

In amassing a collection, it's a good idea to do some long-term planning. If you find a wine you like, buy enough of it to try a bottle every year over a five- to ten-year period so you can track its development. Over time,

"Somehow—I don't know why—people who are really into wine tend to be fascinating in their own right. They are delightful people to meet."
—Bipin Desai, theoretical physicist and wine collector

WHEN FIRST STARTING A COLLECTION, THINK ABOUT FORMING A BASE. JOHN THOREEN, THE WINE TUTOR, SUGGESTED TO ME A GOOD WAY TO BEGIN. START WITH LEON ADAMS'S PREMISE THAT THERE ARE ONLY TWO KINDS OF WINE IN THE WORLD: WEEKDAY WINES AND SUNDAY WINES. FIND ONE GOOD, REASONABLY PRICED WHITE AND A SIMILAR RED FOR WEEKDAY CONSUMPTION AND CALL THEM YOUR HOUSE WINES. THEY BECOME YOUR BASIS FOR COMPARISON. ANYTIME YOU COME ACROSS A WINE THAT'S MORE INTERESTING, MORE CHALLENGING, BETTER-TASTING, MAKE A NOTE. CONSIDER ADDING A FEW BOTTLES OF IT TO YOUR COLLECTION OR, IF IT'S IN THE RIGHT PRICE RANGE, MAKING IT YOUR NEW HOUSE WINE. LET YOUR OWN PALATE BE YOUR GUIDE, NOT YOUR WINE TUTOR, YOUR RETAILER, A SOMMELIER OR SOME WINE JOURNALIST.

you'll learn how age affects your favorite wines. As always, there's no substitute for popping corks. Don't ever forget: Wine is a moving target. It changes. Give it the time and respect it demands and you will be rewarded.

Unless you're buying for investment or posterity, there's no point in accumulating more wine than you and/or your friends can drink in a lifetime. If you're fifty years old and you drink an average of one bottle a week from your collection, for instance, it doesn't make a lot of sense to have two thousand bottles of Bordeaux that need ten more years of bottle age unless you are leaving them to someone in your will. By the same token, if you're collecting something like Burgundy, you should plan to hold at least a portion of it for five to fifteen years before drinking.

Another consideration to keep in mind: You don't have to buy all standard-sized bottles. Magnums, for example, are a lot of fun for special occasions such as fancy dinner parties, and some connoisseurs swear the wines age differently in them, too.

One more important criterion that is often ignored is your geographical location. If you live in the desert, a formula that says your cellar should consist of so many bottles of Port, so many bottles of Burgundy, so many bottles of Bordeaux does not apply. The wines are simply too heavy. If you live at the beach, you are likely to take a different approach toward the composition of your cellar than someone who lives in the city. You'll find that your style of entertainment, your mood and your ideas about food-wine pairings will reflect your environment.

Whether it's big or small, a collection benefits from organization.

HERE IS A BLUEPRINT FOR A START-UP COLLECTION OF BETWEEN 120 AND 150 BOTTLES THAT HAS A FAIRLY TRADITIONAL EMPHASIS WITH AN ECLECTIC NOTE. YOU CAN BEGIN STOCKING A CELLAR BY FOLLOWING THIS GUIDELINE AND CREATING YOUR OWN VARIATIONS. CONSULT THE APPENDIX FOR RECOMMENDED WINES WITHIN THESE CATEGORIES OR ASK YOUR TRUSTED LOCAL MERCHANT FOR EQUIVALENTS. AT AN AVERAGE OF $12.50 PER BOTTLE, THIS FOUNDATION WILL COST YOU A TOTAL OF APPROXIMATELY $1,500—OR JUST UNDER $100 PER WEEK OVER A FOUR-MONTH PERIOD. AT THE HIGHER END, IF YOU AVERAGE $33 PER BOTTLE, IT WILL SET YOU BACK ABOUT $5,000. (SEE PAGE 162 FOR AN EXAMPLE OF HOW ONE WINE ENTHUSIAST WOULD SPEND HIS MONEY.)

A BASE COLLECTION

FRANCE

2 cases red Bordeaux (mix of Cabernet-based Medoc wines and Merlot-based St.-Emilion and Pomerol)
1 case red Burgundy
½ case Champagne
½ case white Burgundy
several bottles each of red Rhône wines, Alsatian whites and Sancerre

THE REST OF THE WORLD

2 cases California Cabernet
1 case Barolo
1 case Supertuscans and/or Chiantis
½ case California Chardonnay
½ case California and/or Oregon Pinot Noir
½ case Australian Cabernet, Shiraz and/or blends
½ case Spanish reds (Rioja and/or Ribera del Duero)
several bottles each of California Rhône and/or Italian varietals, California or Washington State Merlot,
New Zealand and/or South African Sauvignon Blanc, miscellaneous Italian selections

A COLLECTOR'S WISH LIST

WE ASKED SEATTLE PUBLISHING ENTREPRENEUR MICHAEL ROZEK, WHO IS A PASSIONATE WINE LOVER, TO PUT TOGETHER A WISH LIST GIVEN A BUDGET OF $5,000. HERE'S WHAT HE CAME UP WITH:

FIRST LEVEL

1 case each of 4 of the best Bordeaux wines you can find—around $600+ each, definitely bought as futures (*Note:* Châteaus Latour, Margaux, Lafite-Rothschild would be nice, but their prices have been driven so high that you'd probably be able to afford only about 3 bottles each of the mid-1990s vintages. So in order to collect cases, you might choose some less-expensive, lesser-known châteaus.)

SECOND LEVEL

1 case each of Pahlmeyer Merlot (around $600+), Guigal Hermitage or Châteauneuf-du-Pape (around $400+), Leonetti (Washington State) Cabernet Sauvignon or Merlot (around $500+), Peter Michael "Les Pavots" Red Table Wine (around $600+) all in 1990s vintages

THIRD LEVEL

6 bottles of good New Zealand Sauvignon Blanc (for example, Cloudy Bay, Stonleigh, Villa Maria), about $75

6 bottles of inexpensive French Viognier, about $60

3 Didier Dagueneau wines (he makes Sauvignon Blancs, Fume Blancs and Pouilly-Fumes), about $75

3 of Sean Thackerey's (California) "Pleiades" Old Vines Red Table Wine (a blend of Syrah, Grenache, Zinfandel, Carignane, Nebbiolo, Mourvèdre and many other grapes), about $75

3 Steele (California) or Bethel Heights (Oregon) Pinot Noirs, about $60

6 bottles of any wine from Navarro, an amazingly consistent and affordable California vintner that makes good Cabernets, Merlots, Pinot Noirs, Zinfandels, whites and dessert wines, about $80

2 Andrew Will (Washington State) Merlots, about $55

2 Blackwood Canyon (Washington State) late-harvest dessert wines: for example, a twelve-year-old Gewürztraminer the color of prune juice (wow!)

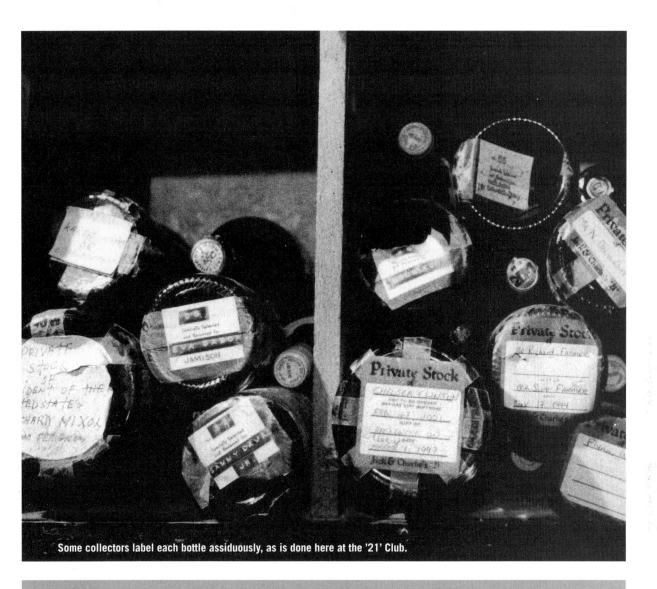

Some collectors label each bottle assiduously, as is done here at the '21' Club.

Michael's comments illuminate his choices: "All of the 'First Level' wines can sit for twenty to thirty years. They will surely go up in price and become scarce during that time. And one can always be sure of their initial and eventual quality. I'd spend half my 'nut' on them alone, grabbing them while I could, as a benchmark, a blue-chip no-brainer.

"My thoughts on the 'Second Level' are more or less the same as on the first. Guigal will hold twenty years, Leonetti ten to twenty, Pahlmeyer ten to twenty, Peter Michael fifteen to twenty. These are four very different reds with very little chance of low quality, to some a step down from the great Bordeaux wines above but still great wines—big, fruity, complex, subtle, pure, masterful—with geographical and personality diversity.

"This leaves about $500 in my budget. How should I spend it? On foolproof wines I can cellar briefly, one to three years (the 'Third Level'). This way, I'll be drinking some nice wine while the other stuff ages. Of course, for this third level to work, it'll need to be constantly replenished or replaced with new items, allowing me to keep reading about, learning about, tasting and buying new wine, too."

BOTTLE SIZES

THE STANDARD WINE BOTTLE SIZE IS 750 MILLILITERS, WHICH IS A LITTLE OVER 25 OUNCES. THE STANDARD WINEGLASS SERVING IS 6 OUNCES, A "RESTAURANT POUR." LARGER BOTTLE SIZES ALL HAVE NAMES AND THEY HOLD THE FOLLOWING EQUIVALENT AMOUNTS:

MAGNUM	2 STANDARD BOTTLES
JEROBOAM	4 BOTTLES
REHOBOAM	6 BOTTLES
METHUSELAH	8 BOTTLES
SALMANAZAR	12 BOTTLES
BALTHAZAR	16 BOTTLES
NEBUCHADNEZZAR	20 BOTTLES

MATCHING THE CELLAR
TO THE CLIENT

Being The Wine Merchant, Beverly Hills, I've been asked to consult with many wealthy, demanding and high-profile clients in putting together their wine cellars. They're usually busy people used to acquiring *the best* and having it *now*. Much more important than following some kind of collecting formula, however, is to judge a client's attitudes and predispositions, then to give them what will make them feel most comfortable. I try to read the signals rather than make the obvious assumption—that they can afford the "name" wines, that they'll enjoy showing them off so I might as well sell them those. You and/or your wine merchant should apply the same sort of criteria—that is, enjoyment as opposed to prestige—in building your own collection.

I remember a few years back, Johnny Carson called and said, "Dennis, I bought a new home and it has an empty wine cellar. I'd like to fill it." The cellar, he told me, was built to accommodate more than twelve hundred cases of wine, more than fourteen thousand bottles. Needless to say, I was thrilled. What a great opportunity, especially with a client who had the resources to fill it immediately. I went over to Johnny's house and he showed me around.

One of the first things I noticed was there were only six chairs at Johnny's dining room table. Before we went down to the wine cellar, he graciously gave us each a jacket so we wouldn't catch a chill. I started to survey the cellar and tried to picture where everything would go. Johnny soon returned with a big bowl of freshly popped popcorn. "You know," he said, "being from Nebraska there are some things I do very well. One of those is popcorn. I know how to make a mean batch and I wanted to share some with you." He went back upstairs. After a while we followed him and went on to discuss what kinds of wines he should have. I told him the most important consideration was what type of entertaining

he would be doing, how he would share his wines. I commented about the size of his dining room table and noted that it seemed he was really a rather private person. I also took into account his sharing of the popcorn, which showed me that regardless of his financial wherewithal he was a person who really knew who he was and what he was. It wasn't as if he'd brought out Champagne and caviar. Here was a person who really enjoyed his life—dining on simple, delicious cuisine with a few close friends. He had nothing to prove to the world. Rather than throw a big, lavish Hollywood party, he would just as soon sit down and enjoy the green flash as the sun set over the Pacific. You certainly don't need Romanée-Conti with that. There was no point in putting together a cellar of trophy wines, wines of tremendous complexity. So we put together a collection of wines that retailed in the neighborhood of $25, adding just a few luxuries for special occasions.

Johnny has stayed in touch over the years. After he retired from "The Tonight Show," he and his wife went on a couple of safaris to Africa. He called me after one of them and said, "We took a Bordeaux wine that you put in our cellar, the Château St.-Georges, and we enjoyed it very much. We opened up a bottle and drank it looking up at a billion stars, hearing the wild animals cry in the night, watching the satellites race across the sky. It was truly a great pleasure." This wine had cost him less than $19 a bottle; it was not Haut-Brion, it was not Mouton. It didn't have to be and it reinforced for me the fact that wine demands a witness, that it's about sharing, that a certain bottle of wine in a certain place at a certain time delivers an incomparable experience. Forget about formulas or quotas, anchors or highlights—*this* is the attitude I'd like to encourage among collectors. Whether you're a wide-eyed novice or a knowledgeable veteran collector of fine wines, focus on quality not price, on the *experiences* not the *appearances*.

CONNOISSEUR

IN ADDITION TO A SOLID FOUNDATION, EVERY CELLAR SHOULD HAVE A DISTINGUISHING STYLE OR CHARACTER THAT SAYS SOMETHING ABOUT ITS COLLECTOR. AS AN ILLUSTRATION, HERE ARE A FEW PERSONALITY TYPES AND THEIR "MUST-HAVE" WINES:

THE CUTTING-EDGE HIPSTER

Clarendon Hills Estrella, a blend of Cabernet Sauvignon and Shiraz (Syrah), a big over-the-top hippie wine from Australia.

Sillex Asteroid, a Sancerre for the new millennium from Didier Dagueneau. Drink it while reading *The Hitchiker's Guide to the Galaxy*.

Château Musar from the Bekaa Valley of Lebanon, just down the road from Hezbollah headquarters. This wine is producer Serge Hochar's homage to Bordeaux: big fruit, powerful tannins.

Randall Grahm's Bonny Doon wines from the Santa Cruz Mountains of California because they make conversational sense at three o'clock in the morning.

Lots of cheap Champagne and Guinness Stout to make Black Velvets, Dublin's favorite drink, which has become très chic in Hollywood.

THE ESOTERIC INTELLECTUAL

Clos Ste.-Hune from the producer Trimbach, known as Charles de Gaulle's favorite wine, an austere and elegant Alsatian Riesling.

Hungarian Tokay Eszencia, the fabulously sweet dessert wine. Pure apricot pits—the essence of laetrile.

Oregon Pinot Noirs: Just as the Bordeaux lover can recite the stellar years of the past two decades—1982, 1986, 1990, 1995 and 1996—so this fine fellow can tell you the Oregon vintages that have been spared the Pineapple Express, which is what they call those nasty, crop-diluting rainstorms that sweep across the Pacific direct from Hawaii. It's only one in four and he'll have them all in his cellar.

CELLARS

THE RESPECTED PROFESSIONAL

Unroll the blueprint! This gentleman has got his cellar impeccably laid out and every bin labeled. These are the doctors and lawyers who make up the wine intelligentsia. They read Parker and *The Wine Spectator.* Their approach is solid, grounded, if a bit conventional.

Classified Bordeaux wines, particularly first and second growths: Château Margaux and Ducru-Beaucaillou would be perfect.

Any of the Domaine de la Romanée-Conti wines. They're a no-brainer, like that big Mercedes in the driveway.

Everything produced by Helen Turley. A quality guarantee.

Bollinger and Krug Champagnes. Big, bubbly and classic.

THE GOURMET HOME CHEF

The obvious angle here would be high-end "food-friendly" wines to go with those perfectly choreographed dinner parties:

He loves the wonderful flavors of the Rhône wines, especially those produced by the master, Guigal.

Budget considerations aside, he should be well-stocked with the wines of Emmanuel Rouget, who has plots in the great Burgundy vineyards of Nuits-St.-Georges, Echézeaux and Vosne-Romanée. These wines are nothing but pure, unblemished fruit, absolutely perfect Pinot Noir grapes that would win any beauty contest they entered.

The Gourmet is a Barolo freak; he's also fascinated by the great German dessert wines, the Auslese, Beerenauslese and Trockenbeerenauslese categories from late-harvested Riesling.

THE SOPHISTICATED WORLD TRAVELER

The Traveler knows where these wines live and how to get there: he's walked the vineyards, sniffed the breeze, seen the Aurora.

For his Champagne corner, I'd bet on Louis Roederer's Cristal and Taittinger's Blanc de Blancs. He often flies first class.

In Bordeaux, he visits St.-Emilion, where he has deployed his antennae to discovered a few small, prized estates such as Châteaus Valendraud, La Mondotte and La Gomerie.

The Traveler has explored South Africa and would want a selection of its wines. The names Constantia, Stellenbosch and Paarl roll off his tongue as easily as Jo'burg and Cape Town. Speaking of the former British Empire, his white table wine would be the classic New Zealander, Cloudy Bay Sauvignon Blanc.

THE COLLECTORS

At The Wine Merchant, there are many collectors among our clientele. The following few stand out in my mind because they lack pretension, are intellectually curious and they truly love wine. I urge you to be like them, to express your love of wine, to embrace the wine lifestyle, regardless of your age, social status or the size of your bank account, with openness and joy. They are by no means exclusively my clients. I can't say for sure how much wine I've sold them or how I've influenced their collections. But I do know that we share the passion, that we all react the same way to a truly excellent wine: It makes us want to jump and shout.

Among my favorite collectors is Greg Gorman. I hesitate to pin any formal label on him because, more than anything, Greg is "just a wine lover," the kind of guy who will give you a bottle of one of his favorite wines right out of his cellar. Greg is Los Angeles's premier celebrity and advertising photographer. He entertains well and often,

preparing gourmet meals in the kitchen of his house on the edge of the Hollywood Hills for an eclectic group of friends that includes many film personalities.

At once relaxed, charming and intense, Greg loves to sample different wines and talk about them. Wine for him is an enabler of conversation, a refreshment during long and arduous photo shoots, a reward after a hard day's work. He loves to share it with friends, staff, clients and business associates. So infectious is his enthusiasm that everyone on his staff has become somewhat of a wine expert. Greg's connoisseurship is totally lacking in pretension, totally informed by enthusiasm.

Greg's passion for wine began in the mid-1960s. Some of his first good wines were the '67 and '68 Riojas, which he drank in the early to mid-seventies. The first serious bottle of wine that got him into collecting was a 1982 Tignanello, which he bought and consumed in 1984. He

BENCHMARK

A MEDIUM-SIZED COLLECTION
AL STEWART'S COLLECTION OF ROUGHLY 1,500 BOTTLES BREAKS DOWN AS FOLLOWS: 850 BOTTLES OF RED BORDEAUX; 250 OF RED BURGUNDY; 25 OF WHITE BURGUNDY; FOUR OR FIVE CASES OF DRY WHITE BORDEAUX, WHICH HE'S LEANING MORE TOWARD THAN THE WHITE BURGUNDY; A COUPLE OF CASES OF CHAMPAGNE (HE ONCE HAD CLOSE TO 500 BOTTLES); A COUPLE OF CASES OF VINTAGE PORT; 100 TO 150 BOTTLES OF ALSATIAN WINES TO WASH DOWN ALL KINDS OF ASIAN FOOD (HE'S A BIG FAN OF ZIND-HUMBRECHT); 50 TO 100 BOTTLES OF CALIFORNIA WHITES; 50 TO 100 BOTTLES OF CALIFORNIA REDS.

became a regular customer at The Wine Merchant after a lunch with Sharon Stone at L'Orangerie, an elegant French restaurant in Beverly Hills. They enjoyed some of proprietor Martine Sauntier's fine Burgundies; Greg was taken by the whole experience and Martine recommended he call The Wine Merchant to find some of the wines, which he did. We love serving impassioned collectors like Greg. When he calls asking us to track down some interesting or rare wines, we consider it a challenge. We don't want to let him down so we'll go to the ends of the earth if necessary to find them.

One of my closest friends, who I met through the wine business, is Al Stewart. He is another totally committed collector who buys wines for the only good reason: because he loves to drink them. He's got an incredible memory for figures and dates and his mind is a catalog of fascinating wines and wine experiences.

Al got into collecting in 1971 when he was in his mid-twenties living in London. He had just begun to make money as a folksinger, moved into a house near an Oddbins wine shop and became a collector virtually overnight after he had his first serious bottle of wine from that shop: a 1961 Château Calon-Ségur. It cost the equivalent of about $7. (You'd have to add at least a few zeroes to arrive at today's price.) Looking into Hugh Johnson's *World Atlas of Wine,* he set out, in his methodical manner, to drink his way through all sixty of the 1855 classified Bordeaux in the outstanding 1961 vintage. It became a quest. Some of them were nearly impossible to get—at least in England. He'd drive hours out of his way to buy a bottle of rare wine and eventually was able to try forty-four out of the original sixty-one *cru* classes. He branched out and continued to experiment through the early seventies.

Al's collection started with a solid foundation of "hot vintages" of first-growth Bordeaux, including the obligatory cases of 1961 Châteaus Mouton-Rothschild, Latour and Lafite-Rothschild. His oldest wine in the beginning was a 1949 Cheval-Blanc, which he found a bit disappointing. The 1953 first-growths were early favorites; other memorable early tastings involved some young 1966 red Bordeaux.

Then he began buying futures. He bought a slew of them for the 1975 Bordeaux, then held the wines for ten years, tasting them every so often. Like many of us, he's come around to the realization that harsh, tannic vintages like 1975 are not the Holy Grail: "When someone says to me, 'This is a great wine because you can't drink it for thirty years,' I don't buy into this argument. I think a great wine is a great wine from the word *go,* the way that a vintage like '53 was. It was drinkable at any time. Another example is 1971. I thought it was a delightful vintage just because it was ephemeral. It came and it went. If you had it at its peak, it was wonderful. I'd much rather have a cellar full of something you could drink rather than 1975, which I'm not sure anyone is ever going to be able to drink."

Al built a 2,400-bottle cellar at his house in Los Angeles. He takes a detailed inventory of his collection about every six months. Lately, Al has shifted his focus to wines that are drinkable *now,* not twenty years hence. The red Bordeaux portion of his collection has shifted from predominantly Medoc wines to mostly Pomerol and St.-Emilion as he has developed a preference for Merlot-based wines. Like many established collectors, he has also begun exploring California wines with the same excitement and curiosity that helped him discover the French ones a quarter of a century ago.

THE CHASE

FOR COLLECTORS OF FINE WINES, AS FOR COLLECTORS OF ANY OTHER PRIZED ARTIFACTS, THE THRILL IS IN THE CHASE. WE LOVE THE CHALLENGE AND ADVENTURE OF TRACKING DOWN FINE WINES. WE RELISH THE PEOPLE WE MEET AND THE CIRCUMSTANCES WE FIND OURSELVES IN. THEY'RE ALL PART OF THE PLEASURES OF WINE, FIXTURES IN A LIFESTYLE.

When you're hunting down wines, you've got to put out some tentacles. Sometimes, you've got to be seriously persistent.

I remember when I went on one of my wine odysseys, this one to St.-Emilion in 1996. The drums were beating about a new "boutique wine" called Château Valandraud. Eager to get my hands on a bottle, I went with a friend into a local shop where a somber-faced clerk told us, "It is impossible to get." Little did he know he had just thrown down the gauntlet. Within a few days we had tracked down eleven bottles and invited the owner, Jean-Luc Thunevin, to dinner. He was kind enough to arrange a tasting for us at the estate and we were able to squeeze it in on the morning of our flight home. In spite of what that clerk said, we managed to taste four of the five existing Valandraud vintages by the time we took off.

MY FAVORITE DINOSAURS

I'm always suspicious about collectors who have cellars full of "names." I have to wonder if they are buying by the label. Then, when I get to know them and discover the ones who are true wine lovers, I'm once again encouraged. With the genuine collector, no matter how experienced, the wonder and enthusiasm never wane. The real ones don't get jaded because they're always on to something new.

Wolfgang Grunwald, Dick Fleming, Bipin Desai—they are the dinosaurs. Sometimes I call them archaeologists or even necrophiliacs. They are into old and often very expensive wines, some of them arguably dead or dying. Do these dinosaurs have a place in the New Wine Revolution? Yes. Why? Because they are helping to set the standards, because they were part of the first wine revolution, because some of them are driving the market in Bordeaux futures and super-premium wines and because they, too, are beginning to collect the new superstar wines, legitimizing the wines among the international collecting elite.

WOLFGANG GRUNWALD

Wolfgang is a major collector who has participated in many legendary tastings. He's a self-made success in the international steel business who remembers going hungry as a teenager in Germany during the war years. When he moved to the United States in the late 1950s, he found, much to his delight, a wider selection of fine wines than in Europe. He settled in Los Angeles in 1967 and we met in the mid-1970s as I was establishing my business.

Wolfgang has Old World manners and charm with none of the stuffiness or pretension that often goes with that territory. Where he's from, one simply does not brag or show off. Wolfgang embodies the generosity inherent in the wine lifestyle. When he's your guest, he always recip-

rocates—and usually in a big way. His private wine dinners at home are memorable, usually with a traditional progression from a Champagne aperitif to white wines, Bordeaux or Burgundies, then to the reds with the oldest one last. He often invites a "newcomer," a younger enthusiast who might not have the means to have tasted some of the rare old wines he serves, and derives a good amount of vicarious pleasure from introducing these people to his inner circle.

For Wolfgang, discovering a new wine is a true aesthetic experience. He moved back to Switzerland in the mid-nineties and has since felt the thrill of discovery several times, ferreting out some unknown Swiss treasures. Among them are Elephant Merlot; the *Gran Riserva* Merlot from Klausener in the province of Ticino, a wine that compared favorably to Château Petrus in a blind tasting; and the wines of Daniel Gantenbein from near St. Moritz, including his superb Blauburgunder (Swiss Pinot Noir) sweet wine.

Wolfgang started out buying California wines for $10 to $12 a bottle in the early to mid-seventies. In the late seventies he bought a case of 1949 Mouton-Rothschild, a turning point that led him into collecting Bordeaux. He got into Burgundies with the '78 vintage, considered a superlative vintage among connoisseurs. Wolfgang's collection of nearly twelve thousand bottles still emphasizes the classic Bordeaux and Burgundies, yet he, too, has been branching out. I remember pressing on him his first bottle of serious Italian wine, a Sammarco from Castello dei Rampolla. Until then, he admits, Tuscan wine was just "Chianti in straw bottles." He discovered New Zealand in the early nineties when Cloudy Bay's Chardonnays and Sauvignon Blancs were blind tasting extremely well against the top French white. He has some Australians, including Penfolds and Taltarni (Shiraz and Sauvignon Blanc), made by Dominique Portet, brother of Bernard, the Bordelais who went to Napa and founded Clos du Val. Wolfgang also has about five hundred bottles of California wines.

DICK FLEMING, M.D.

Soft-spoken, low-keyed and friendly, Dick Fleming is one collector who really knows his stuff. Dick started collecting in the early eighties, when he was establishing his practice as a plastic surgeon. He is a clinical professor at USC, where he encourages young doctors who lament high prices to join tasting groups so they can gain exposure to a lot of good wines without having to buy full bottles of them. He keeps about twenty cases of wine at home and the rest in a warehouse space that he had customized for wine storage.

One of Dick's favorite social activities is to arrange to meet friends for dinners at some of the better restaurants around the country. They send the wines ahead but never specify a menu, allowing the chefs to exercise their creativity and respond to the wines. One New Year's Eve they celebrated with a dinner at Charlie Trotter's in Chicago. On another memorable occasion they had an evening at Emeril's in New Orleans that began at seven o'clock in the evening and lasted until two in the morning, with fifteen courses and fifteen different wines.

Dick is a self-professed "Burgundy freak." Two of his favorite "dinosaur wines" are the '49 La Tache ("One of the finest bottles of wine I've ever had. It's just glorious. All that spice and acid is still there. It's still great.") and

the '49 Musigny from Leroy ("They don't get any better than that."). He also has a good selection of Bordeaux as well as some older vintage Champagnes. Although he grew up in the Bay Area with early exposure to wines, he has a relatively small California collection, concentrating on some of the older wines—Inglenooks from the 1940s, for example. His collection's primary sidelight is Penfolds, really the only significant player in Australia until quite recently, of which he has about sixty cases. In early 1997, he staged a vertical tasting of Penfolds back to its beginnings in 1955.

PROFESSOR BIPIN DESAI

Bipin Desai is as delightful a character as you'll ever meet in the world of wines and has built an immense reputation based largely on the tastings he's organized. The funny thing about Bipin is he was born and raised in India, in a vegetarian culture where alcohol is strictly prohibited. He went from his first taste of alcohol to being a world-class wine collector in about ten years.

Bipin first came to the United States in 1955 as a university student. He earned his Ph.D. in theoretical physics from Berkeley in 1961. It was a good year for Bipin because he also got married *and* it was one of the all-time great Bordeaux vintages. He acquired a taste for fine foods and wines while on sabbatical from his post at UC-Riverside, where he still works today. The Desais were in Geneva and Max Ferluzzi, an Italian colleague, took them to three-star restaurants. Bipin visited Burgundy and the Rhône Valley, both nearby, and began tasting the wines. Being an academic, Bipin also started to read: Edmund Penning-Rowsell's *Wines of Bordeaux*, Harry Waugh's *Wine Diaries*, Michael Broadbent's *How to Taste Wine*.

In 1973 his wife encouraged him to go to a tasting organized by the wine-tasting society Les Amis du Vin in
Fontana, California. There he befriended a number of
connoisseurs and was exposed to some truly great
wines, including a '62 Latour, a '66 Haut-Brion and a '61
Palmer, about which he still rhapsodizes as a silky wine
of almost unbelievable deliciousness and finesse.

I like Bipin's philosophy, which I call the Mt. Everest
approach. Establish your criteria, starting at the top. Go
up to Mt. Everest, take a look at the view and only then
decide where you want to live. "People in my field
always think of themselves as on the cutting edge of
life," he says. "They pride themselves in knowing what's
the greatest, the best and the latest. If I'm interested in
something, the first question I always ask is, 'What is the
best?' My wife is very much into art. We go to a museum
and I ask her, 'Where are the best paintings and why are
they the best?'"

Like any genuine collector, Bipin can't stand the thought
that there's a great wine lurking out there that he hasn't
tasted. He built his collection on a foundation of 1961
Bordeaux, particularly that Château Palmer. In fact, he
and his friends started an informal Palmer Club at one
point. Now he tries to emphasize breadth, keeping two
or three bottles of great wines such as the 1947 Petrus,
but fewer full cases. In the mid-1990s, his inventory of
1961 Bordeaux was still at about thirty cases, the largest
block in the collection. He also had blocks of 1978 and
1949 Burgundies. He has started to collect older Italian
wines and has been discovering wines from South Africa
and Australia. This dinosaur also has spunk; he likes Diamond Creek, Gravelly Meadows, 1978.

EARTHQUAKE WINE

WE USED TO LIVE IN A GLASS HOUSE
UP IN THE HILLS AND I HAD A PRI-
VATE CELLAR THERE. WHEN THE
NORTHRIDGE EARTHQUAKE HIT IN
1994, WE GOT PRETTY SHOOK UP. IN
ADDITION TO SOME OTHER DAMAGE,
THE TREMORS KNOCKED A BOTTLE OF
1893 MOUTON-ROTHSCHILD OFF ITS
SHELF AND I FOUND THE PRECIOUS
OLD WINE DRIPPING ONTO THE FLOOR.
(HOW PRECIOUS? A BOTTLE OF THE
1893 VINTAGE RECENTLY SOLD FOR
$4,500 AT AUCTION.) MY BUSINESS
PARTNER CAME OVER TO COMMISER-
ATE AND WE DECIDED WE HAD TO
SALVAGE THE WINE. WE CAREFULLY
SOAKED IT UP WITH A BIG SPONGE,
FILTERED IT THROUGH SOME CHEESE-
CLOTH AND DRANK IT THEN AND
THERE, TOASTING OUR LUCK THAT WE
LIVED THROUGH THIS ONE.

WE DON'T LIVE IN THAT HOUSE
ANYMORE, AND I NOW MAKE SURE
TO KEEP THE DOORS ON ALL MY
WINE BINS CLOSED.

Chapter Six

THE WINE LIFESTYLE

EVERYTHING THAT CAME BEFORE THIS CHAPTER—AND, FOR THAT MATTER, AFTER IT—BOILS DOWN TO ONE GOAL: MAKING WINE PART OF YOUR LIFESTYLE. WE AMERICANS CAN LEARN A LOT FROM THE EUROPEANS. FOR HUNDREDS, EVEN THOUSANDS, OF YEARS WINE HAS BEEN PART OF THEIR EVERYDAY LIFE THERE. THEY PRACTICE HEDONISM WITHOUT EXCESS. IN THE UNITED STATES, WHERE WE'RE PRONE TO OVERCONSUMPTION OF FOOD AND ALCOHOL AND JUST ABOUT EVERY OTHER NATURAL RESOURCE, WE SHOULD ADOPT THE SAME MODEL. EUROPEANS ARE EXPOSED TO WINE AT A YOUNG AGE, NOT AS A WAY TO GET DRUNK BUT AS PART OF NORMAL SUSTENANCE. THIS IS WHAT IS MEANT BY THE PHRASE "WINE IS FOOD." A GOOD GLASS OF TABLE WINE TO WASH DOWN A HEARTY MEAL...A BOTTLE OF EXCEPTIONAL CHAMPAGNE AS AN APERITIF BEFORE A CELEBRATORY DINNER PARTY...THESE ARE PLEASURES WE CAN ENJOY IF WE MAKE WINE PART OF OUR LIVES. *THIS IS THE WINE LIFESTYLE.*

Accumulating knowledge, experience and confidence, learning by experimentation—these are the pursuits that bring us closer to the goal of living and entertaining effortlessly with wine. In this chapter, I offer some practical advice and some sample meals so you can put into practice the axiom that wine is an enhancement of your meal experience and of your quality of life. The two keys to entertaining with wine are, first, serving them properly and, second, matching them with foods. These are the two main themes of this chapter.

SERVING WINE: PRACTICAL GUIDELINES

Popping the cork and pouring the wine is a wonderful moment of anticipation that can be carried out with as much or as little pomp and circumstance as you like. Obviously you're not going to drink Château Margaux out of paper cups or Château D'Yquem on the rocks. By the same token, you don't want to overdo it. When you're dressed in black tie for a formal affair, it's important, in my opinion, to maintain a relaxed, congenial attitude. Likewise, if you're in the mood to do some serious tasting, even if you're dressed casually, you don't want to lose that laser-beam focus. My motto is "casual elegance." When you dress up, don't act stuffy; when you're wearing your baggies, don't get sloppy. Most important of all is a sense of *balance,* of relaxed, unhurried enjoyment. As you may recall, these are two of Overstreet's Important Principles of Wine: *slow down* and *keep your balance.*

Following are some suggestions. As always, I encourage you to experiment and take your own route so you can eventually arrive at a personal style that makes you and your guests most comfortable.

ACCESSORIES: CORKSCREWS AND GLASSES

There are many companies, some with extensive mail-order catalogs, that are taking advantage of the resurgence of interest in premium wines and offering all kinds of accessories, from neckties adorned with wine-label patterns to elaborate wine racks and storage units. Indulge yourself by buying as many of those toys as you like but bear in mind there are only two items you really need: a reliable corkscrew and a good glass.

The standard-bearers are Screwpull for corkscrews and Riedel for glasses. While the majority of smart, committed

At home, as in restaurants, proper service enhances the enjoyment of wine.

wine people—restaurants and connoisseurs—own these brands, there are others that fulfill the requirements.

When it comes to corkscrews, the size of the screw itself is crucial. It has to be long enough to capture the whole cork without any danger of crumbling or splitting. A Teflon-coated Screwpull is smooth, tough and just the right width to pull out any cork. It is a simple design that burrows solidly into the cork and pulls it out of the bottle with none of the maneuvering and yanking required from the waiter's friend, that familiar folding pocket model you see in most restaurants, or the winged corkscrew, aka the butterfly, with its anthropomorphic figure and two arms that you push down to pull out the cork. The two-pronged screwless butler's friend is good for crumbly corks or if you want to recork a bottle, but it can definitely challenge your manual dexterity. The ultimate corkscrew is the Screwpull Leverpull LX model, a marvel of modern design that yanks out the cork in a decisive up-and-down motion and has a foil cutter included in the package.

Riedel is the best name in glassware (see page 181), but you can get by with standard glasses that retail for about $5 to $12 each from any number of houseware stores or catalogs. Glasses should be large enough to swirl the wine without spilling and to capture its aroma so you can inhale before it dissipates. Glasses should be smooth, clear and transparent so you can see the wine. Etched, engraved or colored glass is pretty but it doesn't work for wine appreciation. Obviously, keeping the glasses clean and free of anything with taste or aroma is paramount. You can wash them by hand (in the case of good crystal) or in a dishwasher with mild soap; if you want them perfectly spotless and sparkling for a special occasion, steam them by holding each one briefly over a pot of boiling water and then wiping it spotless with a linen napkin or a clean paper towel. Another way to avoid water spots is to dip the glasses in a solution of water mixed with vodka or gin before drying them.

MATCHING
THE SHAPE
TO THE GRAPE

INSISTING ON DIFFERENT-SHAPED GLASSES FOR DIFFERENT TYPES OF WINES MIGHT SEEM LIKE A CLEVER MARKETING GIMMICK, BUT THERE IS A SCIENTIFIC BASIS FOR IT. THE RIEDEL PRINCIPLE IS THAT THE SHAPE OF THE GLASS CHANNELS THE WINE TO A PARTICULAR AREA OF THE TONGUE, CREATING A MORE BALANCED TASTE SENSATION. A HEAVIER, MORE TANNIC WINE, SUCH AS A BIG BORDEAUX OR AN AUSSIE CAB, WOULD BE CHANNELED MORE TO THE FRONT AND TIP OF THE TONGUE, WHERE THE SWEET-DETECTING TASTE BUDS ARE, EMPHASIZING THE FRUITY COMPONENTS IN THAT WINE. (REMEMBER, THE TASTING ZONES OF THE TONGUE ARE SWEET ON THE TIP; SOUR ON THE SIDES AND BITTER ON THE TOP IN BACK.)

THE STANDARD IN STEMWARE

"Everybody is the sovereign of his own palate and has to decide if the concept is meaningful to him," says Georg Riedel, who represents the tenth generation of his family in the business. "It's partly scientific and partly emotional."

Riedel uses only the highest quality, thinnest glass possible. This takes the vessel itself out of the equation and puts the focus firmly where it should be—on the wine. Another important feature of Riedel glasses is the polished cut rim; inexpensive wineglasses have rolled rims, which inhibit the smooth flow of the liquid and tend to accentuate acidity and harshness.

"The better the wine, the more important the glass," says Georg. "This is why our glass philosophy is more important today than it has ever been, because of the high quality of wine produced and served worldwide."

The Riedels founded their company in 1756 in the Sudetenland, a part of Bohemia that, in the twentieth century, at one time or another has belonged to Austria, Germany and Czechoslovakia. They were pioneers in many areas of glass production, including early windows, engraving and colored glass; their nineteenth-century perfume bottles were treasured works of art. The Nazis seized the Sudetenland, home to many ethnic Germans, just prior to World War II and the Communists took it back at the end of the war. Like most Germans, the Riedel family was forced out. By 1956, Georg's father, Claus, and his grandfather Walter, the inventor of fiberglass who died in 1974, had reestablished their business by buying a factory in Kufstein, Austria, near Innsbruck. There, Claus created Riedel stemware as we know it, combining his vision of large, unadorned wineglasses with his recognition of the potential of local craftsmen. Several of his designs from the late fifties are still in production; they are also exhibited in museums as exemplars of twentieth-century craftsmanship.

Georg's role has been to transform his father's "genius idea" into a successful business and keep it at the pinnacle.

Riedel's Sommelier series, the top of the line, offers a glass for every wine and for spirits, too; thirty-three total, all handmade, they retail for about $60 each and are a marvel of simplicity, purity, economy of design. Form follows function and is expressed in the highest quality materials.

A classic example is the Bordeaux Grand Cru glass. First introduced in 1959, it is designed for young, full-bodied red, over-12% alcohol, high-tannin, moderate-acid wines. The more modestly priced Vinum series features twenty-two different models made of machine-blown glass.

ENVIRONMENT

"Serious wine tasting" should be done in an environment where the tasters can relax, concentrate and focus on the wines. If you're organizing a formal tasting and you want to be a real stickler, make the setting totally antiseptic, a clean white room with no distractions in terms of sight, sound and especially smell. Sometimes, a formal tasting is called for. But an antiseptic environment can be the antithesis of the conviviality and ease I like to encourage in connection with wine. Most occasions should be about ensuring that your guests feel relaxed, at home, totally at ease, with no pressure to perform. I always find a casual attitude and a sense of humor do wonders to break the ice. The idea is to create a total wine experience for your guests, with good food, company, music and whatever else you feel enhances the occasion.

Some words of advice for getting the most out of what's in your glass: Don't wear any strong perfumes or colognes. Make sure your hands are clean. If you've recently used a perfumed moisturizer or washed your hands with some fancy soap, those aromas can interfere with the wine. Make sure your palate is clear, that there's no taste on your tongue or in your mouth that can confound the taste of the wine. At wine tastings, it helps to offer some neutral-tasting crackers, biscuits or bread and mild cheese to clear the palate. A good mouthful of water, sloshed around and swallowed or spit out usually does the trick. As an alternative, try taking a bite out of a carrot stick or a sip of Champagne.

ORGANIZING A WINE TASTING

Here are some practical considerations for putting together a tasting:

Decide on a theme or focus, for example a "vertical" of seven consecutive vintages of your favorite Burgundy or a "horizontal" of a particular vintage, say ten different 1990 Barolo wines. Another fun theme is "varietal," for instance "Around the World with Pinot Noir," comparing wines from France, California, Oregon and South Africa. Tastings are also often organized by country or winegrowing region.

Consult magazines or books, work with your merchant or a friend who is also a wine maven to amass a selection of five to twenty wines. More than ten is a challenge; more than twenty is confusing. The wines should be similar enough to invite comparison but different enough to make things interesting.

Have plenty of clean glasses available, at least one per wine for every guest. That's a lot of glasses if you have ten guests and ten wines. As an alternative, plan the tasting in stages with a break in between to wash the glasses.

Provide pitchers of water, spittoons (a bowl, jar, crock or pitcher will do) and (optionally) crackers or bread for palate-cleansing. Provide napkins and a tablecloth you don't mind staining—preferably a white one that can be bleached and can also serve as a neutral background for examining the wine's color. If it's going to be a blind tasting, make sure to have paper bags, napkins or some other means of covering the wine's labels when pouring. Also, clearly number the wines for identification and note-taking. It's a nice touch to offer pads or paper and pencils for note-taking. Often, tasters are given blank charts or checklists to fill in, with rows and columns that list the various wines and tasting criteria.

Decide in advance who is going to pour the wines, in what order and at what intervals—or if tasters will be allowed to pour for themselves and proceed at their own pace. Organize the wines in order of vintages or in flights by category or points of comparison. For example, a "vertical" would most likely proceed from youngest to oldest while a "horizontal" might be organized by region or variety or by "weight" of the wine—that is, from lighter wines to heavier ones.

Set the tone for tasting with casual comportment and measured enthusiasm. Don't be pompous.

Preparing for a large professional tasting.

"I'D MUCH RATHER HAVE A BLIND TASTING BECAUSE I DON'T WANT

TO BE INFLUENCED BY WHAT I KNOW ABOUT THIS WINE, WHAT MY

EXPERIENCE WAS LAST TIME I HAD IT. SO WHAT IF YOU'RE

EMBARRASSED? I'VE SEEN THE BEST PALATES IN THE WORLD

TOTALLY EMBARRASS THEMSELVES. WHAT'S THE BIG DEAL?"

—Dick Fleming, M.D., collector

TASTING
LINEUPS

HERE ARE A FEW EXAMPLES OF TASTINGS, ARRANGED ACCORDING TO TYPI-CAL THEMES. WINES SHOULD BE SIMILAR ENOUGH IN SOME WAY—THEY MIGHT BE FROM THE SAME GRAPE OR THE SAME COUNTRY OR REGION—TO INVITE COMPARISON. IN PLANNING YOUR TASTING LINEUPS, TAKE THIS CONCEPT AND RUN WITH IT.

WHITE VARIETIES

French Chardonnay 1: Niellon Chassagne- Montrachet

French Chardonnay 2: Bonhomme Macon-Vire

California Chardonnay: Babcock (Central Coast)

Northern Italian Chardonnay: Alois Lageder

French Chenin Blanc 1: Foreau Vouvray

French Chenin Blanc 2: Huet Vouvray

Austrian Sauvignon Blanc: Tement

French Sauvignon Blanc: Lucien Crochet Sancerre

New Zealand Sauvignon Blanc: Cloudy Bay

California Sauvignon Blanc: Frog's Leap (Napa)

French Viognier: Georges Vernay Condrieu

California Viognier: Alban (San Luis Obispo)

Austrian Riesling: Franz Prager

Alsatian Riesling: Marcel Deiss

German Riesling 1: Kunstler Hocheimer Herrnberg Kabinett (Rheingau)

German Riesling 2: Fritz Haag Brauneberger Juffer-Sonnenuhr Spatlese (Mosel)

Italian Pinot Grigio: Maso Poli (Trentino)

ITALIAN REDS

Barolo: Aldo Conterno

Chianti: Castello di Ama

Brunello di Montalcino: Ciacci Piccolomini "Pianorosso"

Sagrantino di Montefalco: Arnaldo Caprai

Cabernet Sauvignon: Castello di Gabbiano

Merlot: Avignonesi

Taurasi: Mastroberardino

Aglianico del Vulture: D'Angelo

Nero D'Avola: Duca Enrico

"GERMAN" WINES

Gunderloch Nackenheim Riesling (Rheinhessen, Germany)

Egon Muller Scharzhofberg Riesling (Mosel-Saar-Ruwer, Germany)

Willi Brundlmayer Gruner Veltliner (Austria)

Franz Xavier Pichler Riesling (Austria)

Henschke Eden Valley Riesling (Australia)

Petaluma Clare Valley Riesling (Australia)

Marcel Deiss Altenberg Gewurztraminer (Alsace)

Zind-Humbrecht Riesling (Alsace)

AROUND THE WORLD WITH PINOT NOIR

France: Domaine Dujac Morey-St.-Denis

South Africa: Hamilton Russell

Australia: Coldstream Hills

California: Au Bon Climat (Santa Barbara)

Oregon: Ponzi

AROUND THE WORLD WITH SYRAH

France 1: Jean-Louis Chave Hermitage

France 2: Noel Verset Cornas

California: Qupe (Santa Barbara)

Australia 1: Penfolds

Australia 2: Wynns

A TASTING
OF PETRUS

In 1985, I was invited to New Orleans by Lloyd Flatt, the aerospace mogul, who had just renovated two homes in the French Quarter. He had a multimillion-dollar wine collection and half of one of his homes was devoted to a wine cellar while the other half housed a custom-built tasting room. It had a special halogen lighting system that threw a spot of bright light about the size of a quarter onto each place setting and partitions at the tasting table so that each taster could proceed with no distractions. Our host was clearly someone who understood technology and was going to utilize it to the max.

I was flattered to be on a guest list that featured a selection of VIPs in the wine world, including a number of major collectors and journalists, for a vertical tasting of Château Petrus, with bottles dating back to the turn of the century. It was a black-tie event—they do like to dress up in the South—which, unfortunately, was held on a muggy night in April. There were no fewer than twelve flights of wine, with six or seven wines per flight. For every single wine—even the oldest, rarest ones—there were back-up bottles ready in case the first one wasn't right. The wines were grouped according to ratings and age. In other words, stronger vintages went up against stronger ones, weaker against weaker. I remember thinking it was quite an interesting approach, to handicap the wines as if it were a horse race. In other respects, though, the event felt more like a chess tournament. Every time a new wine was tasted, there were at least three minutes of absolute silence.

Despite the partitions, I managed to look around at the other tasters. Here was an impressive panel of experts tasting some great old wines; amid the air of great solemnity, I could tell not everyone was comfortable. It began to border on the ridiculous for me when I noticed one well-known, respected collector who kept putting a finger in his nose. I had to say something. "Excuse me," I said, in my most polite tone, "but does it really help to massage your nostrils like that?" "Oh, yes," came the response. "Many studies of the brain and nervous system have revealed that if you widen the nostrils you get more aroma into the nose so you can recognize the wines more easily."

Another guest at that gathering refused to taste from any of the first three glasses poured from a bottle because he insisted they could not truly represent the wine's essence. After hearing that, I remember remarking to one of the journalists there that we were really in another world. He admitted that things had gotten a little out of hand, yet when I read his column the next week both of those strange assertions were reported as fact.

It's always amazed me how much hocus-pocus seems to creep into such a simple topic as wine.

I went to a tasting party one evening not so long after that. Attempting to give myself a quick shave before I left, I somehow managed to cut my finger. It was one of those sharp cuts that didn't want to stop bleeding, so I just wrapped some white gauze around the hand, taped it up and left for the party. When I got there, lo and behold, I ran into the same columnist. He asked me about the bandage and I told him I had wanted to buy a wine glove on my way over but didn't have time so I just wrapped the hand up. He nodded seriously to indicate his understanding. At the time, word had gone out around the West Coast that people were once again taking up the custom of wearing white gloves at tastings so as not to get their fingerprints on the glasses.

OPENING A BOTTLE OF CHAMPAGNE

THE ONLY TIME YOU SHOULD EVER WASTE A DROP OF THE PRECIOUS BUBBLY IS IF IT'S CHEAP SPARKLING WINE AND YOUR TEAM HAS JUST WON THE SUPER BOWL AND YOU WANT TO SPRAY IT ALL OVER THE COACH WHO'S BEEN DOGGING YOU ALL SEASON. IN THAT CASE, SHAKE IT UP, PRY IT OPEN AND LET IT POP. (JUST BE CAREFUL NOT TO PUT ANYONE'S EYE OUT WITH THE FLYING CORK.)

On any other occasion when you're opening Champagne the old cliché of the loud pop and the fizzy overflow should never happen. To open it properly, make sure your bottle has been resting quietly for at least a couple of hours, that it hasn't been agitated. Place it on a solid surface and, holding one hand over the cork in case of an accidental explosion, slowly and carefully remove the wire and foil. Then grasp the cork firmly in one hand and gently but forcefully twist the bottle underneath, easing the cork out. Keep enough downward pressure on the cork to balance the pressure from inside the bottle. There should be very little pop and certainly no overflow. Once you've mastered it, you can open a bottle silently and surprise your guests with the first pour: "Where did *that* come from?"

When you twist open the wire over the cork, note whether it's five and a half twists. Anything more or less and it was not an authentic French machine that put on that wire. (They do use French machines some places in California but be assured that only the genuine article delivers precisely five and a half twists.)

An additional tip: If the cork doesn't give on the first turn, it probably means that there is a dab of wax holding it. In this case, turn on the hot water and hold the cork under it for about ten seconds, which should be enough to loosen the wax.

SERVING TEMPERATURE

It's a fundamental fact that our perceptions of sweetness and alcohol are suppressed by colder temperatures and enhanced by warmer ones. Cooler temperatures also heighten our perception of acidity and bitterness (tannins). As always, balance is important. This is why lighter, sweeter wines (whites) are served cooler than those with more alcohol and tannins (reds).

If you serve wine that is too warm, you're going to taste too much alcohol. You're going to feel a "burn" on your palate that's liable to wipe out some of the other good flavors and aromas. Alcohol has a very low evaporation temperature, so heating it releases a lot of fumes into the air. We absorb those fumes more quickly than we do the liquid form. (If you've ever had a hot rum toddy you know how quickly it goes to your head.) That's the last thing you want to happen with a fine glass of Bordeaux or Burgundy, because if it made you tipsy right away you'd risk missing most of its charms.

Temperature also affects aroma. Heat speeds up chemical reactions, one of which is the evaporation of volatile compounds from the wine into the air. The higher the temperature, the more aroma you'll smell. This is why relatively aromatic wines like Rieslings or Sauvignon Blancs can be served cooler.

Many wine books give exact temperatures at which different types of wines should be served. This is a perfect example why detailed prescriptions are silly. How would you determine a wine's exact temperature? Stick a thermometer in the bottle? The best way to gauge the approximate temperature is to put your hand on the shoulder of the bottle (be gentle) and compare it to the temperature of the room. Since room temperatures can vary from 65 to 75 degrees F. and sometimes higher, you'll want to check an indoor thermometer. Then you can estimate the temperature of the wine by comparison.

In general, you'll want to bring reds out of the cellar an hour or two in advance of serving so they warm up toward room temperature. Sparkling and light white wines can stay in the fridge all day before serving while fuller-bodied whites can be chilled for an hour or two *or* given a quick bath in a bucket of ice water. (This actually chills the wine a lot more quickly than simply putting it on ice since the ice leaves much less cold surface area in contact with the bottle.)

Some guidelines:

For red wine, the rule of thumb is to serve it a bit above cellar temperature—assuming that's about 58 to 62 degrees F.—and a bit below room temperature. (If your wine seems a little too cold, try quickly warming it up by cupping your hands around the glass.) A fruity, light-bodied red wine might be served at 50 to 55 degrees F. while a fuller, tannic red might be best at 60 to 65 degrees F.

A light white wine should be served coolest, say 40 to 50 degrees F., whereas a full-bodied, dry white would be best slightly warmer, say 55 to 60. Good Champagne should be served at about 45 degrees F. to accentuate its acidity and freshness, the wonderful prickly sensation of those millions of tiny bubbles. Chilling white wines or Champagne in an ice bucket is an aesthetically pleasing bit of ceremony. But if they're left too long they get too cold and you'll miss some of their delightful flavors and aromas.

Professional tasters lean toward higher serving temperatures to ensure a higher volume of flavor and aroma. Pro-

"Oftentimes the idea has been that the bigger, the heavier, the more alcoholic the wine is, the better it is. Now people are beginning to realize that's not necessarily the case. Certain wines that are lower in alcohol, more delicate, work better with food."

—Roger Dagorn, Master Sommelier

WATER AND WINE

fessor Ann Noble recommends about 70 degrees F. for reds and 50 to 60 for whites. If you're staging a tasting, particularly of white wines, don't worry about erring on the side of warmth. But if it's a sparkling wine, make sure it's plenty cold.

There are no absolute right answers concerning serving temperatures. Finding your comfort level is key. I'd recommend the following experiment: Take several reasonably good bottles of white wine—not your best vintage of Corton-Charlemagne—and serve them at three different temperatures, say 45, 50 and 55 degrees F. or, better yet, after 15, 30 and 60 minutes in the fridge. Try some reds at 30, 60 and 120 minutes out of the cellar. Take note of how the temperature affects your perception of the aromas and the taste of the wines. Try the experiment with a few friends and take note of preferences.

TO DECANT OR NOT

This is a subject of much debate among wine lovers and connoisseurs, amateurs and professionals alike. The only hard-and-fast rule is that older wines or vintage Ports, which have sediment, should be decanted.

The act of decanting is simple. Just stand the bottle upright for at least several hours, if not a couple of days, to let the sediment settle. Then carefully pour the wine into a clear glass container using a good source of light behind the bottle so you can see the sediment and avoid pouring any of it into the decanter.

The next question is, how long to decant before serving?

The concept of "allowing a wine to breathe" is overrated. Leaving wine in an open bottle or thin-necked decanter doesn't bring it into contact with much air anyway. Once you pour it, wine aerates and its aromas begin to dissipate, which may be a good thing if they are particularly strong or funky. The problem is some older wines can deteriorate so quickly, they'll lose most of their precious bouquet and complex of flavors after just a few minutes. To my mind, it's much more important to track the development of a wine in the glass. It is absolutely fascinating to see how much some wines can change. Why risk missing that because you decanted unnecessarily? My recommendation is to pour the wine from the bottle, swirl it, smell it and try it right away. If it's harsh or overpowering, go back to it five, ten, fifteen, twenty minutes later and so on.

SERVING SIZE

How much wine to put in the glass? The standard bottle size is 750 milliliters or 25 ounces. As mentioned in Chapter 4, the conventional restaurant pour is between 4 and 6 ounces, yielding between six-and-a-quarter and four-and-a-dribble glasses per bottle. The "restaurant pour" may seem parsimonious for a dinner party or overly generous for a multiple tasting. Use common sense. For a tasting, pour just enough so you can tilt to examine and swirl to sniff without spilling. For a dinner party, pour a bit more, say, just over half full for smaller glasses, around a third full for the larger "balloon" glasses. In a restaurant, if you order by the glass and they fill it full you should be thankful you're getting your money's worth. The downside is that you might have to gulp some of the precious liquid before you can properly tilt the glass and swirl the wine.

THE FRENCH PARADOX AND...

THE HEALTH BENEFITS OF WINE

(In case you were looking for an excuse to drink wine...)

EPIDEMIOLOGICAL STUDIES FOCUSING ON HEART DISEASE HAVE REVEALED A PHENOMENON CALLED THE FRENCH PARADOX. DESPITE A DIET RICH IN DAIRY FATS, THE FRENCH, AND PARTICULARLY THE INHABITANTS OF SOUTHWEST FRANCE, HAVE THE LOWEST INCIDENCE OF HEART DISEASE IN THE WESTERN WORLD. (EPIDEMIOLOGY, BY THE WAY, IS THE SCIENCE OF STUDYING THE HABITS OF LARGE GROUPS OF INDIVIDUALS AND ATTEMPTING TO LINK THEM TO THE PRESENCE OR ABSENCE OF CERTAIN DISEASES OR SYMPTOMS.)

Dr. Serge Renaud, director of the Research Unit on Nutrition and Cardiology at the Institut National de la Santé et de la Recherche, Lyon, burst onto the American scene when CBS-TV's "60 Minutes" broadcast a report about the French Paradox on November 17, 1991. It was a watershed date in American wine history. The segment was rebroadcast in July 1992 and was also featured as part of the show's twenty-fifth-anniversary gala in late 1993. Sales of wine in the United States ballooned 39 percent in 1992. Thank you, CBS!

Dr. Renaud has been researching the French Paradox for more than thirty years. For his patients, he recommends the Mediterranean diet, which has been followed for nearly three thousand years: breads, grains, fruits and vegetables, beans or nuts (for protein) every day; more vegetable fat (e.g., olive oil) and less dairy fat (although cheese is part of the diet); fish, poultry and sweets two or three times a week. Red meat a few times a month and—here comes the good part —moderate consumption of alcohol, preferably red wine. A glass a day keeps the doctor away.

Coronary heart disease is the No. 1 killer in the United States. When the arteries that supply blood to the heart become clogged by deposits of cholesterol, it can result in deadly heart attacks. There are two types of cholesterol: the bad (LDL, or low-density lipoprotein), which clogs arteries, and the good (HDL, or high-density lipoprotein), which actually helps clear away the bad. Many scientific studies point to the fact that alcohol seems to reduce levels of bad cholesterol, increase levels of good cholesterol and help prevent blood clotting, which can lead to either heart attack or stroke.

Like many substances in the body, LDL appears to be more harmful when oxidized. (Hence the new trend toward antioxidants in the billion-dollar vitamin and mineral supplement industry. Vitamin E and beta-carotene are two popular antioxidants.) Fruits and vegetables are good sources of antioxidants. So is wine. After all, what is it but preserved fruit juice with a percentage of alcohol? The phenolic compounds contained in red wine are now believed by scientists to be even better antioxidants than Vitamin E.

Recent studies point to the possibility that certain phenolics may also be natural anticancer agents. According to one theory, resveratol, the grape's natural defense against *Botrytis cinerea* (noble rot), is believed to work against tumors and can only be absorbed through the intestines when consumed in a solution containing alcohol, of which wine, of course, is the best example.

The effects of drinking too much or binge drinking are well documented. Still, scientists are working to explain thoroughly why people who regularly drink small to moderate amounts of alcohol, particularly wine, live longer than those who drink none or who drink too much. One thing is certain: When the French raise a glass of wine and say *"A votre santé"* ("To your health"), they know whereof they speak.

WINE+FOOD

FINDING A HAPPY MARRIAGE

When food and wine find a perfect marriage, it's a magical moment, an unforgettable sensual experience.

Should we match the wines to the foods or the foods to the wines? I'm a wine person, so my answer is forget about the menu, give me the wine list, let's choose a few good bottles then let the chef devise some dishes to complement our liquid entertainment. Since it is a marriage, though, it should be more of a meeting of mutual interests and passions. (Isn't that what marriage is all about?) While not every marriage of man and woman is perfect, there seem to be endless possibilities for superlative food-wine pairings. By taking all relevant factors into consideration—season, ambience, occasion, menu, selection of wines—it is possible to narrow our options and eventually settle on a match that works.

Traditional advice from the experts has been prescriptive. Typically, we find extensive lists or charts of wines that give corresponding foods to be paired with them. The trend toward eclectic, fusion or "world" cuisines, with the new rainbow of flavors, has led to a broad reexamination of conventional food-and-wine wisdom. Accepted rules such as "spicy foods are the enemy of wine" or "only white wine with fish" are being challenged. The field is wide-open and I find this much more exciting than lists, charts or prescriptions.

Has there been a shift in tastes? Sure, it's inevitable. Consumers of fine foods and wines are developing more worldly palates. Will we be drinking Sauternes with poached fish and cream sauce as they did in gourmet restaurants a hundred years ago? Probably not. If we keep our spirit of adventure alive, though, we can have some tantalizing surprises over the horizon.

Following are a few fundamental principles of food-wine pairings, punctuated with some tidbits of conventional wisdom that no longer apply. Use them as your departure point for experimenting with and enjoying the universe of possibilities.

Balance

The principle of balance is as crucial to food-wine pairings as it is to viticulture and viniculture. The weight of the wine should match that of the dish. Neither should overpower the other. A light fruity wine such as a Beaujolais Nouveau, for example, paired with big stews or game will taste watery. A big, rich, oaky Cabernet is too powerful for many dishes; grilled steaks or roast lamb, however, can stand up to it. Make sure you know the weight of the wine and match accordingly.

Be aware of balance with respect to sweetness and acid. With a sweet dish, the wine should always be *at least* as sweet. A medium-bodied wine or even a full-bodied dry one with a sweetly sauced dish or a dessert can taste dull and sour by comparison. The wine should always pack as much punch as the food; put a welterweight in the ring with a heavyweight and all you get is a quick knockout.

Conventional wisdom: It's very difficult to match wines with dessert dishes and *forget about chocolate*. True, very few wines can stand up to the sweetness and richness of chocolate. There are, however, delicious exceptions. A luxurious dessert such as a flourless chocolate cake, dense and fudgelike, can combine beautifully with a twenty-year-old tawny Port, which has the body and the bittersweetness to match the cake's sugar and cocoa. If the cake had a little raspberry sauce drizzled around the edges, you might opt for a ruby Port, which has more age in the bottle, less in the cask and retains more fruity flavors to match the sauce. Another delightful dessert wine is Italy's Moscato D'Asti, a subtle sweet-tart, lightly sparkling wine that marries well with light fruity desserts, such as peach compote.

More conventional wisdom: Salads are another classic enemy of wine, because the acid in the dressing, whether vinegar or lemon juice, easily overwhelms the relatively low acid in the wine, making it taste flat. If you choose a crisp, acidic wine, however, it can actually taste *less* acidic alongside a mildly tart salad dressing. Once again, it's all about balance.

PERSONAL PREFERENCE

SOMETIMES IT'S HARD TO ARGUE WITH INDIVIDUAL TASTE.

I recall a certain high-profile celebrity client, who has since become notorious (sorry, no names), asking for Château Margaux with his caviar. Of course, my No. 1 priority is to keep the customer happy. Unfortunately, in this case, it came down to a choice between what would make him least unhappy: explaining to him that this was a bad food-wine pairing, or saving him the embarrassment of being contradicted. I chose to warn him and I thought I did it very politely. He didn't like it. (Nice try, Dennis.)

One prominent sommelier we know likes to keep his mother-in-law, who's not a big wine drinker, happy with her favorite sweet wines. Sometimes she'll even drink Port with her meal, a highly unorthodox choice. "Who am I to argue?" he says with a shrug.

Apart from keeping one's treasured customers or mother-in-law happy, there are plenty of examples of, shall we say, interesting personal preferences. Roger Dagorn recalls a regular customer who used to drink first-growth Bordeaux wines chilled: "He was a Frenchman who certainly knew his wines, because I used to have great conversations with him. I finally asked him why he wanted these wines chilled. He explained to me that a number of years back he had moved to Tahiti. He was so used to drinking great wines that he had to have them, but in Tahiti you can't drink them at room temperature. They would be so heavy. It made sense to him. Perhaps somebody gets used to caviar and Château Lafite. Fine, although it's not an ideal marriage. I know some people who say that Champagne and caviar do not marry. Other people swear by it." As the French say, *Chacun a son gout* ("to each his own").

An elegant wine dinner at Chateau Pontet-Canet in Bordeaux.

Dominant Flavors

Food and wine guru Josh Wesson makes the important point that we shouldn't think in terms of rules, which are rigid, but rather principles, which are flexible. His approach is like all great science: He breaks a problem down into its fundamentals. Every wine, like every food, has a dominant flavor. Once you've determined that, you can make an informed choice based on the two important principles of contrast and similarity.

The dominant flavor of raw oysters is—*salt!* What better way to balance this than with the refreshing, cool bubbles of a fine sparkling wine? And why not the finest—Champagne?

One reason why rules such as "no red wine with fish" don't work is that they ignore these important principles. Often, it's the sauce that provides the dominant flavor of a dish, so the wine needs to be matched accordingly. If it's a meaty, mild-flavored fish such as sea bass with a red wine sauce, then you would naturally look for red wine with your fish. It's usually more a matter of matching the style of the dish to the wine. A heavy tannic red wine such as a young Bordeaux with a mild white fish might indeed yield an unpleasant metallic taste. Yet take a piece of good, fresh, simply prepared tuna, grilled or seared. It's like a piece of steak, not too fishy, and it pairs nicely with a light, fruity red wine such as Beaujolais, but also with a smooth, round Cabernet-based one.

Conventional wisdom: Certain vegetables simply clash with wine. The usual culprits are asparagus, artichoke, fennel and spinach. To a certain extent this is true. As with the red wine–fish conundrum, these foods on their own can produce strange metallic, or "off," tastes in combination with wine. A sauce or a condiment, however,

can help. For example, artichokes seasoned with lemon or a mild vinaigrette dressing to cut its latent bitterness can pair very nicely with a lighter-bodied, acidic wine. Spinach with butter sauce can work with a medium-bodied Chardonnay; the more creamy or buttery the sauce on the spinach, the richer and more buttery the matching Chardonnay can be.

Similarity and Contrast

Men who struggle with matching their ties to their suits and shirts do well to apply the KISS Principle (Keep It Simple, Stupid). They shouldn't try to get fancy, to mix and match complicated patterns or color combinations. Instead, they should rely on fundamental principles such as similarity or contrast: Wear a white shirt and red tie with a navy blue jacket (contrast) or a light blue shirt and blue striped tie (similarity). The same goes for wines: Look for either similarity or contrast between your foods and wines. Keep it simple and basic.

If the dish has flavors of herbs and spices, choose a wine whose flavor and aroma can complement them. If the wine has hints of citrus, choose a dish with lemony, orange or fruity flavors. Determine the dominant flavors in your foods and wines, then try to find pairings based on similarities.

Contrast is the opposing principle to similarity. Put another way, opposites attract. The old Bordelais custom of drinking Sauternes—what we think of as a sweet dessert wine—with foie gras is a good example. The sweetness and acidity in the wine contrast with the saltiness and fattiness in the foie gras. Opposites attract: salt works with sugar, acid with fat. The result? Perfect harmony! A lip-smacking Sancerre (Sauvignon Blanc) might have the acidity to match with a goat cheese salad, but a classic California Chardonnay, much fruitier and oakier, might not have the bite to cut through the dense texture of the cheese. The contrasting acidity of the wine and chalkiness of the cheese—base versus acid—need to be in balance for the pairing to succeed.

Conventional wisdom: Spicy food is another sworn enemy of wine. Master sommelier Roger Dagorn recalls his three and a half years working in a Chinese restaurant: "It was a lot of fun because I got to see what pairings would work best. One thing I noticed in Chinese cuisine is how they intensify the flavors by adding salt *and* sugar to a dish." A wine with some sweetness to contrast the salt and some acidity to balance out the sweetness in the food, for example, an Alsatian Gewürztraminer, can work well with spicy Asian-type cuisine.

At EOS in San Francisco, where the dishes often feature bold, spicy flavors with an Asian influence, Debbie Zachareas noticed a lot of customers ordering the proverbial glass of Chardonnay. In this particular instance, spicy food *is* the enemy of wine. When a relatively full-bodied dry white wine like Chardonnay is paired with spicy dishes, the flavors of the food kill the fruit in the wine, leaving you with a dull alcoholic taste that is not at all pleasurable. But a sweeter, lighter, more acidic wine, say an Austrian Grüner Veltliner, is just the ticket.

One of my favorite luncheon spots is Yeung, a Chinese restaurant in West Los Angeles; there's nothing better than washing down their tasty Hong Kong and Szechuan specialties with a glass or two of Zind-Humbrecht's Alsatian Riesling. I've often heard the opinion that those wines are too garish, nothing but "day-glo." It may be true that they are difficult to drink unaccompanied, but they certainly make an excellent match for this type of food.

COCKTAIL ANYONE?

I'M NOT A COCKTAIL PERSON. MAYBE, IF I'M SITTING AT ONE OF THOSE LOVELY OUTDOOR CAFES IN VENICE'S PIAZZA SAN MARCO AND THE MOOD IS RIGHT, I'LL HAVE A CAMPARI AND SODA. WINE PURISTS SAY YOU SHOULD ESCHEW HARD SPIRITS ALTOGETHER AS THEY NUMB YOUR PALATE SO YOU CAN'T TASTE THE WINE. WHETHER OR NOT YOU ADHERE TO THIS POINT OF VIEW, THERE *IS* AN ARGUMENT FOR THAT PREMEAL COCKTAIL: IT LOWERS YOUR BLOOD SUGAR AND MAKES YOU HUNGRY. THE WORD *APERI-TIF* COMES FROM THE LATIN ROOT *APERT,* WHICH MEANS TO OPEN. YOU CAN OPEN THE MEAL WITH A COCKTAIL OR OPT INSTEAD FOR A GLASS OF CHAMPAGNE, WHICH HAPPENS TO BE MY PERSONAL PREFER-ENCE. IN FACT, I OFTEN LIKE TO PERUSE THE MENU AND WINE LIST OVER A GLASS OF THE BUBBLY AND, MUCH LATER, END THE MEAL WITH IT, TOO.

Regional Pairings

When in doubt, pair wines of a particular region with foods from that region. There's a good reason why they complement one another; they come from the same soil and they evolved together down through the decades. Enjoy the hearty, olive oil–based cuisine of Provence with the spicy full-bodied wines of that region—a classic ratatouille with a Bandol wine. Match a Tuscan dish of Paparadelle all Lepre, the wide, thick homemade noodles topped with a rustic rabbit-meat ragu, with a fine Chianti Riserva. Savor the smoky, lemony, salty Greek appetizers *taramasalata, tzatziki* and hummus with a piney-tasting Retsina wine; or a bracing Portuguese Vinho Verde with one of their innumerable Bacalhau (salt cod) recipes; or a classic meat-and-potatoes feast—rack of lamb, prime rib—with full-bodied red Bordeaux or California Cabernets.

Putting It All Together

As is the case with wine-tasting, once you've mastered the fundamental building blocks of food-wine pairings—balance, matching dominant flavors, similarity or contrast—you can begin to master some more complex or challenging match-ups. Most fine foods feature an interplay of flavors and textures, with several themes underlying the dominant one. With a salty, oily, spicy dish, you'll want a light and refreshing beverage, a "palate cleanser." Most Americans, when confronted with such a choice, reach for a frosty cold mug of beer. What's the wine most like beer? A sparkling one, like Champagne, which is dry to medium-dry and pleasingly acidic.

Take, for example, a mildly spicy curried shrimp appetizer, served on a bed of spinach, seasoned with sesame oil and garnished with slices of ripe papaya. A cool, bubbly Champagne, with its fruity, mildly sour taste, would be a nice match. The Champagne, whose dominant flavor is acidic, can cut through the sauce on the shrimp dish, whose dominant flavor is sesame oil. It refreshes the palate after the hint of saltiness and spice in the cur-

ried shrimp, creating a nice contrast. Another nice complement might be a crisp Sancerre. With hints of peach and melon flavors and aromas along with a pleasant chalky, minerally quality, it provides a nice contrast with the flavors of the shrimp dish as well as a complement to its fruit garnish.

PROGRESSION

Deluxe wine dinners, multicourse tasting extravaganzas, are more work and more fun than most of us can manage on a regular basis. They can feature five to seven, ten or even fifteen wines and an equal number of food courses. Some hosts like to serve two or three wines per course for comparison tasting, say verticals of a certain producer or horizontals of a particular region or international expressions of a grape (e.g., a Syrah from California, a Rhône wine from France, a Shiraz from Australia or South Africa).

The classical progression of a multicourse always builds from light to heavy, from dry to sweet, from white to red, from young to old. Often, the cocktail or aperitif is treated as an item apart and served with appropriately matched hors d'oeuvres, which is why it's allowed to be more substantial—heavier, sweeter, more alcoholic—than the initial wine selection.

A typical sequence would go something like this: Champagne or dry sherry or a light white wine from Germany or Alsace as an aperitif; white wines with first (fish) courses and/or appetizers; red wines with main courses, possibly a Gamay or Pinot Noir first then moving to a Cabernet or even a Syrah or Zinfandel; for dessert and/or the cheese course, a late-harvest or fortified (sweet) wine.

In principle, the wines should complement each other and no one should overshadow the others, particularly the ones that go before it. And, as always, I encourage experimentation.

BODY CHART

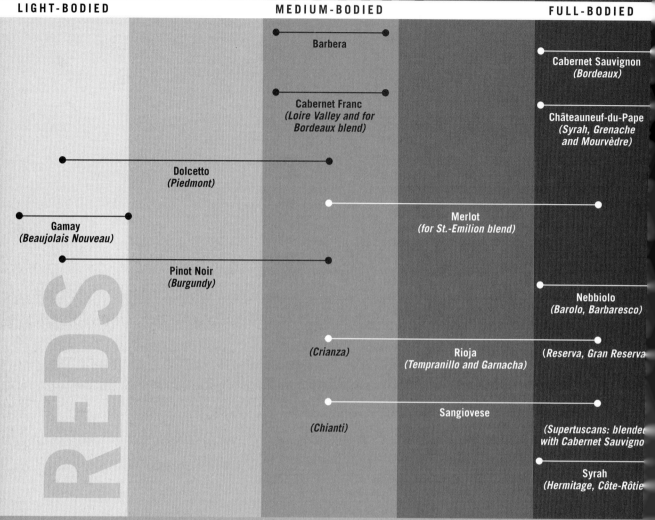

Barbera

Cabernet Franc
*(Loire Valley and for
Bordeaux blend)*

Cabernet Sauvignon
(Bordeaux)

Châteauneuf-du-Pape
*(Syrah, Grenache
and Mourvèdre)*

Dolcetto
(Piedmont)

Merlot
(for St.-Emilion blend)

Gamay
(Beaujolais Nouveau)

Pinot Noir
(Burgundy)

Nebbiolo
(Barolo, Barbaresco)

(Crianza)

Rioja
(Tempranillo and Garnacha)

(Reserva, Gran Reserva)

Sangiovese

(Chianti)

*(Supertuscans: blended
with Cabernet Sauvigno)*

Syrah
(Hermitage, Côte-Rôtie)

REDS

TANNINS IN RED WINES
(LIGHTEST TO HEAVIEST WITHIN EACH CATEGORY)

Light: Gamay

Medium: Dolcetto, Barbera, Pinot Noir, Merlot

Medium-heavy: Sangiovese, Syrah, Zinfandel

Heavy: Cabernet Franc, Cabernet Sauvignon, Nebbiolo

N o t e : As is the case with body, sweetness and other characteristics, the strength of the tannins in a given grape variety will vary depending on *terroir,* viticulture and viniculture.

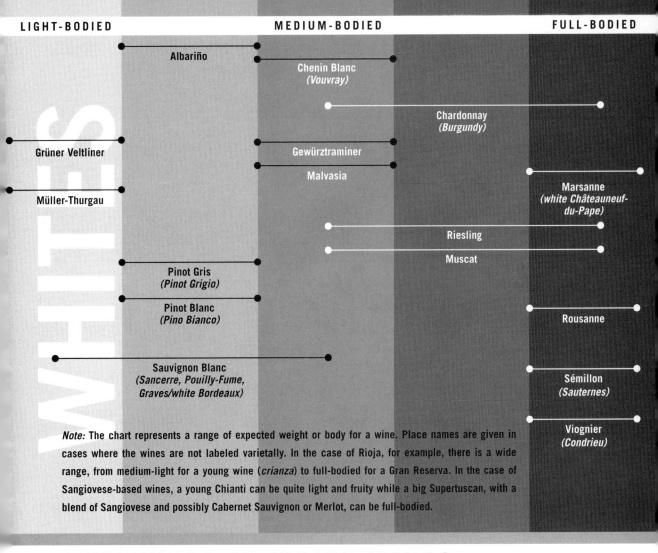

LIGHT-BODIED **MEDIUM-BODIED** **FULL-BODIED**

Albariño

Chenin Blanc
(Vouvray)

Chardonnay
(Burgundy)

Grüner Veltliner

Gewürztraminer

Malvasia

Marsanne
*(white Châteauneuf-
du-Pape)*

Müller-Thurgau

Riesling

Muscat

Pinot Gris
(Pinot Grigio)

Pinot Blanc
(Pino Bianco)

Rousanne

WHITES

Sauvignon Blanc
*(Sancerre, Pouilly-Fume,
Graves/white Bordeaux)*

Sémillon
(Sauternes)

Viognier
(Condrieu)

Note: The chart represents a range of expected weight or body for a wine. Place names are given in cases where the wines are not labeled varietally. In the case of Rioja, for example, there is a wide range, from medium-light for a young wine (*crianza*) to full-bodied for a Gran Reserva. In the case of Sangiovese-based wines, a young Chianti can be quite light and fruity while a big Supertuscan, with a blend of Sangiovese and possibly Cabernet Sauvignon or Merlot, can be full-bodied.

SWEETNESS IN WHITE WINES

Very dry: Sauvignon Blanc, Albariño, Chardonnay (Premier Cru and Grand Cru Burgundies), German Trocken wines

Dry to medium-dry: Pinot Blanc, Viognier, Grüner Veltliner, Chenin Blanc (Vouvray Demi-Sec), Gewürztraminer, Riesling Spatlese

Medium-sweet to sweet: Moscato D'Asti, White Zinfandel, Vouvray Moulleux (late-harvested Chenin Blanc), late-harvested Riesling Auslese, Beerenauslese and Trockenbeerenauslese, Sauternes (late-harvested Sémillon), Tokay 5 Puttonyos, Sherry, Marsala

Thomas Keller, one of America's greatest chefs, orchestrates multi-course meals with precision at The French Laundry.

WINE

MEALS

Wine is the focus of this book and it's usually the first thing I think of when planning a dinner, either professionally or at home with friends and family. Once you've found a comfort level with wine, you'll begin fitting it effortlessly into your meal planning. It may not play the starring role in your meal or gathering, but I'd like to think that fine wine is always an important piece of the puzzle. For all but the most serious connoisseurs and collectors, a formal wine tasting—with or without an accompanying sit-down dinner—is a rare occasion. By the same token, a celebratory dinner at home or a special picnic in a beautiful spot would be . . . well, empty without a nice bottle or two of wine.

In the following sections, we've taken a couple of tacks in order to illustrate successful food-wine pairings based on the principles I have outlined. First, a wine-tasting dinner at The French Laundry in Napa Valley specially devised for this book, then the Sommelier's Challenge, where we "ordered" meals from some of my favorite restaurants, ranging from romantic dinners for two to a multicourse dinner for six, asking their sommeliers to suggest matching wines and explain their choices. Lastly, I offer my own picks for two informal outdoor meals. I encourage you to try some of these pairings and then branch out and create your own matches.

WINE-TASTING DINNER

The French Laundry, Yountville, California,
Chef's Tasting Menu by Thomas Keller
Wine Selections by Laura Cunningham

THE FOOD		THE WINES
"Oysters and Pearls": Sabayon of Pearl Tapioca with Poached Malpeque Oysters and Sevruga Caviar	1	1989 Schramsberg Blanc de Blanc, Napa Valley
Salad of Marinated Kadota and Mission Figs with Roasted Peppers, Shaved Fennel, Balsamic Glaze and Wild Fennel Seed Oil	2	1995 Araujo Estate Sauvignon Blanc, Napa Valley
Filet of Gold Coast Pompano "Amandine" with Preserved Lemon-Infused Orzo	3	1995 Araujo Estate Sauvignon Blanc, Napa Valley
Sweet Butter-Braised Maine Lobster with Baby Arrowleaf Spinach and a Saffron-Vanilla Sauce	4	1994 Clos du Ciel Chardonnay, Peter Michael Winery, Napa Valley
Medallion of "Ris de Veau" with Potato Gnocchi, Forest Mushrooms and White Truffle Emulsion	5	1990 Gary Farrell Pinot Noir, Allen Vineyard, Sonoma Valley
Filet Mignon of Prime Beef with Melted Green Leeks, "Confit" of Tomato and Seared Moulard Duck "Foie Gras"	6	1992 Paradigm Cabernet Sauvignon, Napa Valley
"St. Agur" Cheese with Quince Marmalade and Candied Walnuts	7	1991 Swanson Late Harvest Sémillon, Napa Valley
Caramelized Tartlette of "Heirloom" Apples with Sweetened "Crème Fraîche"	8	1991 Swanson Late Harvest Sémillon, Napa Valley

1 The Schramsberg Blanc de Blancs is a classic aperitif, especially with this canape. It has a balance of sharp acidity and finesse to create a clean combination with the rich sabayon while its honey overtones provide an attractive contrast to the saltiness of the caviar.

2 An elegant, nuanced white wine from Napa Valley's famous Eisele Vineyard, the Araujo Estate Sauvignon Blanc offers hints of melon and herbs which pair nicely with the figs and balance the acids from the fennel and balsamic vinegar.

3 The Araujo Sauvignon Blanc worked well with this mild, firm, moderately fatty fish and its citrus accompaniments. The lemon-infused orzo enhanced the aromas of the Araujo, increasing the intensity of its finish.

4 The well-crafted Clos du Ciel Chardonnay offers an excellent match for the rich butter-braised lobster. The sauce's vanilla component gives a leaner appearance to the wine, which nevertheless retains its succulent, creamy finish.

5 The Gary Farrell is a super-concentrated Pinot Noir with great depth and earthiness. Its silky palette and raspberry fruit added an intriguing layer to the unique texture of the sweetbreads; the mushrooms and hint of truffle emulsion rounded out the dusty characteristics of the wine's *terroir*. Layers of fruit and raspberries with a touch of oak cut through the extremely rich textural components of the dish.

6 Produced by an Oakville estate, the Paradigm is a well-balanced Cabernet featuring bright fruit, mild tannins and herbal qualities that proved to be a good match for this meat course. The wine's deep purple fruit, firm structure and hint of peppery spice meshed well with the tomato confit. It found a perfect balance with the weight of the beef while its silky, fleshy overtones complement the richness of the seared foie gras.

7 A silky, slightly smoky, viscous wine, the Swanson Late Harvest Sémillon has delightful honey and sweet spice qualities. Like a Sauternes, it pairs well with this full-flavored cheese. Add the slightly bittersweet quince along with the candied walnuts and you have a myriad of flavors and textures.

8 The somewhat sticky finish of this Sémillon is calmed by the crème fraîche and fruity ripe apples, striking an appropriate dessert balance.

THE SOMMELIER'S CHALLENGE

To illustrate how even the most knowledgeable wine connoisseurs must confront issues of conflict and compromise when making a selection to pair with diverse food flavors, we picked a few of my favorite wine-destination restaurants, ordered meals from their menus and challenged their sommeliers to recommend matching wines from their lists. In one case we assumed a party of two diners, in other cases four or more, all ordering different meals. We asked these food-wine experts to be adventurous with the aim of exciting and stimulating the palates of these hypothetical diners. Rather than taking a formulaic approach or suggesting a specific wine for each individual dish, they were asked to make real-world recommendations that would please each customer equally.

DINNERS FOR FOUR

Manfred Krankl, Campanile, Los Angeles

My good friend Manfred is skeptical about the concept of restaurants carefully matching wines with foods, other than generally coordinating the style of cuisine with the wine-list theme. "When you talk about matching wines with dishes," he says, "I find it almost rhetorical. In the real setting that's almost impossible to achieve." This may be true, unless you have a large party and can order two, three or even four different wines. Most people, when they go out to a meal at a special restaurant, order a variety of dishes. What happens if you order foie gras for an appetizer and your dinner partner orders tuna tartar, then for the main course you have the lamb and he or she has the scallops? Manfred points out that if you want to be precise in your matchings, then it makes more sense to pick the wine first and then decide what dishes you feel go with it. If not, you may want to opt for by-the-glass orders or half bottles.

APPETIZERS
Grilled sardines with peperonata and shaved fennel salad
Steamed mussels with spicy sausage, swiss chard and roasted tomato
Lima bean puree with escarole, treviso and grilled rustic bread
Crimson lentil soup with crème fraîche and apple-smoked bacon

ENTRÉES
Eggplant Parmesan with mozzarella and tomato sauce
Braised chicken with saffron, couscous, roasted tomato and garbanzo beans
Grilled swordfish with green lentils, spinach, currants and pine nuts
Pork loin with long-cooked greens, black-eyed peas and mashed potatoes

For the appetizers, Manfred would recommend an Austrian white wine: "The Grüner Veltliner Alte Reben 1995 from Fred Loimer would be a terrific match for most of these dishes. The wine has sufficient body and a creamy, rich texture to stand up to the somewhat spicy quality of the mussels. It has flavor tones that would match wonderfully with the lima bean puree and cool length to beautifully cleanse and prepare the palate for each spoonful of crimson lentil soup. The guy with the grilled sardines should have a pilsner. Sorry, but sardines just don't go with any wine."

For the main course: "The Pinot Noir Shea Vineyard Ken Wright Cellars, 1994, is the ticket here. This is an absolutely gorgeous Oregon Pinot that should be tried no matter what you're having—except, of course, the sardines. It would enhance the already delicious braised chicken with its smoky, meaty, Asian spice character. The swordfish would also wave its tail, once wrapped in the incredibly deep velvety blanket of this wine. The smooth richness of this wine will also underline the soft tenderness of the pork loin. The guy with the eggplant Parmesan—the same guy who had to have the sardines—should take a sip of mineral water before every sip of wine so that this super Pinot won't get the metallic treatment from the eggplant."

APPETIZERS

Grilled seafood sausage

Asparagus flan with fresh morels

Millefeuille of Louisiana crayfish

Cold consommé madrilene with grilled quail salad

ENTRÉES

Peppered tuna with sauteed greens and Banyuls sauce

Diver-caught Maine sea scallops with duck fat, tomato and basil

Sauteed red snapper on a ragout of vegetables with pig's feet and red wine

Breast of muscovy duck with Chinese spices and sweet soy glaze

AN ASSORTMENT OF CHEESES

DESSERT

A duo of rhubarb desserts

Ice creams and sorbets

All of the appetizer dishes are quite aromatic, so Roger looks for something that can match those aromas, a medium-bodied wine without too much oak. Two grape varieties come to mind immediately, a Viognier and a Tokay Pinot Gris. He offers us two recommendations: first, a Viognier from the Château Grillet appellation, produced by Neyrat Gachet, 1991. "It has a fairly intense aroma but is not necessarily full-bodied. You may detect violets, tropical fruit or melon, all of which would work well with the seafood sausage, as well as with the crayfish. This wine also stands up to the asparagus flan, which is fairly aromatic and rich, not too pungent like some asparagus dishes." The second recommendation is an Alsatian Tokay Pinot Gris Vieilles Vignes from Domaine Zind-Humbrecht (1993). "This wine is more aromatic and has more body than the Viognier. It also has what we call in French *eau de petrol,* oiliness, which is a typical characteristic of the older-vine Alsatian wines."

For the main course, Roger recommends Quail Hill Vineyards' 1994 Lynmar Pinot Noir from Russian River Valley, California: "It has a fair amount of earthiness, good fruit and intense aroma but it's not too heavy or tannic. It will certainly stand up to the spices and glaze of the duck and the pig's feet and red wine with the red snapper."

To accompany Chanterelle's delicious cheese plate, Roger suggests something "a little out of the ordinary": The Commandaria Saint John, which is a fortified wine from Cyprus that is made by the *solera* system, the same as sherry, but tastes more like a tawny Port. Its sweetness provides a nice contrast to the cheeses. (Roger notes that this wine comes from one of the oldest vineyards in the world, dating back to at least 1190, when Richard the Lionhearted conquered the island during the Crusades.)

The challenge with dessert is to match the tartness of the rhubarb with a wine that has plenty of acidity but a balance of sweetness. Roger recommends a late-harvest Loire Valley wine from the Quarts de Chaumes appellation, Domaine de Baumard, 1993, made from the Chenin Blanc grape: "It has aromas of quince and honeysuckle with a nice long finish."

"I really rotate wines like crazy—especially my Austrian, German and Alsatian wines—because I want to expose people to a lot of those different flavors. Once I get people to try those wines with our food, they come back and many times they'll order a two-ounce pour of each wine. They'll compare the wines and consider which ones go with what dishes."—Debbie Zachereas

Debbie Zachareas, EOS, San Francisco

APPETIZERS
Black mussels, green curried coconut broth in a clay pot
Grilled Thai bread salad, organic mixed greens and aromatic herbs
Rock shrimp cakes, spicy gingered aioli
Shiitake mushroom dumplings, san bai su

ENTRÉES
Organic "Paro Valley" Bhutanese red rice risotto, chanterelle mushrooms and ginger, roasted red peppers
Blackened Asian catfish, lemongrass risotto
Grilled Thai-spiced smoked natural double-cut pork chop, sweet black rice, fresh local Granny Smith applesauce
Poussin stuffed with sweet sticky rice and Chinese sausage, bok choy

For the appetizers, Debbie would suggest a medium-dry Riesling, perhaps the Boxler Grand Cru Sonnenberg, which she calls "exceptional." "It's medium-dry with amazing complexity and can stand up to more assertive dishes like the mussels and the dumplings. The wine's slight sweetness and bright acidity complement the spiciness of the mussels perfectly." Another option to accompany the appetizers would be to order by the glass: "With the mussels, try a rose. The Etude is a good choice because it has solid fruit on the midpalate that isn't overpowered by the spice and coconut curry.

"The Thai bread salad is very clean and fresh and goes well with a wine of the same character, say the Huet Vouvray Demi-Sec, which offers a hint of sweetness but has the bright acids to pair beautifully with that dish, or the Hiedler Grüner Veltliner, which is refreshing and lively like the salad. The shiitake mushroom dumplings do benefit from richer, sweeter wines so you might try an Alsatian Gewürztraminer, an aged Tokay Pinot Gris or a Riesling.

"The shrimp cakes are pan-fried, so a wine like the Hippolyte Reverdy Sancerre, light with bright acidity, will keep the dish alive.

"There are also several options with the main course. The best wines for our dishes are usually Pinot Noirs and Red Rhônes—both domestic and foreign. I like the more gutsy Pinots; one of the best on our list is the 1995 W.H. Smith Hellenthal Vineyard made by Bill and Joan Smith of La Jota Vineyards. Some other great choices for New World Pinots, in a wide price range, are Au Bon Climat, Domaine Serene, Brick House and Bass Phillips (from Australia). If you want to return to Burgundy, try the '91 Rouget Echézeaux.

"If you want to order by the glass, the red rice goes well with the Vouvray Demi-Sec from Huet, the J.J. Prum Riesling Spatlese Wehlener Sonnenuhr or the D'Arenberg Grenache/Shiraz. The same can be said for the catfish. The pork chop would be most enjoyable with a glass of Vieux Telegraphe Châteauneuf-du-Pape. I like the rustic, gamy edge to the wine with that dish. The poussin works well with a bright fruity red, such as the Qupe Reserve Syrah, Quintarelli's Valpolicella Superiore or Alban's Grenache, which can stand up to the dominant flavors in the Chinese sausage."

TWO ROMANTIC
DINNERS FOR TWO

Windows on the World, New York

Andrea Immer, a master sommelier, succeeded another star, Kevin Zraly, as the beverage director at Windows on the World. She was named Best Sommelier by the Sommelier Society of America in 1997 and cohosted the TV series "Quench." She is now with Starwood Hotels and Resorts. These were her suggestions:

APPETIZERS
Hudson Valley foie gras with roasted squash-potato hash, sherry vinegar-pepper sauce
Beluga caviar service in crystal garnished with capers, onions, chopped egg, dill and sour cream

ENTRÉES
Porcini-crusted Atlantic halibut with toasted barley risotto, basil oil, oven-dried tomatoes
Roasted filet mignon with green peppercorn sauce, Yukon gold mashed potatoes

DESSERT
Red berry crème brûlée tart

For the first course, here's Andrea's suggestion: "It's hard to resist the temptation to pair luxury with luxury, and the Krug Grande Cuvée Champagne is an indulgent choice. Happily, we have it by the glass or bottle. The rich foie gras begs for Krug's expansive flavor and refreshing sparkle, both of which are a terrific foil for the tender, plump Beluga."

For the main course: "A 1992 Volnay Cailletrets from Pousse d'Or has the silken texture to complement the halibut, as well as Burgundian earthiness to match the heady flavor of the porcini crust. The Volnay's bright cherry fruit is also fearless with the meaty, velvety filet, whose peppercorn sauce coaxes out the wine's elegant spice notes."

For dessert: "Our by-the-glass Sauternes is Château Rieussec 1989, showing a luscious, creamy honey-caramel richness in perfect keeping with the flavors of the crème brûlée. The berries in both the crème brûlée and the wine counterbalance the sweetness with a bright tang of acidity."

APPETIZERS
Wild mushroom casserole with creamy Gorgonzola polenta
Chilled Gulf shrimp with homemade ketchup-horseradish sauce

ENTRÉES
Roasted Maine lobster with Putnam County clabber cream, upside-down root vegetable pot pie
Rack of lamb with rosemary-mustard crust, Yukon potato-leek gratin

DESSERT
Valrhona chocolate cake, served warm, with pistachio ice cream

For the first course: "Anyone for a flavor riot? There is one perfect wine for both dishes, each of which reveals a different side to the wine—Condrieu Coteaux de Poncins, Villard 1994, an exotic wine. The earthy-rich flavors of mushrooms and corn in the polenta fuse with the wine's mineral notes, unlocking the rich tropical fruit underneath, which is met head-on by the almost fruity pungency of the Gorgonzola—wow! The fleshy-sweet shrimp are also a natural partner to this rich wine, which shows its exotic spicy side with the horseradish ketchup."

In this meal, there's a conflict between the main courses, so Andrea chooses the sensible route: "Go with glasses here: the lobster dish is all about rich flavors, with the undernotes of sweetness (lobster, braised root vegetables, puff pastry), all of which call for a ripe, concentrated Chardonnay that wears its oak with subtlety: the Torres Milmanda Estate, Penedes 1994. The meat entrée has three of the Cabernet-friendliest flavors in the world: lamb, rosemary and leeks. Here, the elegance and faintly herbal scent of Jordan Cabernet, Alexander Valley 1993, will demonstrate the virtues of a classic pairing."

For dessert: "Our Blandy's ten-year-old Malmsey Madeira with its nutty, caramel-like richness is the ultimate combination with the dark intensity of Valrhona chocolate—the rich flavors of each weave together into a decadent and endless finish."

DINNER FOR SIX

One of New York's top restaurants for the better part of two decades, the Gotham features the superb cuisine of executive chef Alfred Portale, a colossal figure in the American culinary revolution who manages to maintain, year in and year out, his magic touch. Alfred is known for his architectural creations—towering salads, multilayered entrées, painstakingly sculptured desserts —whose succulent flavors are matched by their stunning presentation. He created the style and it has been widely imitated. Alfred is a wine lover, world traveler and published author (his *Gotham Bar & Grill Cookbook* came out in the fall of 1997). His sommelier for many years was Scott Carney, who was succeeded by Joseph Nase, who was in turn succeeded by John Gilman.

APPETIZERS

Seafood salad: Scallops, squid, Japanese octopus, lobster and avocado, dressed in lemon vinaigrette

Goat cheese ravioli: In minestrone with Monini olive oil and Reggiano Parmesan

Grilled octopus: Chickpeas, new potatoes, leeks and charred tomato

Yellow fin tuna tartare: Herb salad, cucumber, lime, scallion and ginger

Sweetbreads: Fried crisp with arugula, glazed cippolini, pancetta and Pommery mustard sauce

Chicken, foie gras and black trumpet terrine: Haricots verts, green lentil salad, pickled onion and Port glaze

ENTRÉES

Grilled New York steak: Crushed white peppercorns, marrow mustard custard and Vidalia onion rings

Shellfish bouillabaisse: Scallops, prawns, mussels, squid, lobster in a saffron shellfish stock

Atlantic salmon: With morels, wild leeks, sweet peas and chervil

Sauteed softshell crabs: Creamer potatoes, broccoli rabe, baby arugula and brown butter

Saddle of rabbit: Grilled, with steamed spinach, white beans and young fennel

Roast pheasant: Marinated in ginger and juniper, with potato puree, braised red cabbage and poached Lady Apple

DESSERT

Gotham chocolate cake: Served warm with espresso ice cream

Lemon tart with warm blackberry compote

Pineapple pound cake: Served warm with toasted coconut ice cream, kumquats and pineapple caramel sauce

Vanilla bean crème brûlée with warm red and black berries

John's suggestions for the dinner: "With a table of six, there are always going to be difficult combinations. The temptation is to find a bottle of wine that works for the majority of the guests, then cover the one or two more difficult dishes with one of our wines by the glass. I only like to explore this option as a last resort, however, as I love the appreciative feedback that comes when finding a wine that works beautifully with each seemingly disparate dish. Here, the sweetbreads, terrine and goat cheese ravioli call out for Pinot Noir, but as much as I love Pinot with tuna, I prefer tartare with a crisp white. The seafood salad really needs white wine as well, though the octopus can swing both ways.

"The wine that will cover everything well is a Chablis, where the earthy flavors will play off the trumpets in the terrine and the white truffle in the ravioli. Chablis is the least understood great Chardonnay in the world; I also find it by far the most flexible at the table. The advantage of six or more at the table is we can create impromptu tasting lineups. I would suggest a flight here, opening with the brilliant 1995 Chablis Fourchaume from Domaine Boudin, and following it up with the 1989 Chablis Les Clos from Raveneau. The sweetbreads will reach unbelievable heights when paired with these two wines.

"With the second courses, the right Pinot Noir will work beautifully. The bouillabaisse and the softshell crabs might work even better with a white, and we could delve into our half-bottle selections here for a richer style of Chardonnay to follow up the Chablis. The Talbott 1995 Sleepy Hollow Chardonnay from Monterey or white Burgundies such as the 1995 Chassagne-Montrachet Morgeots from Jean Noel Gagnard or the 1988 Puligny-Montrachet Truffieres from Etienne Sauzet would match well with these dishes.

"If everyone at the table decides to explore the Pinot option, I would recommend a wine with plenty of 'red fruit' character. A few possibilities: 1995 Etude Pinot Noir from Carneros, 1994 Domaine Drouhin Pinot Noir from Oregon, 1992 Williams & Selyem Russian River Pinot Noir or 1995 Savigny les Beaune Les Peuillets from Maurice Ecard. All of these wines possess bright, tangy acidity to pair with the seafood dishes, but also pack the requisite stuffing to keep our steak-eater happy."

John might make a handful more Pinot suggestions, spurring his table of six to continue exploring what this noble grape has to offer: the 1988 Morey-St.-Denis Clos de la Bussierre from Roumier, the 1988 Clos de la Roche from Dujac, the 1994 Dehlinger Pinot Noir Reserve or the 1995 Martinborough Pinot Noir (New Zealand's answer to Echézeaux). "All offer deeper, plummier fruit and kaleidoscopic soil and herb tones. I would lobby hard for the Dujac Clos de la Roche. This wine just explodes from the glass; diners at five tables around will strain their necks to see where all the excitement is coming from. It would be a stupendous follow-up to the two Chablis.

"For dessert, the chocolate cake is the obvious odd man out. Here I'd recommend two glasses of the Taylor-Fladgate 20-Year-Old Tawny Port. I like Madeira or Banyuls as an option, but the Taylor 20-Year-Old is the more gentle landing after the Concorde trip their palates have taken with the Chablis and the Dujac. For the four diners with the good sense to order fruit-based desserts, the ride can last a little longer. A half-bottle of Sauternes such as the 1988 Château Lafaurie-Peyraguey, the 1988 Château Climens or the 1986 Château de Fargues are great choices. Not quite as perfect a match with the crème brûlée but an equally stunning bottle would be the 1995 Inniskillin Icewine from Ontario. Great acids provide freshness and snap, and this wine's wonderful depth and great tropical notes of pineapple and guava would certainly start the pulse racing."

Something different for dessert: a Moscato D'Asti with the pie

OUTDOOR
LATE-SUMMER DINNER

This is a simple home-cooked meal that was stretched into a four-course celebration. It utilized local fresh produce such as tomatoes, corn on the cob, berries and seafood. A few simple touches, such as adding curry powder to the lemon vinaigrette for the lobster salad and roasted red pepper to the aioli for the fish, lend the dishes a veneer of sophistication.

THE FOOD   THE WINES

Steamed mussels with white wine sauce	1	1995 Sancerre, Clos de la Crele, Thomas Lucien et Fils
Lobster salad with lemon-curry vinaigrette	2	1994 Guigal Condrieu
Tuna steaks with red pepper aioli; ratatouille; corn on the cob	3	1994 Chinon, Alan Lorieux
Three-berry pie with peach sorbet	4	1993 Moscato D'Asti, Giacomo Bologna

1 The Sauvignon Blanc–based Sancerre is a classic accompaniment to seafood. (By the way, we used a cup of it in the sauce for the mussels. Drinking the same wine that's used in the sauce is a shortcut to a good food-wine pairing, though if it's a very expensive or rare wine, you may want to use a similar but less expensive substitute for the sauce.) The mussels are salty; the wine is a chalky, dry refresher. The broth was reduced over high heat and some cream was added, yielding a smooth, slightly thick sauce. The wine's pleasant nip of acidity cut right through that.

2 Made from the Viognier grape, Condrieu is an enchanting wine that gives off a host of delightful and surprising fruit and floral aromas. Very often, you'll encounter apricot along with different types of melon and sometimes even that wonderful bittersweetness of orange rind that you find in orange marmalade. It's got enough heft and a pleasing bite to stand up to the richness of the lobster; it also has a hint of exoticism to complement the lemon-curry vinaigrette.

3 The Chinon is a smooth, medium-bodied red wine made in the Loire Valley from the Cabernet Franc grape. It matches nicely with the grilled rare tuna's red flesh and mild fishy taste. The Chinon has a balance of fruitiness, sweetness and acid to go with the ratatouille, whose dominant flavor is sweet-and-tangy tomato. The red pepper aioli has a sharp, garlicky flavor; again, the Chinon's hint of lip-smacking acidity stands up well to it.

4 If I can't have Champagne for dessert, I'll take a flute of Moscato D'Asti. It has the dryness and pinprickly bubbles but it also has a mouth-watering sweetness. The primary flavor here is peach. The sweet-tart berry pie speaks well to the Moscato's sweet-dry balance while it works in perfect concert with the peach sorbet—they amplify each other.

Note:

The first two white wines are served chilled, but not too chilled. You don't want to kill their wonderful flavors and spoil their interaction with the food by overchilling. About fifteen or twenty minutes in the bucket of ice water will do, *or* you can refrigerate them overnight, then take them out a half hour to an hour before the meal. If they get too warm, just plop them back in the ice bucket for a while. The Chinon is served a few degrees below "room temperature," which in this case was about 70. It was simply removed from the cellar storage unit about an hour before serving. The Moscato was served chilled right out of the fridge.

BEACH PICNIC

What better illustration of "casual elegance" than a picnic,
punctuated by a couple of delicious wines, on a quiet sunny day at the beach?

THE FOOD
Celery sticks with salt and pepper
Deviled eggs with dill and pimiento
Tuna salad sandwiches with lettuce and tomato
Grilled eggplant sandwiches with tomato or roasted red pepper

THE WINES
Marcel Deiss 1995 "Bergheim" Pinot Blanc
Laurent-Perrier 1988 Brut Champagne

The Pinot Blanc is a light, refreshing low-alcohol wine that contrasts beautifully with the saltiness in the tuna sandwiches and the smoky flavor of the grilled eggplant. Its freshness also complements the crispy, crunchy celery sticks and cleanses and refreshes the palate after the smooth, rich, luxurious texture of the eggs. The Pinot is really all you need for a perfect picnic, but if you want to splurge, pop open a bottle of the Laurent-Perrier Champagne, an excellent bottle of vintage Brut —dry and delicious, the quintessential palate cleanser and an exciting way to wind down a beautiful afternoon at the beach. This is a fun variation on the classic combination of Champagne with eggs or omelettes at a brunch.

"Nothing more excellent or valuable than wine was ever granted by the gods to man." —Plato

FOOD

"The discovery of a new wine is a greater moment than the discovery of a constellation. The universe is too full of stars." —A. Brillat-Savarin

"One of the problems people seem to have is that they can be very good at quantitative analysis, judging heft and alcohol and force, but from a qualitative standpoint they are sometimes missing it. The more intangible ideas of balance, length of flavor, depth of flavor, complexity, things like that, sometimes take more time to develop." —Scott Carney, Master Sommelier

"I do believe that wine is now being made better and good wine is being made in larger quantities than at any other time in the history of the stuff." —Al Stewart, musician and collector

FOR

"True *terroir* declares itself across vintages, even grape varieties, in an unmistakable way. Each variety of wine expresses the fullness and character associated with the vine and the soil in which it grows. We are barbarians if we don't enjoy the symphony of all the elements coming together in the wine. Stop and listen to the music!" —Jean-Michel Deiss, Domaine Marcel Deiss

"I like to think of a great vineyard as a great race car. You can win the Indy 500 with it or you can run it right into the wall. You can't win the Indy with a lousy car. You can make a great wine from great grapes but you'll never make a great wine from lousy grapes." —Randy Lewis, proprietor, Lewis Cellars, former professional race car driver

"I love the artistry of the flavor. It's like I'm painting with flavor. My canvas is the winery." —Mark Aubert, Peter Michael Winery, Knights Valley, California

"The fundamental thing is the balance. Wine is a great symphony. I'm the conductor and I've got to create a harmony with five hundred different elements." —Elio Altare, Barolo winemaker

"Old Mondavi said to me, 'I don't think you can properly ripen Cabernet grapes in L.A.' I said, 'Do you think the vine knows its address?' He said, 'Touché.'" —Tom Jones, Moraga Vineyards, Bel Air

THOUGHT

THE WINE MERCHANT'S SELECTIONS

THE WORLD OF WINE SEEMS TO HAVE BECOME BIGGER AND SMALLER AT THE SAME TIME. EVERYONE INTERESTED IN WINES—FROM THE TOP EXPERTS TO THE MOST CASUAL CONSUMERS—IS HEARING ABOUT AND TASTING WINES FROM "EXOTIC" PLACES LIKE NEW ZEALAND AND CHILE MORE QUICKLY THAN EVER BEFORE. DISTANCES HAVE SHRUNK, OUR OPTIONS HAVE MULTIPLIED.

A greater variety of high-quality wines is now available to a wider audience than ever before. Many people are just opening their eyes to the wonderful world of wines; others have explored all the obvious places and now they want to find some intriguing, out-of-the-way ones. New producers and winemakers have taken the world by storm; old ones have revived themselves.

Blessed with so many delicious options, we should be grateful. We must also be selective. In this chapter, I suggest some wines of subtlety, complexity and flavor, wines that go well with food, that complement the wine lifestyle. I am not looking for trendy; I am looking for winemakers and wines that will be around in ten, fifteen or twenty-five years. Some of them have already been around longer than that. Provided they're still pushing the envelope, they're included. I refuse to rule anyone out because of age. The only discrimination I will practice is in favor of the best and most exciting wines.

I'm in favor of all the new trends: globalization; the flying enologists; the festivals and conventions; the cooperation, communication and exchange of ideas. These wonderful resources have opened up new frontiers. They've also created a barrage of information, much of it hype, that can quickly become overwhelming. In the new millennium, we should focus on the only thing that matters: what's in the bottle. We should encourage diversity and resist homogenization. We should demand wines that express their grape variety, their regional character, their unique *terroir*.

A few years ago, I took part in a tasting banquet of top wines from Italy. After dinner, a poll was taken and one of the experts, announcing his choice for the top wine of the evening, held up a glass and exclaimed, "This is great, just like a Bordeaux." Whoa! Time out! When we start to confuse a Château Margaux with an Ornellaia or vice versa, then we've got a problem. Don't misunderstand me. I have nothing against blending Cabernet Sauvignon with Sangiovese; in fact, I love the result. I would just hate to see an "international style" overshadowing all the delightful individuality of the world's finest wines.

The best wines possess individual personality. Imagine throwing a soiree for 150 of your closest friends where everyone showed up wearing the same Armani suit. Not to take anything away from Armani, but variety is the spice of life, and nowhere so much as in the realm of wine. In an age when winemakers rush to make crowd-pleasing, front-loaded wines with "gobs of fruit" and the more oak the better, it's increasingly difficult to find the vintners from whom the idea of *terroir* is more than an advertising slogan.

Whether you take a trip down the block to your favorite wine merchant or halfway around the world to one of the great growing regions, there's always the exciting possibility that you'll fall in love with a wine you've never had before. Life is a journey; sometimes there's an incredible surprise around the corner.

If you're interested in wine, it's crucial to expand your horizons, to be adventurous, to try as wide a variety as possible. Most important, don't settle on any favorites until you've tried a little bit of everything. Even if you love Burgundies and Pinot Noirs, don't leave all those Zinfandels or Rhône wines on the shelf. If you're tired of the classic-style Chardonnay, then try a Sauvignon Blanc. If you've had some good California Sauvignon Blancs, try some from South Africa or New Zealand. Experiment with Rieslings from Alsace, Austria, Australia and Germany; check out a Viognier—from Condrieu in the Rhône and from one of California's "Rhône Rangers."

The following wines are a few of *my* favorites, the ones I consider standard-bearers, based on *my* opinions. Try them, form your own judgments, then use this information as a ticket to your own wine adventure. Remember, if your merchant or supplier can't obtain the wines on this list, they should at least be able to help you find equivalent or comparable ones.

AUSTRALIA

Australia is hot—literally and figuratively. There are some tremendous wines coming out of the island continent, which is a huge, hot, dry country with several pockets of cool winegrowing paradises, the majority on its southeastern flank, dotted through areas surrounding the cities of Sydney, Melbourne and Adelaide. Over the past decade or so, Australia has been a sleeping giant awakening, much like California. The traditional Australian grape variety is Shiraz, which is their name for Syrah. There is also a good deal of excellent Cabernet Sauvignon as well as the white varieties Chardonnay, Sémillon, Sauvignon Blanc and Riesling. Australian (sweet) fortified wines, Muscat and Tokay (made from Muscadelle), have a world-class tradition dating back nearly two hundred years. A more recent tradition is for Champagne-style sparkling wines.

The leader in premium wines since the mid-fifties has been Penfolds. Its Grange Hermitage, a Shiraz varietal, begun by winemaker Max Schubert (d. 1994) after he learned French techniques in the early fifties, is a major world-class wine, built to age, suitable for collecting. It was named for the great Rhône wine Hermitage, but has recently become known simply as Grange to avoid conflict.

The Australian market is dominated by four big producers who rely mostly on blending wines from different regions, moving the grapes from vineyards to distant wineries in refrigerated trucks. There is a blossoming subculture of more than eight hundred small producers following the credo of *terroir* and producing vineyard-designated wines. In most areas, the Aussies rely heavily on irrigation, another similarity with California. They also use a good deal of American oak for barrel-aging. Australians place great weight on competitions, hence the frequency of prize listings on the labels.

Among the top growing regions are Barossa Valley, McLaren Vale, Adelaide Hills, Upper Hunter Valley, Lower Hunter Valley, Yarra Valley, Coonawarra, Padthaway, Pemberton, Rutherglen, Heathcote and Margaret River in the southwest.

SOME FAVORITE AUSSIE PRODUCERS: Bass Phillip; Chambers Rosewood (for fortified wines); Clarendon Hills; Green Point (Möet & Chandon's Australian winery for sparkling wines); Richard Hamilton; Hardys; Henschke (a family concern in Eden Valley, above Barossa Valley, producing superior Shiraz): Cape Mentelle; Chapel Hill; Cullen; Hill-Smith; Jasper Hill; Peter Lehmann; Leeuwin Estate; Lindemans; McGuigan Brothers; Mount Mary; Penfolds; Penley Estate; Petaluma (known for an excellent Chardonnay; winemaker Brian Croser is also a partner in Oregon's Argyle winery); Rosemount; Salitage; Seppelt; Taltarni; Virgin Hills; Yeringberg and Yarra Yering. Three of the biggest premium producers, Penfolds, Lindemans and Seppelt, are owned by the industry giant Southcorp.

Like Terry Theise (for Germany), Kermit Lynch or Bobby Kacher (for France), importer Rob McDonald of Old Bridge Cellars in San Francisco has become one of America's foremost proponents of super-premium Aussie wines. He has assembled an excellent group of smaller producers who turn out some stellar, world-class wines. Try any of his wines.

AUSTRIA

Spurred on by the efforts of forward-looking wine buyers and sommeliers, both Austrian and German premium wines have enjoyed a surge in popularity in recent years. Yet there are still a few sources of resistance: First, the names are often multisyllabic and nearly unpronounceable to most English speakers. Second, the wines suffer from a preconceived notion that they are all sweet, cheap and badly made. These are two beer-drinking countries, the reasoning goes, so how could they make great wines? Cognoscenti know it's quite the contrary.

Germanic wine-labeling is actually among the most consistent and informative anywhere. Yes, the names are hard to pronounce, but if you take a little time and focus on the key words, you can conquer them. The wines themselves are some of the best handcrafted premium-quality examples in the world. They are not uniformly sweet, but instead possess great balance and subtlety. They often do have a lot of residual sugar in them, but it's offset by a fresh, crisp, fruity acidity. It's almost become a cliché that these wines, as well as those of Alsace, go well with spicy Asian foods. Their sweetness can match the sweet-and-sour flavors of Chinese dishes; their acidity can cut through some of the heavier sauces; their cool, luscious fruity tastes can counter the heat of spicy peppers. But they also go with many other types of foods. The wines of Germany and Austria cover a broad spectrum, from light with biting acidity to smooth and balanced to heavier, luscious rare dessert wines that rival the great Sauternes, Vouvray Moelleux or Hungarian Tokays.

Austria's most famous grape is Grüner Veltliner, which makes a delightfully crisp, spicy white wine. There is also a great deal of very fine Riesling along with Müller-Thurgau, generally a more neutral, less-exciting variety. The large majority of Austrian vineyards are planted with white varieties, but they also make some reds. Austria has some of the world's toughest quality standards, which were instituted after a wine-doctoring scandal in the mid-1980s.

RECOMMENDED PRODUCERS: Brundlmayer, Josef Jamek, Kracher, Nigl, Pichler, Prager, Tement.

EASTERN EUROPE

The Bordelais are going into Hungary and Bulgaria, where there are ancient vinelands and a fifteen-year tradition of Cabernet Sauvignon. Over the next couple of decades, we will see international enological consultants such as Michel Rolland lending a hand to make the Eastern European premium wine industry into a presence on the international scene. These will be among the best inexpensive wines of the future, wines to explore into the twenty-first century.

Hungarian Tokay Aszu is among the finest sweet wines in the world, made from *Botrytis*-affected grapes and similar to a Sauternes.

FRANCE

The amazing kaleidoscope of French wines is impossible to cover in an entire lifetime, let alone in one chapter of a book. It's an endless quest, a lifelong adventure to taste and learn about the incredible richness of what this country's soil has to offer.

Change comes slower in established regions such as Bordeaux and Burgundy, but there are still courageous small producers leading the way. Likewise, there is the driven, uncompromising Old Guard, operations such as Guigal and Château Margaux, who never seem content to rest on their laurels. They somehow rise to the challenge each year, producing spectacular wines in good vintages and very good wines even in poor vintages. All are to be saluted.

ALSACE

This region bordering Germany and featuring cross-cultural influences not surprisingly harbors winemakers who specialize in white wines with a Germanic precision and versatility. Some of the finest premium producers work with eight or nine different grapes varieties, from Pinot Gris to Riesling, and as many vineyard designations, producing stellar examples of each—delightful, food-friendly wines across the spectrum from crisp and dry to sweet and luscious. Alsace is a gorgeous place that produces equally beautiful wines.

RECOMMENDED PRODUCERS: Domaine Lucien Albrecht, a family estate since the eighteenth century that makes Pinot Blanc, Riesling, Gewürztraminer, Tokay Pinot Gris, Muscat, Pinot Auxerois ("Fatter than Pinot Blanc, more honey and butter, spicy character with natural richness and low acidity") and a sparkling wine called Cremant from a blend of their other grapes as well as four different late-harvest sweet wines; Domaine Marcel Deiss, where *terroiriste* winemaker Jean-Michel Deiss bottles from as many as ten different Riesling vineyards; Domaine Zind-Humbrecht—Olivier Humbrecht is the only Master of Wine in France who's also a winemaker and many people feel he's the world's greatest.
ALSO TRY: Albert Boxler, Ostertag, Charles Schleret, Schlumberger, Trimbach, Domaine Weinbach.

BORDEAUX

The gravelly soil, the proximity to both the Atlantic Ocean and the largest estuary in Europe—the Gironde, which is called "the River" by the Bordelais—the hundreds of years of tradition, the old Cabernet Sauvignon vines, the dignity, determination and pride of its people, the *terroir*—all this adds up to the world's greatest winegrowing region.

Remember, this is just a selection, a *ménu de degustation* (tasting menu) if you will—a few of my favorites. Volumes have been written and will continue to be written about this wine paradise. Has Bordeaux fallen behind in the New Wine Revolution? Are its great producers self-satisfied? Do they believe they've achieved perfection? Arguably, yes, but you can't argue with *terroir* and you can't help but marvel at institutions like Château Margaux, a national treasure, or Château Cheval-Blanc, a personal favorite, or Château Ducru-Beaucaillou, deserving of the utmost respect. These and others like

THE CLASSIFIED GROWTHS OF
BORDEAUX

IN 1855, SIXTY-ONE OF THE GREAT WINEGROWING ESTATES OF BORDEAUX WERE RANKED IN FIVE CLASSIFICATIONS: FIRST THROUGH FIFTH GROWTHS. IT'S A REFLECTION OF THE POWER OF TRADITION AND *TERROIR* THAT THESE CLASSIFICATIONS HAVE REMAINED UNCHANGED FOR NEARLY A CENTURY AND A HALF. THE LONE EXCEPTION CAME IN 1973: BARON PHILLIPE DE ROTHSCHILD FINALLY CONVINCED THE AUTHORITIES TO PROMOTE HIS ESTATE, CHÂTEAU MOUTON-ROTHSCHILD, FROM SECOND TO FIRST GROWTH. BUT THEN, THAT WASN'T THE ONLY THING THE BARON DID TO ASTOUND THE WINE WORLD. . . .

There are five first growths or *premiers crus*, as follows:

ESTATE	APPELLATION
CHÂTEAU LAFITE-ROTHSCHILD	PAUILLAC
CHÂTEAU MARGAUX	MARGAUX
CHÂTEAU LATOUR	PAUILLAC
CHÂTEAU HAUT-BRION	GRAVES
CHÂTEAU MOUTON-ROTHSCHILD	PAUILLAC

There are fourteen second growths (*deuxiemes crus*), among them Châteaus Ducru-Beaucaillou, Cos D'Estournel, Gruaud-Larose, Montrose and Léoville-Las Cases; fourteen third growths, including Châteaus La Lagune, Palmer, Calon-Segur and Kirwan; ten fourth growths, among them Châteaus Talbot and Lafon-Rochet; and eighteen fifth growths, including Pontet-Canet and Grand-Puy-Lacoste.

Any classified growth estate is likely to produce a superb—and very expensive—wine.

them continue to turn out superlative wines and to make subtle improvements on near-perfection, year in and year out. If you're at the top of the mountain, it's tough to keep from sliding down. *Warning:* If you're looking for bargain prices and ready availability, don't shop here!

CHÂTEAU ANGELUS, St.-Emilion: As of 1996, Angelus became only the third Premier Grand Cru Classé of St.-Emilion, joining Ausone and Cheval-Blanc. This winegrowing site is believed to be at least two thousand years old. The estate has been in the family of winemaker Hubert de Bouard de Laforest since the mid-nineteenth century. Hubert studied under the great Emile Peynaud at the University of Bordeaux in the 1970s, began working at Angelus in 1980 and has been fully responsible for the winegrowing since 1986. He believes in minimal interference and defines his approach as "neoclassical."

CHÂTEAU AUSONE, St.-Emilion: Alain Vauthier, the proprietor-winemaker consults with Michel Rolland and epitomizes the hands-on winegrower. Like his friend Jean-Luc Thunevin at Valandraud, he's returning to the old ways to improve his wines. Ausone is a wine of character and subtlety, with hints of caramel in the aroma and a long, satisfying aftertaste. I love Cheval-Blanc and always will, but in my humble opinion Château Ausone is the new standard-bearer in St.-Emilion.

CHÂTEAU LE BON PASTEUR, Pomerol: Michel Rolland is one of the world's great flying enologists. From this, his own estate on the border of St.-Emilion, he is spreading the gospel to the corners of the wine world—California (where his clients include Simi, Merryvale, Newton, St. Exupery and Harlan Estate), Spain, Italy, Hungary, South Africa, South America and even China. Michel is understated and humble, belying his mammoth and well-deserved reputation. There's a twinkle in his eye that tells you he *knows* how to make a great wine.

CHÂTEAU CHEVAL-BLANC, St.-Emilion: If I were forced to pick my favorite wine in the world, this would probably be it. It's a consistently alluring, enchanting wine, the quintessential St.-Emilion, magic in a bottle year after year, a real thoroughbred (pun intended). I love it. There's nothing more seductive. It is without question the Brigitte Bardot of French wines. (Did I forget to mention it's not cheap?)

CHÂTEAU DUCRU-BEAUCAILLOU, St.-Julien: Owner Jean-Eugene Borie, who also owned Grand-Puy-Lacoste, another wine of perfect pedigree, passed away in 1998 and his son took over. Monsieur Borie lived at the château for close to forty years, overseeing each and every vintage, and was known throughout the wine world for his warmth, dignity, lack of pretension and for his devotion to this special property. Ducru is the name of the family that owned the property when it was named a second growth in the 1855 classification and built the present château. *Beaucaillou* means "beautiful little stones." They're peppered liberally throughout the vineyard and if you examine them closely, they are indeed beautiful and diverse in shape, size, color and lustre. They define this *terroir* and therefore the wine. Ducru-Beaucaillou, one of the "super seconds" along with Léoville-Las Cases, Pichon Lalande and Cos d'Estournel, is a classic Bordeaux blend of 65 percent Cabernet Sauvignon, 25 percent Merlot, 5 percent Petit Verdot and 5 percent Cabernet Franc, renowned for its consistency and long aging potential.

CHÂTEAU LA CONSEILLANTE, Pomerol: This neighbor of Petrus and Cheval-Blanc is owned by Bernard Nicholas, a wonderfully generous man. Here they eschew the formality of the Medoc; these are real people and they're making a great wine with the Merlot–Cabernet Franc blend. I recall a luncheon not so long ago at the Nicholas home by the Dordogne River in Fronsac. It was a sunny June afternoon and they welcomed us with open arms, fitting at least twenty-five people into the dining room for a delicious meal and some great vintages. Friendship, hospitality, fine wine—an unbeatable combination.

THERE'S NO PLACE LIKE...ST.-EMILION

THE GENTLY UNDULATING HILLS AROUND THE PICTURE-PERFECT MEDIEVAL TOWN OF ST.-EMILION, TO THE EAST OF THE CITY OF BORDEAUX, ARE A MAGICAL PLACE FOR MAKING WINE. EVERY TIME I GO THERE TO VISIT THE CHÂTEAUS, TO TASTE THE WINES, I'M MORE CONVINCED THAN EVER THAT ST.-EMILION IS *THE* PLACE. SMALL "BOUTIQUE WINERIES," OFTEN FAMILY OPERATIONS LIKE TROPLONG-MONDOT, RUN BY CHRISTINE VALETTE, OR, NEXT DOOR, LA MONDOTTE, RUN BY COUNT STEPHAN VON NEIPPERG OF CHÂTEAU CANON-LA-GAFFELIÈRE, ARE RAISING THE STANDARDS. THE MERLOT–CABERNET FRANC BLEND OF ST.-EMILION PRODUCES, FOR MY MONEY, AN UNMATCHED BALANCE AND COMPLEXITY, A SWEETNESS, FEMININITY AND CHARM WITHOUT SACRIFICING DEPTH AND POWER, THAT IS UNBEATABLE. HUBERT DE BOUARD DE LA FOREST AT CHÂTEAU ANGELUS IS MAKING SOME OF THE BEST WINE IN ST.-EMILION. WE CAN'T LEAVE THE AREA WITHOUT MENTIONING CHÂTEAU VALANDRAUD AND CHÂTEAU LE PIN, TWO SUPERLATIVE EXPRESSIONS OF *TERROIR*. AND THEN THERE'S CHÂTEAU AUSONE, WHICH COULD BE THE MOST IMPORTANT WINE IN THE REGION AND MAYBE THE BEST IN THE WORLD.

CHÂTEAU LAFLEUR, Pomerol: A neighbor of Petrus, with only twelve acres, that produces one of the most sought-after and expensive wines in the world, a cult wine among collectors.

CHÂTEAU LAFON-ROCHET, St.-Estèphe: One of two major Bordeaux properties owed by the Tesseron family. An excellent classified Bordeaux (see Pontet-Canet, below).

CHÂTEAU LATOUR, Pauillac: Latour is one of the original first growths, a definitive Medoc estate, situated within sight of the Gironde, on land whose soil is half made up of large pebbles. The blend is approximately 75 percent Cabernet Sauvignon, 20 percent Merlot and the rest divided between Cabernet Franc and Petit Verdot. The second wine is Les Forts de Latour; the table wine is called Pauillac. While Latour is, by world standards, a small to medium-sized operation, it has seventy full-time employees and brings in another hundred local workers at harvest time; in other words, those precious grapes are getting a lot of attention. As they should.

CHÂTEAU LA MONDOTTE, St.-Emilion: This small vineyard next door to Troplong-Mondot is owned and operated by Count Stephan von Neipperg, a brilliant and energetic young winemaker from Franconia in southern Germany, whose family has been in the business for 750 years. Stephan believes strongly in traditional methods of winegrowing and concentrates on developing ripe tannins in the grape skins. The family's base in St.-Emilion is Château Canon-la-Gaffelière, whose wines are also highly recommended.

CHÂTEAU LÉOVILLE-LAS CASES, St.-Julien: The proprietor of this second growth, Michel Delon, is a Bolshevik by Bordeaux standards. In a recent vintage, he made a radical selection, using only 25 percent of his crop, and then charged what some thought were exorbitant prices for his wine. He's been called a hero and a lion as well as many unprintable names.

CHÂTEAU LE PIN, Pomerol: The quintessential boutique wine (only about five hundred cases are made), it is fabulously expensive with a taste to match.

CHÂTEAU MARGAUX, Margaux: Corinne Mentzelopoulos, who's been in charge since the death of her father, Andre, has the energy, brains and commitment to live up to her role as curator of this French national treasure, the king of the Bordeaux first growths. It's one of those jobs where millions of people are waiting for you to stumble, where even if you perform exceedingly well you've only lived up to expectations. Had she inherited the Boston Celtics, you can be sure they'd be hoisting a few more banners by now. Corinne has brought modern technological improvements in viticulture, vinification and marketing to Margaux. Margaux's second wine is Le Pavillon Rouge de Margaux.

CHÂTEAU PETRUS, Pomerol: From the Mouiex family, the millionaire's wine, the pinnacle of Pomerol. It is also known as the Cyrano of wines—more than a nose, it is the distinguished example of the Merlot blend of Pomerol, which was once considered no more than "that place across the river" from the Medoc.

CHÂTEAU PICHON-LALANDE, Pauillac: The name has been shortened from the original: Château Pichon-Longueville, Comtesse de Lalande. This "super second," a neighbor of Château Latour, produces consistently one of the best wines in the region under the capable and dynamic ownership of Madame Mae-Elaine de Lencquesaing.

CHÂTEAU PONTET-CANET, Pauillac: Alfred and Michel Tesseron are keeping a close eye on this superior estate, which is located right next door to Château Mouton-Rothschild. The family also owns Château Lafon-Rochet in St.-Estèphe as well as extensive interests in the Cognac region. Both Pontet-Canet and Lafon-Rochet were part of the 1855 classification, the former as a fifth growth, the latter as a fourth. Since father Guy took over Pontet-Canet in 1978, the Tesserons have done a lot of work to bring the vineyards back up to standard. Every year they launch a major capital investment project. In 1996, for example, they completely reorganized the pressing area. As a result, Pontet-Canet is now consistently among the top fifteen wines of the Medoc.

CHÂTEAU ST.-GEORGES, St.-Georges: The château was originally a medieval stronghold, as evidenced by its dominant position on a hill within sight of the town of St.-Emilion. Most of the current structures date from the reign of Loius XVI. The château also dominates the smallest Bordeaux appellation, St.-Georges, with fifty out of a total of one hundred hectares. Its current owners, Petrus Desbois along with his brother Georges, work closely with Michel Rolland in a continuing quest to improve their already-superior wines. I'm proud to say that Château St.-Georges is our house wine at Overstreet's Wine Bar in Beverly Hills. The blend is 60 percent Merlot, 20 percent Cabernet Sauvignon and 20 percent Cabernet Franc.

CHÂTEAU TROPLONG-MONDOT, St.-Emilion: Christine Valette is the youthful proprietor of this splendid super-premium estate on a hill just a short distance from the town of St.-Emilion. A relatively large holding for these parts—thirty hectares—it has been in the family since the early 1900s. Christine took over at the beginning of the eighties and began to institute the real changes about five years later.

CHÂTEAU VALANDRAUD, St.-Emilion: Another of the spectacular boutique wines of Bordeaux—heavenly taste and an equally lofty sticker price. Proprietor-winemaker Jean-Luc Thunevin is a star, a leader by example. As his friend and neighbor Stephan von Neipperg of La Mondotte says, "Perhaps he doesn't have the best site, but he makes the best wine and his neighbors can learn a lot from him."

CHÂTEAU VIEUX MAILLET, Pomerol: I very much admire the spunk and chutzpah of proprietor-winemaker Isabelle Motte. It isn't easy to launch oneself as a high-quality producer in an established appellation, but Isabelle has given herself as good a chance as anybody. Her wine is a velvety blend of 80 percent Merlot and 20 percent Cabernet Franc.

CHÂTEAU D'YQUEM, Sauternes: This beautiful château, built around the remains of a medieval castle, is the source of the world's greatest and most famous dessert wine. Count Alexandre de Lur-Saluces has shepherded this old family estate into the modern era—though he angered many family members when he sold the controlling interest to the Louis Vuitton company. While one would imagine Yquem to be a brand-name bonanza—at least from its starting prices of around $150 to $300 a bottle—production at this rarefied level of Sauternes is extremely costly, making it difficult to maintain as a viable business. Alexandre has done that and he deserves credit. Has the struggle been worthwhile? Try a glass of the '88 Yquem and decide for yourself.

MORE RECOMMENDED BORDEAUX CHATEAUS: Mouton-Rothschild, Pauillac (Baroness Philippine, daughter of the great Baron Philippe, has inherited much of her father's flair and kept the legacy alive); Lafite-Rothschild, Pauillac (Baron Eric); Le Tetre-Roteboeuf, St.-Emilion; Château Palmer, Cantenac; Haut-Brion, Pessac-Leognan/Graves (Jean Delmas has been capably in charge since 1961, a vintage of the century); Cos-d'Estournel, St.-Estèphe; Figeac, St.-Emilion; La Fleur-Petrus, Pomerol; Lynch-Bages, Pauillac; Pichon-Longueville, Pauillac (also run by Jean-Michel Cazes of Lynch-Bages); Rieussec, Sauternes (neighbor to D'Yquem; owned by Lafite-Rothschild); Trotanoy, Pomerol.

BURGUNDY

This superb growing region, where Pinot Noir and Chardonnay reign, produces arguably the world's greatest wines. It can be confusing, to say the least. There are hundreds of appellations and thousands of producers. Geographically, it parallels the Saone River, which eventually empties into the Rhône, stretching from the city of Dijon in the north toward the city of Lyons in the south. The majority of the *grand cru* vineyards are in the Côte d'Or, just south of Dijon, which is in turn divided into the Côte de Nuits in the north, around the village of Nuits, and the Côte de Beaune in the south, around the town of Beaune, which is the unofficial capital of Burgundy's wine country.

The best red wines are generally produced in the northern Côte de Nuits section of the Côte d'Or (literal translation: "golden hillside") whereas the whites generally come from the southern Côte de Beaune section. South of the Côte d'Or is a less-celebrated Burgundian region known as the Côte Chalonnaise, which produces some superb, less expensive wines. Continuing south, along the banks of the Saone, is the Maconnais, with its famous Pouilly-Fuissé white-wine appellation, followed by Beaujolais, which produces the famous *nouvelle* wine of the same name. Chablis is a separate Burgundy appellation northwest of Beaune, where Chardonnay is also king.

There are so many villages, vineyards and producers with so many difficult-to-pronounce names that they demand a detailed atlas to do them all justice. To confuse matters further, AC (appellation) status is awarded not just to villages but also to top vineyards—*premier crus* and *grand crus*. Vineyards are named after villages, but villages also take on the names of their famous vineyards. Vineyards can also

SUBREGIONS OF BURGUNDY

CHABLIS
CÔTE D'OR (DIVIDED IN TWO: CÔTE DE NUITS AND CÔTE DE BEAUNE)
CÔTE CHALONNAISE
MACONNAIS
BEAUJOLAIS

cover one or more villages. So, for example, the villages of Chassagne and Puligny become Chassagne-Montrachet and Puligny-Montrachet since they share parts of the world-famous Montrachet vineyard. Further compounding the overlapping of names is the fact that many different producers can own or lease small portions of top vineyards. Families intermarry, they feud, the sons and daughters inherit different plots of land...and so forth. In short, it's all a natural consequence of a long, rich history of winemaking on relatively small plots of some of the best winegrowing land on earth.

The independent growers and producers of Burgundy represent many of the great old traditions. Whenever appropriate, the best of them have also applied modern science and technology to make great wines even greater. Here are the gold-plated names of Burgundy. They are not everyday wines; many of them are quite expensive. If you have the resources and the desire, they're all worth trying—if for nothing more than to experience an established standard.

VILLAGES IN THE CÔTE DE NUITS: Chambolle-Musigny, Gevrey-Chambertin, Morey-St.-Denis, Nuits-St.-Georges, Vougeot, Vosne-Romanée.
TOP RED BURGUNDY VINEYARDS: Bonnes-Mares, Clos des Lambrays, Clos de la Roche, Clos de Vougeot, Corton (this is the only red *grand cru* in the Côte de Beaune, an exception to the rule), Echézeaux, Grands-Echézeaux, La Tache, Musigny, Richebourg, Romanée-Conti.
VILLAGES IN THE CÔTE DE BEAUNE: Aloxe-Corton, Chassagne-Montrachet, Meursault, Pommard, Puligny-Montrachet, Savigny-les-Beaune, Volnay.
TOP WHITE BURGUNDY VINEYARDS: Bâtard-Montrachet, Chassagne-Montrachet, Chevalier-Montrachet, Corton-Charlemagne, Montrachet.

As in other important regions of France, the wines of Burgundy are ranked in order of specificity: regional ACs are on the lowest rung, followed by the village wines (the AC uses the village's name), then the *premier crus,* based on a nineteenth-century classification (as in Bordeaux) and finally the tip-of-the-iceberg, exalted *grand crus.*

SOME TOP BURGUNDY PRODUCERS: Robert Arnoux, Ghislaine Barthod, Vincent Bitouzet, Bouchard Père et Fils, Jean Chauvenet, J.-F. Coche-Dury, Edmond and Pierre Cornu, Joseph Drouhin, Domaine Dujac, Regis Forey, Domaine Jean Grivot, Louis Jadot, Louis Latour, Domaine des Comtes Lafon, Domaine Leflaive, Domaine Leroy (Lalou Leroy-Bize is also part owner of DRC), Hubert Lignier, Denis Mortet, Michel Niellon, Jacques Prieur, Domaine Ramonet, Remy Rollin, Domaine de la Romanée-Conti (DRC), Emmanuel Rouget (Henri Jayer retired and left Emmanuel, his nephew, in charge), Domaine Roumier, Domaine Etienne Sauzet, Verget.

DOMAINE JEAN-MARC JOBLOT, Givry, Côte Chalonnaise: Joblot, whose family has been in the wine business for many generations, has a Ph.D. in enology from the University of Dijon. At $25 to $30 a bottle, Joblot's wines rival many of the more expensive and hard-to-get Burgundies.

DOMAINE CLAUDE ET MAURICE DUGAT, Gevrey-Chambertin: Like many Burgundian growers, they used to sell the vast majority of their crop to *negociants*. Now they are doing their own estate bottling and the wines are superior. Claude is the fifth generation of his family in this famous appellation.

DOMAINE CHRISTIAN SERAFIN, Gevrey-Chambertin: They practice organic farming on old vines with low yields, no filtration. Another superb winegrower.

DOMAINE ROBERT JAYER-GILLES, Nuits-St.-Georges: Winemaker Robert Jayer is of the famous Jayer clan of Vosne-Romanée (Henri, Georges and Lucien); in fact, he is Henri's first cousin. Whereas someone like Jean-Marc Joblot went to school and learned how to make great wine by the age of thirty, Robert was a farmer who learned through years of trial and error—by about the age of fifty. They came from different generations and took different routes to the top. Robert's rich, perfumed wines are made with 100 percent new oak, no fining, little filtering.

DOMAINE JEAN-JACQUES CONFURON, Côtes de Nuits Villages: Jean-Jacques Confuron passed away, and his daughter and son-in-law, Sophie and Alain Meuniere, are responsible for the renaissance of this excellent small estate. They employ modern winegrowing techniques while respecting age-old traditions to make the most of their lovely fruit.

DOMAINE CHOPIN-GROFFIER, Clos Vougeot: Robert Parker, Jr., called Daniel Chopin "the true heir apparent to the great Henri Jayer." He works a small plot, concentrates on old vines with low yield and produces a modern classic Burgundian Pinot Noir.

CHAMPAGNE

My personal passion is for the bubbly. Champagne is a special gift, a token of passion, affection or esteem. It marks any occasion with an exclamation point. Pop the cork and let the fireworks begin! Champagne sparkles in the bottle, in your glass, your mouth and your throat. There's nothing like it. It's my desert island drink. Give me a case of the stuff in a cooler and I could wait a very long time for my rescue ship.

Whether it's as a thirst-quenching aperitif, refreshing accompaniment to a salty seafood appetizer or delicious *digestif* with dessert, a glass of fine Champagne delivers taste and texture that's hard to match. Champagne means lightheartedness and luxury, fantasy and romance. The wine itself is made by an age-old process that smacks of alchemy. The word alone conjures the ultimate in high style—as in "She has Champagne taste and a beer budget." No wonder it's the beverage of choice in all the world's jet-set spots, including Beverly Hills.

Champagne is the northernmost growing region of France, surrounding the towns of Rheims and Epernay, not far east of Paris. Thousands of small farmers grow the grapes that make up the *cuvée*. They supply the great houses that vinify the wines and embark on the lengthy, detailed process of fermenting, blending and cellaring the neutral-base wines until they've mellowed into that Something Special. Some smaller growers make their own single-vineyard Champagnes. Ripening grapes in this northern latitude is problematic, which is why vintage Champagne is the less common, more expensive option.

MY FAVORITE CHAMPAGNES: Krug, Bollinger, Louis Roederer (Cristal), Pol Roger, Charles Heidsieck, Perrier-Jouet, Dom Perignon (Möet & Chandon), Ruinart, Taittinger, Veuve Clicquot, Deutz, G.H. Mumm, Guy Larmandier, Laurent-Perrier.

LOIRE VALLEY

When I think of the wines of the Loire, I always think of Sancerre. It's a delightfully crisp white wine made from Sauvignon Blanc. Like its Sauvignon Blanc–based neighbor, Pouilly-Fume (not to be confused with Pouilly-Fuissé in the Macon area of Burgundy), Sancerre has a drier, more restrained character than Chardonnay-based wines, a pleasant acidity and herbal taste that will make you want to smack your lips. It's hard to beat a glass of Sancerre to accompany a light lunch or with a seafood appetizer. Next time you go to a business lunch and can't be bothered to consult the sommelier or the wine list, try a new line: "I think I'll have a glass of Sancerre" instead of the old standard: "I think I'll have a glass of Chardonnay."

Savennières is another top Loire appellation, west of Sancerre, toward the Atlantic and close to the town of Anger, where they make excellent dry white Chenin Blanc wines. In Vouvray, Chenin Blanc is made in different grades of sweetness from the dry (*sec*) and medium-dry (*demi sec*), all the way to the

SANCERRE

TO ME, THERE ARE TWO GREAT AMERICANS: THOMAS JEFFERSON AND COLE PORTER—AND BOTH WERE WINE CONNOISSEURS. JEFFERSON, BY THE WAY, WAS FAMOUSLY FRANCOPHILE, SPOKE THE LANGUAGE FLUENTLY, COLLECTED WINES WHEN HE LIVED THERE AND ALSO GREW VINES AT HIS VIRGINIA ESTATE, MONTICELLO. PORTER, THE GREAT TWENTIETH-CENTURY SONGWRITER WHO WROTE HE GOT "NO KICK FROM CHAMPAGNE," ALWAYS DEMANDED THAT AN ARRANGEMENT OF FRESH-CUT FLOWERS AND A CHILLED BOTTLE OF SANCERRE AWAIT HIM WHEN HE CHECKED INTO HIS HOTEL ROOM. HE GOT THAT RIGHT.

sweet long-lasting *Moelleux* or *Liquoreux,* depending on the conditions of the vintage. Vouvray Moelleux is one of the most intriguing sweet wines of the world and has very long aging potential.

Around the town of Saumur are a number of appellations—Saumur-Champigny, Chinon, Bourgeuil and St.-Nicolas de Bourgueil—where they make some soft, delicious, accessible red varietals from the Cabernet Franc grape, normally used only for blending in other regions.

RECOMMENDED PRODUCERS: Didier Dagueneau in Pouilly-Fume is doing everything right, down to biodynamic growing practices; in Sancerre, Jean Reverdy at Domaine de Villots, also Lucien Crochet and Paul Cotat; in Savennières Pierre-Yves Tijou, Domaine de la Soucherie; for Vouvray Moelleux, Philippe Foreau.

RHÔNE VALLEY

The Rhône Valley winegrowing region stretches from the outskirts of Lyon south nearly to the Mediterranean, where it gives way to the Languedoc in the west and Provence in the east. Even if they're not to one's taste, one has to admit that Rhône wines are among the world's best. They have variety, spice and bite; they are built on a rustic foundation and layered with a sophisticated worldly veneer.

Among the Rhône's world-famous appellations are Côte-Rôtie (Syrah), Condrieu (for superb expressions of the Viognier grape), Hermitage (white), Crozes-Hermitage, Tain l'Hermitage, St.-Joseph, Cornas, Côtes-du-Rhône-Villages, Châteauneuf-du-Pape (Grenache with Syrah, and Mourvèdre), Gigondas, Vacqueyres, Tavel (rose) and Muscat de Beaumes-de-Venise (a sweet/dessert made by adding alcohol during fermentation). The so-called Rhône varietals, Syrah—Mourvèdre and Grenache for reds, and Rousanne, Marsanne and Viognier for whites—are becoming increasingly popular with worldwide producers, particularly in California.

DOMAINE SANTA DUC, GIGONDAS, Southern Rhône: Young winemaker Yves Gras, who's taken over the property from his father, Edmund, is quickly attaining legendary status in the appellation of Gigondas, right next to Châteauneuf-du-Pape. The wine is made up of roughly 60 percent old-vine Grenache (for the fruit), 40 percent Syrah (for backbone and longevity) and some Mourvèdre. It features deep, dark colors and rich, concentrated flavors—an authentic Rhône product.
DOMAINE BELLE, Larnage: This family operation—Albert Belle and his son Philippe—is located in the hamlet of Larnage, behind the hill of Hermitage, an ideal microclimate for the Syrah grape within the Crozes-Hermitage appellation. They began bottling their own wines in 1989, previously having sold their fruit to the nearby Tain l'Hermitage cooperative.
E. GUIGAL, CHÂTEAU D'AMPUIS, Vienne: Marcel Guigal and his son Philippe carry on the tradition of their father/grandfather Etienne with their world-renowned wines, grown on the banks of the Rhône south of Lyon. Their single-vineyard Côte-Rôties, La Landonne, La Mouline and La Turque, are pinnacle wines, superlative expressions of the Syrah grape and of the steep, hilly *terroir* where vines have grown for over 2,300 years. (Consider yourself lucky if you can get your hands on a bottle of any one of the three.) Guigal also produces Hermitage white and red, Châteauneuf-du-Pape, Gigondas, Tavel and Côtes-du-Rhône, red, rose and white. His Condrieu white wine from Viognier grapes is also top drawer. Overall, an impressive lineup.

DOMAINE JOSEPH JAMET, Côte-Brune: In the northern part of the Côte-Rôtie, not far from Lyons, Jamet's sons Jean-Luc and Jean-Paul produce delicious spicy, dark, fruity, full-bodied, rich wines. About 30 percent of the wine comes from the legendary La Landonne vineyard site, popularized by Guigal.

DOMAINE DE LA MORDORÉE, Côtes-du-Rhône: The name means "home of the woodcock" (*mordorée*), which is pictured on the label. This wine is made in a fresh, fruit-driven style while maintaining the typical spicy, black pepper regional character. A cousin to the broader, richer, higher alcohol Châteauneuf-du-Pape wines, it's priced in the $8 to $10 range as compared to Châteauneuf-du-Pape, which runs from $25 to $35.

MORE FAVORITES: Andre Brunel (Les Cailloux, Châteauneuf-du-Pape), M. Chapoutier, Jean-Louis Chave (Hermitage), Michel Ferraton (Hermitage and Crozes-Hermitage), Paul Jaboulet (Hermitage), Domaine du Vieux Telegraphe (Châteauneuf-du-Pape).

OTHER INTERESTING FRENCH WINES

LANGUEDOC-ROUSSILLON

These are actually two regions often listed as one, both in the extreme south of France, the latter bordering on Catalonia in northeastern Spain, and the former west of the city of Montpellier. Carignan is the ancient indigenous vine; more recently the Rhône varieties Grenache, Syrah and Mourvèdre have thrived. The Languedoc historically produced a large amount of low-quality table wine, but there is potential to produce dark, rich, concentrated red wines in appellations such as Corbieres, Fitou, Menervois and Costieres de Nîmes. Banyuls, like Muscat de Beaumes-de-Venise is a *vin doux naturel* produced in the southernmost tip of France, often referred to as France's answer to Port.

DOMAINE DE COUSSERGUES in the Côteaux du Languedoc AC, makes a terrific Sauvignon Blanc with aromas of pineapple and melon, and a zesty, citrus flavor in the finish that is priced around $8 to $10 a bottle. **MAS JULLIEN,** also in the Côteaux du Languedoc, is where Olivier Jullien makes a very fine red.

PROVENCE

Provence—a magical land that draws hoards of northern tourists desperate to soak up the summer sun. Bandol, near the coast and the city of Toulon, is generally acknowledged to be the best appellation in the region. **DOMAINE TEMPIER** and **CHÂTEAU PRADEAUX** are among the best premium producers. The wines are made from the Mourvèdre grape, which is typical of this area and is also planted all over southeastern Spain.

DOMAINE RICHEAUME: A sixty-acre property in a hot, dry microclimate, in the heart of the Côte de Provence in the foothills of St.-Victoire, a familiar landmark in Paul Cezanne's paintings. Henning Hoesch, the proprietor since 1972, practices organic farming. His wines include the Cuvée Tradition (half Grenache and half Syrah, full-bodied and spice-scented) as well as Cuvelle Columelle, a reserve wine made in selected vintages with a typical blend of 50 percent Syrah, 25 percent Merlot and 25 percent Cabernet Sauvignon.

SOUTHWEST

CHAPELLE LAURETTE: Tucked away in the appellation of Madiran on the edge of Gascoigne, which is where they make Armagnac, toils an award-winning winemaker named Patrick Ducournau. His wine, which is made from the local variety Tannat with about 10 percent Merlot for smoothness, is big and robust and has been compared to two Bordeaux heavyweights, Château Latour and Château Montrose.

GERMANY

The main winegrowing regions are along the Rhine, Mosel, Necker and Main Rivers in southwestern Germany, an area that borders on Switzerland, France (Alsace), and Luxembourg. The top region is the Mosel-Saar-Ruwer, named for its three rivers, the largest being the Mosel. Premium winegrowing artisans in these areas work the steep south- and southwest-facing hillside vineyards tirelessly, making the best of a relatively cool climate. They do have the advantages of good soil drainage and the moderating climatic effect of the river. Other top regions include the Rheingau, the Rheinhessen and Pfalz. Riesling is by far the dominant grape variety in Germany. There is some Müller-Thurgau, another white variety, and a few red varieties in the southern Baden region, around the famous spa town Baden-Baden, including Spätburgunder, which is German for Pinot Noir.

Of the fine white wines of the world, the Germans are always among the best. They possess legendary balance, complexity, aroma and aging potential. They have plenty of acid and relatively low alcohol. The trick in Germany is to ripen the grapes. Many of the finest German wines are late-harvested, left with residual sugar after fermentation.

RECOMMENDED PRODUCERS: Burklin-Wolf, Maximin Grunhauser, Gunderloch, Fritz Haag, Karthauserhof, von Kesselstat, Egon Muller, J.J. Prum, Robert Weil, Zelbach.

ITALY

Italy excites me because it's both a hotbed of innovation and a bastion of tradition. The Italians are masters of technology and technique. They bring a Renaissance touch to their winemaking, a passion and commitment to their love of wine. It's an ancient part of their culture and a lightning rod for their tremendous energies.

Italy's wine revolution caught fire in the late seventies and early eighties, in Piedmont and Tuscany. The new revolution is spreading all over the country, thanks to an increasing number of winemakers of character and integrity.

Some years ago, when I thought of launching a serious wine tour of Italy, I was almost afraid to betray my first love—French wines. How would I find space in my heart for the Italians? Once I arrived there, though, I knew space would have to be made. Everywhere I looked, I found enchanting landscapes, intriguing people and fascinating wines. Marc de Grazia, the distinguished exporter, is fond of saying that it's hard to find something new in a country as old as this, but the producers are doing just that. Established areas such as Barolo and Barbaresco and Chianti are soaring to new heights. New areas like the South and Sardinia, where the wines have always been rustic, are vying for supremacy.

There are two noteworthy trends in Italian premium wines: the "international style" of blended table wines, exemplified by the Supertuscans, and the new expressions of ancient varieties. Among Italy's more than two thousand indigenous varieties of vines, the most famous are Nebbiolo, which makes Barolos and Barbarescos, and Sangiovese, which makes Chiantis. In the new millennium, Nebbiolo's neighbor, Barbera, will be widely hailed as a world-class grape as will Sangiovese's cousin, Morellino di Scansano. The list of "emerging" varieties goes on and on: there's Teroldego from around Trent in the Alpine foothills; Sagrantino from Montefalco in Umbria; Grechetto from the Viterbo area in Lazio; Negroamaro, which makes the Salice Salentino, in Puglia; Aglianico, which makes Taurasi in the mountains of Campania east of Naples.

The Italian wine scene is brimming with richness and variety. Over the coming years, I believe it will come to be seen as a model for the rest of the wine world.

ABRUZZI

EDOARDO VALENTINI, Loreto Aprutino (Pescara): Valentini is one of Piero Selvaggio's favorite winemakers and Piero is one of our great Italian wine experts. A traditionalist, Valentini works with two indigenous grapes, Trebbiano D'Abruzzo, the white, and Montepulciano D'Abruzzo, the red, neither to be confused with the Tuscan grapes of the same names. In some years, Valentini's Trebbiano is said to rival a fine white Burgundy. Take note: Montepulciano d'Abruzzo wines are among the best in Italy—balanced, rich, with good aging potential—and they come at bargain prices, many under $10 a bottle.

DOC AND DOCG

A NOTE ON DOC'S (*DENOMINAZIONE DI ORIGINE CONTROLLATA*) AND DOCG'S (*GARANTITA*): THE ORIGINAL DOC LAWS BEGAN TO TAKE EFFECT IN 1966. THEY DEFINE ZONES OF PRODUCTION, MINIMUM AND MAXIMUM GRAPE VARIETY CONTENT AS WELL AS SOME PARAMETERS OF VINIFICATION; THEY ORIGINATE WITH PRODUCERS' ORGANIZATIONS BUT THEY MUST BE APPROVED BY THE MINISTRY OF AGRICULTURE TO GO INTO EFFECT. THERE ARE HUNDREDS OF DOCS IN ITALY AND FAR FEWER, BUT STILL AN INCREASING NUMBER, OF DOCGS. THE TWO GRADES ARE ANALOGOUS TO BURGUNDY'S *PREMIER CRU* AND *GRAND CRU* DESIGNATIONS—GUARANTEES OF SUPERIOR QUALITY.

APULIA

The heel of Italy's boot, which is the Salento Peninsula of Apulia, is another area to watch for inexpensive, high-quality wines over the coming decades. Distinguished enologist Severino Garofano is consulting with a number of wineries all over the south, including two top ones in this area. There is **D'ANGELO,** from Rionero in Vulture, near Potenza in the arch of the boot, which produces a wine called Aglianico del Vulture from the Aglianico grape. And there's **COSIMO TAURINO,** which makes Salice Salentino, a DOC wine, as well as Patriglione and Notarpanaro, both table wines, from the Negroamaro and Malvasia Nera grapes. Garofano and his producers are bringing to market sophisticated worldly wines made from grapes that were traditionally used as components in blends for their punch and power. Fran Kysela recommends **MOCAVERO'S** Puteus, Salice Salentino.

CAMPANIA

Olivier Humbrecht, "The Alsation Sensation," is consulting for a winery called **FEUDI DI SAN GREGORIO,** in the area known as Irpinia, surrounding the town of Avellino east of Naples, in a cool, mountainous microclimate. They're making noteworthy wines from local grapes: Taurasi reds from Aglianico and Greco del Tufo (fruity and crisp) and Fiano (dry) whites.

By far the dominant producer in the area is the **MASTROBERARDINO** family in Atripaldi, also in Irpinia. They rebuilt after a devastating earthquake in 1980 and are producing about half the good wines in the area. They also produce premium wines in the Fiano di Avellino, Greco del Tufo and Taurasi categories. Taurasi is often referred to as "the Barolo of the South" and is considered one of the best wines in Italy with great aging potential. All of these superb wines are priced about $12 to $15 per bottle.

FRIULI

Rumblings began to be heard in the early eighties and continued throughout the decade. Friuli put Italy on the world map for white wines. Soon other regions such as Alto Adige, Orvieto and Lazio quickly came into the picture to compete against this leading area.

In Friuli, you don't really feel as though you're in Italy anymore; it looks more like Austria. Across the rolling hills you can see the Slovenian Alps looming big and dark. Some of the vineyards literally straddle the border. It's a quiet, peaceful area where the winemakers work hard, with Italian industriousness and Germanic precision, to make some stunning wines despite a difficult, humid climate. The Collio, Isonzo and Colli Orientali DOCs are the hot spots.

VINNAIOLI JERMANN, Villanova di Farra (Gorízia): Silvio Jermann reigns over this family winery, established in 1881 by immigrants from the Austro-Hungarian empire. There are a lot of good winemakers; Silvio is a master. Known for his artistry and imagination, he has brought out the best in a variety of white-wine grapes, including Chardonnay, Pinot Blanc, Sauvignon Blanc, Gewürztraminer, Riesling, Ribolla Gialla, Müller-Thurgau and Malvasia. His flagship wines are Vintage Tunina, which blends Chardonnay, Sauvignon Blanc and other varieties (Malvasia, Ribolla, Tocai, Pinot Bianco, Picolit), and Dreams, named in honor of the Irish rock group U2. "Vintage Tunina is the best white wine from Italy that I've ever had," says Roger Dagorn of Chanterelle, in New York. He is not alone in holding this opinion.

MARIO SCHIOPETTO, Capriva del Friuli (Gorízia): Schiopetto, like Aldo Conterno, is a veteran producer who has been at the head of the pack for thirty years. He established his winery in the Collio zone in the mid-sixties, and it's very much a family business. Both his wife, Gloria, and his children are involved. Daughter Maria Angela handles the sales and marketing, while sons Carlo and Giorgio are responsible for the winegrowing. They cultivate Tocai, Pinot Bianco, Pinot Grigio, Sauvignon Blanc, Malvasia, Müller-Thurgau, Ribolla Gialla and Riesling for varietals and also make a blend of Tocai, Pinot, Sauvignon and Malvasia called Blanc des Rosis.

MORE RECOMMENDED FRIULI PRODUCERS: Josko Gravner for his Sauvignon del Friuli, Chardonnay and Ribolla Gialla; Edi Kante for Chardonnays and Sauvignon Blancs; Ronco del Gelso for Tocai, Pinot Grigio, Sauvignon Blanc and Chardonnay as well as Merlot; Villa Russiz for Tocai Friuliano, Sauvignon, Pinot Bianco and Merlot. (Note: The Friulian Tocai grape produces a delightfully refreshing light and smooth wine and is no relation to that of the famous Hungarian sweet wine, Tokay.)

LAZIO

CANTINA FALESCO, Montefiascone (Viterbo): The Cotarella name carries a great deal of clout in Italian wine. Renzo is head winemaker for all of Antinori's operations (see Tuscany, below) and brother Riccardo is one of the top consultants in the country, the man largely responsible for putting Umbria and Lazio on the world map of premium wines. The brothers represent the sixth generation of their family involved in winegrowing. This is their home winery, built in 1979 and located just outside of Montefiascone in the Est! Est!! Est!!! appellation, which for years relied on its catchy name as a marketing gimmick to sell wines that were not representative of the area's true potential. Falesco's top wines are: Poggio dei Gelsi, representing the rejuvenation of Est! Est!! Est!!! wines, made from the local varieties Trebbiano, Roscetto and Malvasia and first released in the 1990 vintage; Grechetto D'Umbria, another indigenous grape worthy of rediscovery that, like Chardonnay, can support malolactic fermentation in French oak and produces a more full-bodied wine; Montiano, Falesco's flagship red (80 percent Merlot, 20 percent Cabernet); and Vitiano, a delicious and versatile table wine from equal parts Merlot, Cabernet Sauvignon and Sangiovese that sells for $8 to $10 a bottle.

Riccardo consults for nearly thirty other wineries and co-ops in the Umbria and Lazio area, including small producers like Montevetrano, Capri; Colle Picchione (Paula di Mauro, outside of Rome); La Carraia, near Orvieto, which makes a fine eight-twenty Merlot-Cabernet blend called Fobiano; La Palazzola, near Terni in Umbria, which makes a Cab-Merlot blend called Rubino; the large Colli Amerini co-op, with four hundred producers; and Le Pupille in the Maremma, which makes fine wines from the Morellino grape. All recommended, on the strength of Riccardo's influence.

LOMBARDY

This region encompasses the city of Milan and Lake Como and extends east as far as Lake Garda, where it borders on the Veneto near Verona.

Maurizio Zanella is the acknowledged master of the Franciacorta DOC, which is known as Italy's hotbed of sparkling wines made in the *methode champenoise*. His estate, **CA' DEL BOSCO**, whose name translates as "house in the woods," features Champagne-style cellars. Look for his Dosage Zero, Brut Millesimato and Cuvée Annamaria Clementi. He also makes some fine still wines outside of DOC regulations from Cabernet Sauvignon, Merlot, Pinot Noir and Chardonnay.

LE MARCHE (THE MARCHES)

ALESSANDRO MORODER, Ancona: Made in consultation with Franco Bernabei, who also works with Giuseppe Mazzocolin at Fattoria di Felsina in Tuscany, the Rosso Conero Dorico is an outstanding expression of the Montepulciano grape. (This has nothing to do with the Tuscan town of the same name and its famous Vino Nobile, which comes from the Sangiovese grape family.)

PIEDMONT

The most important grape here is Nebbiolo, which for years yielded Barolo and Barbaresco wines featuring harsh tannins. These wines demanded long barrel aging—four or five years—and often emerged somewhat oxidized. Beginning in the mid-1980s, with the advent of modern techniques—lower yields, more concentrated fruit, harvesting for ripe tannins, shortening the fermentation time, eliminating the grape pits and better sanitation in the vinification process—the wines saw a vast improvement.

In Barolo Country, known as The Langhe, you wind your way up and down steep little hills topped with medieval castles and Renaissance villas, the snow-covered Alps providing a spectacular backdrop. Everywhere you look, there's a picture-postcard view. Not a bad place to get lost.

With their abrupt contours, these hills offer a variety of different exposures to the vines, ultimately giving the wines complexity and balance. The Barolo DOCG production zone is 3,200 acres, while the Barbaresco DOCG is a mere 2,700; these wines, however, are the tip of the iceberg, because there are many other equally intriguing wines of lesser classifications from the area.

In Barolo, the dynamic, opinionated Italian-American exporter Marc de Grazia, has been a driving force since the early 1980s. Marc has mustered a group of *grand cru* producers to create wines that are among the finest in the world. Although there has never been an official ranking of *cru* and *grand cru*, first, second and third growths as in France, there is a tacit acknowledgment of the outstanding spots —especially in Piedmont and Tuscany.

Marc has pushed his "Barolo Boys" to employ modern practices and oak barrels for aging. With pride, care and determination, they are achieving wondrous single-vineyard expressions of their grapes.

Following are some choice producers and wines from Barolo Country.

ELIO ALTARE, ALTARE WINERY, La Morra: Among the smaller independents, it was Elio Altare who first joined the revolution in the late seventies and early eighties. The rest soon followed. Elio was among Marc de Grazia's first "Barolo Boys," the first to travel to France in the footsteps of the great Gaja. His energy and commitment are a thing of beauty and they are reflected in his superb wines: Barolo Cru Arborina (100 percent Nebbiolo); Vigna Arborina (100 percent Nebbiolo); Vigna Larigi (100 percent Barbera); Barbera D'Alba; Dolcetto D'Alba and Nebbiolo D'Alba. He also produces a blend of 60 percent Barbera and 40 percent Nebbiolo called La Villa.

ANTICHE CANTINE DELL'ABBAZIA DELL'ANNUNZIATA, La Morra (Cuneo): Renato Ratti, the patriarch, died in 1988, but his sons, Piero and Giovanni, continue to produce superior wines in the Barolo DOCG as well as Barberas, Dolcettos and Nebbiolos. The company name, by the way, translates as "Old Cellars of the Abbey of the Annunciation."

BRAIDA, Rocchetta Tanaro: The charming and brilliant pioneer Giacomo Bologna, who helped bring the Barbera grape to the forefront with his Bricco dell'Uccellone and Bricco della Bigotta wines, is gone now, but his family continues the legacy. They built a new winery in 1996 and there are high hopes that they will restore the two Bricco wines, as well as Bologna's fine Pinot Nero–Barbera blend called Baciale, to their former glory.

FILLI CERETTO ("CERETTO SONS"), Alba: Brothers Bruno and Marcello Ceretto produce a fine Barolo, Bricco Rocche, as well as a Barbaresco, Bricco Asili, maintaining high standards with careful selection. For example, they declassified the 1993 and 1994 Barolos and only released the Barbarescos.

AZIENDA AGRICOLA DOMENICO CLERICO, Monforte d'Alba: Domenico Clerico and his wife, Giuliana, are established stars, their wines in demand at the finest establishments worldwide. Yet they remain humble and devoted to the task of producing great wines. Clerico has worked closely with Marc de Grazia since the early 1980s and was one of the first to use French *barriques*. One of his major innovations was a red table wine called Arte, blending about 90 percent Nebbiolo and 10 percent Barbera grapes from the Ginestra and Bussia crus, begun in 1985 and now considered one of the finest Italian wines. Clerico produces Barolos from the Ciabot Mentin Ginestra, Pajana and Bussia vineyards, all judged to be *grand crus*. The wines have spicy aromas with a hint of herbaceousness and are in many ways reminiscent of Cabernet Sauvignon. They are rich with a lingering finish. All in all, a superior expression of the Nebbiolo grape and the Barolo *terroir*.

PODERI ALDO CONTERNO, Monforte D'Alba: Aldo led his own revolution within the Conterno family when he left his father Giacomo's winery in 1967. The business, which had been in the family for five generations, eventually went to Aldo's brother Giovanni. Meanwhile Aldo created a new blueprint for making Barolos. He cut the fermentation time, cleaned up the winemaking and concentrated on extracting sweet, ripe tannins. He started using French *barriques* in the early eighties and has never stopped experimenting and innovating. In 1995 he was among the first Barolo producers to use rotating fermenters to enhance color extraction and drop the grape pits, which contain the bitter tannins, out of the solution. Aldo's wines are: Barolo Granbussia, a reserve selection; Barolo Bussia Soprana, a regular Barolo; Il Favot, a red table wine—all three from the Bussia Soprana vineyards. There

KEY TERMS IN BAROLO

AZIENDA AGRICOLA "agricultural firm," an independent wine producer. The colorful Piedmontese dialect, which is more guttural and French-sounding than standard Italian, often appears on labels denoting wine or vineyard names.

BRIC OR BRICCO "hilltop."

SORI "a hilltop with southern exposure."

COSTA "a hillside that faces the sun."

---

are also two other vineyard-designated Barolos, Bricco Bussia Vigna Colonello and Bricco Bussia Vigna Cicala; a Nebbiolo Langhe, a Dolcetto D'Alba and a Barbera D'Alba; one red sparkling wine from Freisa grapes and two Chardonnay wines, Printanie (Piedmontese dialect for "spring"), a fresh young wine made in stainless steel, and Bussiador, which is fermented in *barriques* and aged in oak.

CONTERNO FANTINO, Monforte D'Alba: Their flagship wine is Monpra, a blend of Nebbiolo, Barbera and a small amount of Cabernet Sauvignon. They also make an excellent classic Barolo from the Sori Ginestra vineyard and another fine Barolo from the Vigna del Gris vineyard as well as a pleasing Dolcetto D'Alba from the Bricco Bastia vineyard.

LUIGI COPPO & FIGLI, Canelli (Acqui Terme): The four Coppo brothers produce a wide variety of wines, especially sparkling, and are known for their technical prowess. Their best wines, however, are two Barbera D'Astis: the Camp du Rouss and the Pomorosso, which have earned them, in some circles, the title "Kings of Barbera."

LUIGI FERRANDO & FIGLIO, Ivrea: Ferrando is guru to a number of small producers in Northern Piedmont. He's based at his *enoteca* in Ivrea, about eighty miles from Alba and Barolo country, north of Turin. His best wine is the Ferrando Carema Etichetta Nera ("Black Label"), from Nebbiolo grapes, and its reputation is building internationally. It's lighter than Barolo but with plenty of complexity and aging potential. Ferrando also makes an interesting white wine from the Erbaluce grape.

ANGELO GAJA, Barbaresco: Gaja is a towering figure of international stature who stands shoulder to shoulder with Marchese Piero Antinori of Tuscany. A consummate winegrower and marketer, he represents the fourth generation of his family in the business. He almost single-handedly put Barbaresco, younger brother to Barolo, on the international wine map. Gaja pioneered the use of French-style *barriques* and was also the first to plant Cabernet Sauvignon, Chardonnay and Sauvignon Blanc in his region. In 1988, Gaja expanded his holdings to include a Barolo *grand cru* estate in Serralunga d'Alba. Then he branched out into Tuscany with the Pieve di Santa Restituta, an ancient abbey and winegrowing estate near Montalcino that produces Brunello, and more recently to a property near Bolgheri to produce Supertuscans. Gaja's wines are: three superlative single-vineyard Barbarescos called Sori Tildin, Costa Russi and Sori San Lorenzo; a Cabernet Sauvignon varietal called Langhe Rosso Darmagi ("Darmagi" in Piedmontese means "What a shame," which was the phrase muttered by Angelo's father, Giovanni, every time he walked past that vineyard of foreign grapes his son had planted); Barolo Sperss ("Sperrs" is Piedmontese for "nostalgia," and the wine is so named because it represented a return to Barolo production for the Gaja family after a hiatus of twenty-seven years); Chardonnay Gaia & Rey (named after Angelo's sister and grandmother). Gaja also makes a Barbaresco DOC wine, Dolcetto D'Alba, Barbera D'Alba and Nebbiolo D'Alba DOC wines, a Sauvignon Blanc, two grappas and two table wines.

BRUNO GIACOSA, Neive: Bruno Giacosa, the great Barolo and Barbaresco producer, is patriarch of the firm and another giant in Italian wine. His daughters Bruna and Marina are the fourth generation in the business. Dante Scaglione is their talented young winemaker. Their red wines are Dolcetto D'Alba, Barbera D'Alba, Nebbiolo D'Alba, Barolo from three different *crus* and Barbaresco, also from three different *crus*. Their whites are a Roero Arneis, a Spumante made from Pinot Noir in the traditional champagne method and a Moscato D'Asti. Their 1991, 1992 and 1994 Barolos and Barbarescos were declassified and sold in bulk due to poor conditions. In good vintages, they produce reserve wines—look for the red-highlighted labels.

AZIENDA AGRICOLO PARUSSO ARMANDO, Monforte D'Alba: This family operation, run by the brother-sister team of Marco and Tiziana Parusso, encompasses a total of eight hectares of prime vineyards in Monforte D'Alba and Castiglione Falletto planted to Nebbiolo, Barbera, Dolcetto and Freisa grapes. Their Nebbiolo-based wines are a regular Barolo *assemblaggio* ("assembly," or blend) from the Bussia vineyards in Monforte and the Novello vineyards in Castiglione Falletto, and three vineyard-designated Barolos—Bussia Vigna Munie, Bussia Vigna Rocche and Mariondino. In addition, they produce a Barbera D'Alba called Ornati, a Dolcetto D'Alba, a Bricco Rovella Rosso (Langhe DOC, 60 percent Nebbiolo, 40 percent Barbera) and a Bricco Rovello Bianco (Langhe DOC, mostly Sauvignon Blanc with 5 to 10 percent Chardonnay). The Munie Barolo, which benefits from a long, slow maturation of the grapes, is a beautifully balanced wine with abundant fruit and acidity; the Rocche Barolo is equally delightful, with a pronounced aroma of cinnamon that jumps right out of the glass.

AZIENDA AGRICOLA E. PIRA & FIGLI, Barolo: Chiara Boschis is an independent businesswoman with a Ph.D. in economics who, in the early nineties, began devoting her efforts full-time to this winery, located in the village of Barolo. Her family owns a larger producer in the village, Borgogno, but this is her pet project, drawing its grapes from two and a half hectares in the Cannubi *cru.* Coinciding with the great 1990 vintage and in consultation with Giorgio Spinetti, she began to break away from the old style of winemaking. Pira is turning out among the best examples of the new-style Barolo, with plenty of fruit, penetrating aromas, round ripe tannins, a long finish and structure for aging.

LA SPINETTA, Castagnole Lanze: Giorgio Rivetti of La Spinetta is a leader among the independent producers of the Langhe. Rivetti has always been an instigator and organizer. He spearheads a tastings and travel group that includes Clerico, Altare and Scavino plus friendly competition and the exchange of valuable information. Ironically, Giorgio's reputation is based neither on Barolo nor Barbaresco but on Moscato D'Asti, the light, sweet sparkling wine that requires a tremendous mastery of technique. As a longtime Champagne drinker, I feel I'm qualified to make a categorical statement: Forget about the other sparkling wines of Italy and try some of this Moscato—preferably from La Spinetta or a comparable producer. It's a real treat. Among cognoscenti, Rivetti is considered the best Moscato producer. In the late 1980s, he branched out to produce red wines, including a superstar Nebbiolo-Barbera-Cabernet blend called Monferrato Rosso Pin.

AZIENDA AGRICOLA ROCCA ALBINO, Barbaresco: Rocca is a hands-on family operation in Barbaresco. On a recent visit, father Albino was down in the vineyard driving the tractor. Angelo, Albino's son and the winemaker, has three daughters, Daniella, Monica and Paola, each involved in the business. The Roccas are also members of Rivetti's "Group of 16" producers called

"Punto Langhe." They have about nine hectares of vineyards with southeast and southwest exposure, about four in Nebbiolo and five split between Barbera and Dolcetto.

LUCIANO SANDRONE, Barolo: Luciano Sandrone's winery is located in the shadow of the village of Barolo, with its castle precariously perched on an outcropping that overlooks some of the best vineyards in Italy. He comes from a family of carpenters and learned the winemaking trade working for many years in the cellars at Marchesi di Barolo, a big producer. Luciano works with his wife, Maria, and his brother, Luca, who quit carpentry and learned viniculture at the University of Alba. Sandrone's international reputation is built on the Barolo Cannubi Boschis, which he's been producing with continued success since 1978 from grapes grown in the Cannubi *cru*, known as "the hill where Barolo was born." The Sandrones also make a Dolcetto D'Alba, a Barbera D'Alba, a Nebbiolo D'Alba and Barolo Le Vigne, from four vineyards in Barolo and Monforte, including the famous Bussia *cru*. Over the years, Sandrone has gradually accumulated, by purchase and lease, an impressive collection of small vineyard parcels in the top *crus* of the Barolo region. This is no mean feat for a small independent producer, especially when the price of land as of this writing is around 500 million lire per hectare ($120,000 per acre) and rising. Along with Elio Altare, Sandrone is one of Marc de Grazia's original "Barolo Boys."

PAOLO SCAVINO, Castiglione Falletto: Enrico Scavino has taken his father Paolo's operation to the pinnacle of the New Wine Revolution. In 1982, Scavino, whose daughter Enrica is now involved in the business, began to institute changes in his vineyards, which consist of twelve hectares of prime sites in the villages of Castiglione Falletto, La Morra and Barolo. Castiglione, in the Barolo appellation, was always known for its harsh, tannic wines, due not only to the quality of its Nebbiolo grapes but also to long maceration (up to thirty days) at high temperatures. The style has changed. Maceration is shorter, fermentation temperature is controlled in steel vats and aging in *barriques* is carefully monitored. Scavino's wines are Vigneto del Fiasc, a Dolcetto varietal from Castiglione; Barolo Cannubi, Barolo Rocche Annunziate and Barolo Bric del Fiasc, three classic *grand cru* Barolos; and a regular Barolo, made from a blend of the best of several small plots. His newest wine is a Barolo called Vignane.

SARDINIA

Giacomo Tachis, the famed consultant largely responsible for giving us Sassicaia and Tignanello, is working with the producer **ANTONIO ARGIOLAS** on his native island. As Piero Selvaggio says, "If Antinori is the Robert Mondavi of Italy, Giacomo Tachis is the Andre Tchelistcheff." Argiolas makes excellent red wines from the indigenous Cannonau grape and also a Vino Da Tavola called Turriga.

SICILY

TENUTA DI CASTIGLIONE, Acireale (Catania): On the steep slopes of Mt. Etna, which, at nearly eleven thousand feet, is by far the tallest volcano in Europe, are the terraced vineyards of this estate where the Benanti family has cultivated grapes since the late nineteenth century. In 1988, Giuseppe Benanti began to rejuvenate the property. The reds, both part of the Etna Rosso DOC, are Rovittello, the *grand vin,* and Rosso di Verzella, the second wine, both primarily from Nerello Mascalese grapes with Cappuccio rounding out the blend. The whites are Pietramarina, an Etna Bianco Superiore DOC from old vines (circa 1915), and Bianco di Caselle, an Etna Bianco DOC from thirty-five-to fifty-year-old vines. Both whites are made from 100 percent Caricante grapes.

CONTE TASCA D'ALMERITA-REGALEALI, Sclafani Bagni (Palermo): The Tasca family's estate is an established producer that forges ahead into the twenty-first century. It offers some very fine wines, a white made of Sauvignon Blanc called Nozze D'Oro and an excellent red at about $10 a bottle called Regaleali Rosso from the local Nerello Mascalese and Perricone grapes. More recently, they've brought out some superior vintages of Cabernet Sauvignon and Chardonnay.

DUCA DI SALAPARUTA, Casteldaccia (Palermo): For years, this giant of Sicilian wines has been known for its Corvo reds and whites, one of the most popular wines at trattorias and pizzerias the world over. This saddled the company not only with multiple billions of lire in profits with which to build their new state-of-the art winery but also with a mass-market reputation. Beginning in 1984, they began producing a premium wine from the Nero D'Avola grape called Duca Enrico. For seven years running, the *Gambero Rosso*, Italy's answer to *The Wine Spectator*, has rated it among the very best. Deservedly so. We compared it to a hundred other top Italian wines at a tasting at the Hotel Bel Air in the spring of 1997 and it was definitely in the top ten.

TRENTINO-ALTO ADIGE

FORADORI, Mezzolombardo (Trent): The proprietors are Gabriella Foradori along with her daughter Elisabetta, a trained enologist who, beginning in 1984, successfully revived an indigenous red variety called Teroldego, which had been used to make local table wine in the co-ops. The Foradoris make two highly rated wines from Teroldego, the Granato and the Teroldego Rotaliano Sgarzon—Sgarzon being the vineyard name—as well as a regular Teroldego Rotaliano. They also make a Chardonnay Trentino, a Pinot Bianco and have recently introduced a Sauvignon Blanc called Myrto. The Teroldego has hints of floral aromas, along with toasted almond and sweet citrus; a rich, complex taste with plenty of black fruit and cherry, and a long, satisfying finish.

AZIENDA AGRICOLA POJER & SANDRI, Faedo: Maro Pojer and Fiorentino Sandri are among the best winegrowers of the Trentino. Their Rosso Faye, a blend of 50 percent Cabernet Sauvignon, with the remainder equal parts Cabernet Franc, Merlot and Lagrein, is quickly gaining international renown. Luca Moroni, the Italian Robert Parker, is rumored to have called the 1993 Faye the best wine he ever tasted; he gave it 99 points. Pojer, Sandri and seven workers farm twenty-three hectares from which they vinify and distill an astounding array of wines and spirits. The whites: varietals of Nosiola, Chardonnay, Müller-Thurgau, Sauvignon Blanc, Gewürztraminer; an oak-aged blend of Chardonnay and Pinot Bianco also called Faye. Two roses: Schiava and Vin dei Molini. Three reds: the aforementioned Faye along with a Pinot Nero and a reserve Pinot Nero, as well as an outstanding *spumante* and a German-style late-harvest *eiswein*. They also distill just about every imaginable flavor of grappa, including apricot, prune, quince, raspberry and blackberry.

TWO MORE FINE PRODUCERS: Normally cooperatives are suspect, but there are exceptions to every rule. The Cantina Sociale San Michele Appiano and the Cantina Viticoltori di Caldaro, both located near Bolzano, offer strong lineups. Look for any of their wines, particularly Sauvignon St.-Valentin from the former and the Cabernet Sauvignon Riserva from the latter.

TUSCANY

What can you say in praise of Tuscany that isn't God's Honest Truth? The Sangiovese grape is king of this promised land, but the spirit of the Florentine Renaissance is alive, which means there are plenty of other luminaries. Tuscany is about ancient noble families who pursue the endless quest for perfection; it's also about humble, dedicated farmers who work the land. Although the tile roofs are maybe five hundred years old instead of fifty, it reminds me of California in that there is a plethora of superb wines waiting to be discovered.

There are a couple of important trends. First, the Consorzio del Marchio Storico, Gallo Nero, which is the consortium of Chianti producers, continues to promote experimentation in the vineyards for the purpose of furthering everybody's knowledge. The Consorzio oversees Project 2000, headed by enologist/agronomist Dr. Stefano Porcinai, which assigns vineyard experiments to each of its producers then collects, analyzes and disseminates the results. The other important trend is expansion—particularly into the coastal hills of Tuscany south of Bolgheri going toward Grossetto, in the region known as the Maremma. Again, this brings echoes of California, where producers are expanding into the northern coastal areas of Sonoma and the Lake Counties. There will be many exciting new wines coming out of these new vineyards in the coming decades.

ANTINORI, Florence: The premier name in Tuscan wines, the Antinori family has been in the business since 1385. That's twenty-six generations and counting (and I thought twenty-five years was a long time...). The current scion is the Marchese Piero Antinori, a man of considerable social charm, not to mention business acumen. Antinori properties now include three classic *tenute* (farms or estates, literally "holdings") in the heart of Tuscany: Santa Cristina, Peppoli and Badia a Passignano. There is a new acquisition in the Maremma, Tenuta Belvedere, along with the most recent addition, Le Maestrelle, near Montepulciano and Cortona. There is also the Castello della Sala, a spectacular fourteenth-century castle in Umbria south of Orvieto managed by Marchese Piero's daughter Albiera. (Daughter Allegra has also joined the business.) Antinori's red wines are Santa Cristina (100 percent Sangiovese), a fine fruity table wine; Chianti Classicos from Badia a Passignano, Villa Antinori and Peppoli; a Chianti Riserva from Badia as well as Tenute Marchese Antinori Chianti Classico Riserva, a reserve blend of the best of the estates; Tignanello, the original Supertuscan (80 percent Sangiovese, 15 percent Cabernet Sauvignon, 5 percent Cabernet Franc); Solaia (70 percent Cabernet Sauvignon, 20 percent Sangiovese, 10 percent Cabernet Franc). Their white wines: Galestro "Capsula Viola" (purple capsule), a light Trebbiano-Chardonnay-Pinot Bianco blend; Orvieto Classico "Campogrande," an improvement on the traditional white Orvieto; Villa Antinori Bianco Toscano, a Trebbiano-Malvasia-Chardonnay blend; Castello della Sala Orvieto Classico, a single-vineyard expression of the traditional Procanico grape, which is the local name for Trebbiano Toscano, with the highest percentage of Grechetto allowed by law; Borro della Sala (80 percent Sauvignon Blanc and 20 percent Procanico) and Cervaro della Sala (80 percent Chardonnay and 20 percent Grechetto).

BIONDI-SANTI, Montalcino: Jacopo Biondi-Santi is the son of Franco, longtime leader of the family firm whose grandfather presided over Il Greppo, known as the vineyard where Brunello di Montalcino was born. Unfortunately, father and son have been involved in a drawn-out legal dispute, but meanwhile, Jacopo has been able to break from a tradition that perhaps grew stagnant. He has made two great new wines, Schidione, a Cabernet-Sangiovese blend, and Sassoaloro, from Sangiovese, in consultation with Vittorio Fiore.

PIEVE DI SANTA RESTITUTA, Montalcino: Angelo Gaja's first venture outside his native Piedmont, acquired in 1994, this estate near the ancient abbey of Santa Restituta is one of the *grand crus* of Montalcino. It gives Gaja a presence in all three of the oldest and most prestigious Italian appellations, Brunello di Montalcino, Barbaresco and Barolo. The Pieve produces two Brunellos: Rennina, from three vineyards on the property, and Sugarille, a vineyard that dates back to 1547. It also produces a Supertuscan, Promis (90 percent Sangiovese and 10 percent Cabernet Sauvignon).

TENUTA SAN GUIDO, Bolgheri: Marchese Mario Incisa planted Cabernet Sauvignon vines of French origin on this estate in the mid-1940s. In consultation with his nephew Marchese Piero

Antinori and enologists Giacomo Tachis and Emile Peynaud, he eventually produced Sassicaia, a Bordeaux-style blend of approximately 75 percent Cabernet Sauvignon and 25 percent Cabernet Franc first released in the late 1960s. It quickly became a cult wine the world over and still is. It also put Bolgheri on the map; the village was awarded DOC status in 1994.

TENUTA DELL'ORNELLAIA, Bolgheri: Piero Antinori's younger brother Lodovico, with Andre Tchelistcheff's advice, developed this property near San Guido, home of Sassicaia, and has made its flagship wine, Ornellaia (Cabernet Sauvignon, Merlot and Cabernet Franc), into a world-class, international-style Tuscan Vino da Tavola. He's also making a Merlot varietal called Masseto as well as a Sauvignon Blanc–based white Poggio alle Gazze.

PODERE POGGIO SCALETTE, Greve: Consulting winemaker Vittorio Fiore, a force to be reckoned with in Tuscany, along with his wife, Adriana Assje de Marcora, and their son Jurij, an enologist by training, farm their own estate in the Ruffoli section of Greve in Chianti, which they bought in 1991 and expanded in 1996. It's a classic Tuscan winegrowing site, about fifteen hundred feet up on a hillside. The view toward Siena is breathtaking; according to legend, it was the background for Leonardo da Vinci's Mona Lisa. The wine, Il Carbonaione, has an intense deep ruby color, hints of wild berries (blackcurrant, blackberry) in its aroma, ripe soft tannins and a smooth, delicious finish. The name refers to the traditional sheds where *contadini* (farmers) burned log wood to make charcoal. Vittorio is consultant to more than twenty-five smaller, high-quality wineries, mostly in Tuscany, including Caparzo, Colle al Matrichese, La Gerla, Poggio Salvi in Montalcino, Monteverdi, Valtellina and Castello di Meleto in Gaiole in Chianti; La Madonnina, Le Bocce, Terre di Montefili and Viticcio in Greve; Capaccia and Terrabianca in Radda in Chianti. If you have trouble finding the flagship wines produced by top consultants like Fiore, have your wine merchant locate others of the same pedigree.

CASTELLO DI FONTERUTOLI, Castellina in Chianti: When you talk about tradition in Tuscany, you have to talk about the Mazzei family, which has been in the wine business since 1435. One ancestor, Ser Lapo Mazzei, was a notable citizen of Florence in the fourteenth century and wrote the earliest-known reference to Chianti. Another ancestor, Filippo Mazzei, took vines to his friend Thomas Jefferson to plant at Monticello in Virginia. Their base in Chianti country is Fonterutoli, near Castellina, about ten miles north of Siena. Once a fortified castle, the southernmost Florentine outpost in the age of warring city-states, it is now a tranquil little village. Lapo Mazzei is the current patriarch. Two of his five children, sons Francesco and Filippo, are involved in running the company. (Filippo is also working to revive Brolio, another famous family firm in the region.) The Mazzei are keeping the revolution alive by producing three outstanding Supertuscans: Siepi (50 percent Sangiovese, 50 percent Merlot,), Concerto (80 percent Sangiovese, 20 percent Cabernet Sauvignon) and Brancaia (85 percent Sangiovese, 15 percent Merlot). The Siepi is a big mouthful of a wine with cherry aromas and hints of chocolate, mint and spice that begins to develop a velvety smooth Merlot signature within a year or two of its release. The Concerto and Brancaia are equally delicious. Take your pick, these are superb wines, smooth, complex, with body, power and plenty of aging potential—pleasing to the international palate but also expressive of their Tuscan *terroir*. The Mazzei also make a Chianti Classico (100 percent Sangiovese) as well as the Poggio alla Badiola (90 percent or more Sangiovese with small amounts of Merlot and Cabernet Sauvignon), a good bargain at about $10 per bottle.

FATTORIA DI FELSINA, Castelnuovo Berardenga: Giuseppe Mazzocolin, a former high school humanities teacher, manages this estate for his father-in-law, Domenico Pogialli, an industrialist from Ravenna. Giuseppe works with winemaker Franco Bernabei, who came on board in 1982 after working at a number of major Tuscan producers and traveling to Bordeaux frequently. They are turning out some stellar examples of Tuscan *terroir*. The flagship wines are Chianti Classico Vigneto Rancia and Maestro Raro Cabernet Sauvignon. In addition, the winery produces a Chianti Classico, a Chianti Classico Riserva, an excellent table wine called Fontalloro and a Chardonnay called I Sistri. Twenty kilometers away in Sinalunga, the family's new estate, Castello di Farnetella is producing a Sauvignon Blanc, a Pinot Noir called Nero di Nubi and a Chianti Colli Senesi.

MONTECALVI, Greve in Chianti: Bernadette and Renzo Bolli are the proprietors of this beautiful little estate, with a restored early-seventeenth-century farmhouse, in the heart of Chianti country. Stefano Chioccioli, a respected young enologist/agronomist with an impressive list of clients, is the consulting winemaker. Working together since the early 1990s, they've created a wine of increasing balance and finesse. They call it Montecalvi, Rosso dell'Alta Valle della Greve, Vino Da Tavola ("red table wine from high in the Greve Valley"). Stefano also consults for Tenuta Bonzara, Monte San Pietro, Colli Bolognesi (Bologna); Le Farnete, Carmignano (Firenze); Matroneo, Greve in Chianti; Tenuta Cantagallo, Capraia (Firenze), Chianti Montalbano, among others.

PODERE IL PALAZZINO, Gaiole in Chianti: Since the mid-1980s, proprietors Andrea and Alessandro Sderci have been improving their Chianti Classico wines, particularly the Riserva, which has had impressive results in blind tastings.

SAN FELICE, San Gusme, Castelnuovo Berardenga: Leonardo Bellaccini, a dynamic young enologist trained at the University of Florence, is responsible for production at this, the biggest, most ambitious boutique winery in the Chianti Classico region. San Felice, one of the larger members of the Gallo Nero consortium, has 18 acres of experimental vineyards, called the Vitarium, created by its late viticulturist and manager Enzo Morganti. It contains nearly 300 indigenous varieties—about 160 reds and 130 whites, including the likes of Pugnitello, Abrostine, Colorino and Malvasia Nera —not exactly household names. San Felice's wines include a Chianti Classico; a Chianti Classico Riserva called Il Grigio, after the Titian painting that adorns its label; Vigorello, a Supertuscan blend of about 20 percent Cabernet Sauvignon with Sangiovese; Poggio Rosso, another Chianti Classico Riserva; Belcaro, a white blend of 40 percent Vermentino, 30 percent Riesling and 30 percent Pinot Bianco; Ancherona, a Chardonnay from the vineyard of that name. They also make a young red of Primanno, a rosé of Canaiolo, a white blend and a Chardonnay as well as a vin santo and a grappa. There is also a Brunello di Montalcino from the Campogiovanni estate in Sant'Angelo in Colle. Overall, an impressive portfolio.

TENUTA DI GHIZZANO, Peccioli: The Venerosi Pesciolini family, ancient Tuscan nobility originally from Pisa, preside over this breathtaking estate about forty miles to the west-southwest of Florence that is producing one of my favorite Italian wines. Veneroso, named after their ancestor Veneroso Venerosi, is a blend of approximately 45 percent Cabernet Sauvignon, 40 percent Sangiovese and 15 percent Merlot. The count and countess have retired from the business, which is now in the hands of their daughter Ginevra who works with the brilliant, young enologist Luca D'Attoma. The estate also produces a Chianti Colline Pisani (meaning "Chianti from the little hills around Pisa"), which is about 90 percent Sangiovese with equal parts Cabernet Sauvignon and Cannaiolo.

TUA RITA WINERY, Suvereto: Proprietors Virgilio and Rita Tua work closely with consulting enologist Luca D'Attoma to bring out the best of this small, unpretentious family farm in the Maremma, south of Bolgheri. The soil has lots of rock, sand and clay. It is an excellent habitat for Cabernet Sauvignon and Merlot, which is why Luca calls it "a little piece of the Medoc in Suvereto." Their star is the Giusto di Notri, a strikingly delicious blend of roughly 60 percent Cabernet Sauvignon and 40 percent Merlot with deep, rich color and hints of cassis, currant and chocolate among its complex aromatic components. They also make an excellent 100 percent Merlot called Redigaffi along with several other reds and whites.

UMBRIA

This region, sharing its western border with Tuscany, is home to Perugina chocolates, Monini olive oil, white and black truffles and, of course, more great wine.

CASTELLO DELLA SALA, Ficulle (Terni): See Antinori, above.

ARNALDO CAPRAI WINERY, Montefalco (Perugia): Consulting winemaker Attilio Pagli works with Marco Caprai to produce Sagrantino di Montefalco, a wine of tremendous distinction and character that, I'm convinced, is Italy's new international superstar. It gives off aromas of caramel, spice and mint, and features a full extraction of delicious, rich fruit, soft, ripe tannins and a long, delicious finish that predicts aging potential of twenty years or more. Piero Selvaggio characterizes Sagrantino, a great example of Italy's little-known indigenous varieties, as "very rich, intense, very inky—like a cross between a Syrah and a Pinot Noir." Right on the money. Pagli, who specializes in Sangiovese and Brunello projects, also consults for more than twenty wineries, including Angelo Gaja's Pieve di Santa Restituta, Montalcino; Il Poggiolino, Sambuca Val di Pesa, Chianti Classico; Rascioni Cecconello, Fonteblanda (Grosseto); Solatione, Mercatale Val di Pesa, Chianti Classico; Tenuta La Fuga, Montalcino. He also consults for a number of distinguished Brunello di Montalcino producers; for Staglin, Benessere, Seghesio and Amador Foothill in California on Italian varietal projects; and for two wineries in Argentina, where he's working on Sangiovese and Malbec projects.

VENETO

The region is named after Venice but extends to include the hills around Verona, a well-known and popular winegrowing region called Valpolicella. While there are producers working hard to bring traditional Valpolicella wines up to modern premium standards, the most interesting wines of the area are the Reciotos: Recioto della Valpolicella and Recioto della Valpolicella Amarone, usually referred to simply as Amarone. Reciotos are made from air-dried grapes, a process known as *appassimento*, which concentrates the flavor, giving the wine weight, viscosity and sweetness and also the aromas and tastes of dates, plums, wild berries, raisins, cocoa and much more. It's a unique and complex wine. The regular Recioto is sweet, with about 14% alcohol and 2% residual sugar, somewhat reminiscent of Port, suitable for sipping after dinner or with gamy dishes or strong cheeses. The Amarone is the dry version, also 14% alcohol, delicious with a good concentration and a pleasant bitterness that is offset by an underlying sweetness.

GIOVANNI ALLEGRINI, Fumane (Verona): The winery, now in the capable hands of the brother-and-sister team of Franco and Marilisa Allegrini, is applying modern techniques to revamp the way Vapolicella is made. They produce a Recioto Classico as well as a highly regarded Amarone, also a superb wine called La Poja from 100 percent Corvina, a local grape variety similar to Sangiovese.

DAL FORNO WINERY, Illasi (Verona): Romano Dal Forno is another master capable of making superior wines even in off vintages. His flagship wines are the Amarone and the Recioto della Valpolicella, both from the Vigneto di Monte Lodoletta vineyard.

SERAFINI & VIDOTTO, ABAZIA DI NERVESA, Nervesa della Battaglia (Treviso): Their Rosso dell'Abazia has come into its own as one of the finest wines in Italy. It's a blend of Cabernet Sauvignon, Cabernet Franc and Merlot. Francesco Serafini and Antonello Vidotto are both the owners and winegrowers.

GIUSEPPE QUINTARELLI, Negrar (Verona): Quintarelli is known for his artistry with Amarone and Amarone Riserva as well as his Recioto della Valpolicella. The bottles have distinctive labels printed in a "handwritten" typeface.

NEW ZEALAND

This island country, even farther down under than its neighboring continent, Australia, is known for its Sauvignon Blanc, which is crisp, "veggie-tasting" and emphasizes fruit over oak. Because of New Zealand's extreme southerly latitude, its grapes, like those of northern Europe, don't ripen as conclusively. Consequently they maintain plenty of acid to add zest to the fruitiness of the wines. The big name in Sauvignon Blanc is Cloudy Bay, which is from the Marlborough region and has successfully gone head-to-head with some major French wines in blind tastings. Other top Sauvignon Blancs come from Hunter's and Selaks. Stonyridge (reds) and Te Mata (reds and whites) are two other recommended producers. New Zealand produces some good Chardonnays as well and is also getting into Cabernet Sauvignon, Pinot Noir and Riesling. It is an exciting winegrowing region with emerging developments, definitely worth exploring—at least via your taste buds.

PORTUGAL

Portuguese wines, which have been popular in Britain and the Scandinavian countries for years, are just coming into focus in the United States. They are made from traditional local varieties such as Touriga Nacional, Tinta Cao and Tricadera with small amounts of Cabernet Sauvignon, Merlot or Syrah for additional complexity. There are many fine wines selling for around $10. The dashingly handsome half-English, half-Portuguese winemaking consultant Joao Portugal Ramos, is leading the revolution there. From his base in Estremoz in southern Portugal, he oversees the winemaking at eighteen wineries and is responsible for about eighty-five different wines.

One of Portugal's most intriguing wines is its Vinho Verde, an acidic, sometimes lightly sparkling young wine that comes in both red and white and is delicious with seafood. Of course, Portugal is the land of Port, the world's most famous fortified wine, the grapes for which are grown in the Douro Valley. This region, along with Dão to the south as well as Bairrada and Alentejo, is home to a developing premium wine industry thanks to people like Mr. Ramos. The Portuguese island of Madeira produces another famous (eponymous) fortified wine that is said to be able to age indefinitely.

SOUTH AFRICA

Although wine has been made by European settlers in South Africa's Cape of Good Hope since the seventeenth century, modern international wine connoisseurs have had little exposure to it. With the end of apartheid and the lifting of boycotts in 1994, the wines of South Africa, predictably, experienced a boom. Things settled down and in the shakeout we see the establishment of certain producers as world players.

The South African varieties are Shiraz, as in Australia the same as Syrah; Pinotage, a local cross between Cinsaut, a B-level grape once very common in southern France, and Pinot Noir; Chenin Blanc, mostly for bulk wines and also referred to as Steen; and Chardonnay as well as some Merlot, Cabernet Sauvignon and Sauvignon Blanc.

Like Australia, most of the country is hot and dry, so the main challenge is to find cool growing areas where European varieties can thrive. Look for the wines of the top growing regions, Constantia, Stellenbosch and Paarl. Franschhoek Valley is a beautiful subdistrict of Paarl which was home to Huguenot (French) settlers. Some of South Africa's top producers are Delheim (Shiraz), Klein Constantia (Sauvignon Blanc), Grangehurst (Pinotage), Mulderbosch (Sauvignon Blanc), Rheeboksloof (Merlot) and Villiera (Merlot).

SOUTH AMERICA

For years, international winemakers have seen potential in Chile. Due to lower costs, plentiful land and disease-resistant vines, the Europeans have invested. The Rothschilds of Lafite are in a joint venture there with Los Vascos. The great Catalan producer Miguel Torres has had a presence there since the late seventies. The other Rothschilds (Mouton) are working with the producer Concha y Toro. Michel Rolland consults with Casa Lapostolle, owned by the same family that makes Grand Marnier, to produce a world-class Merlot. All of these are wines worthy of serious attention.

Some distinguished Chilean producers are Cousino-Macul, Concha y Toro, Santa Rita, Errazuriz and Undurraga for Sauvignon Blanc. Maipú, near Santiago, the capital, is the most famous growing region; other areas are Aconcagua, in the shadow of that towering peak, and the newer Casablanca. Chile has shown itself capable of producing excellent Cabernet Sauvignon and Merlot wines, but the industry is still relatively rustic.

In Argentina, Catena, Bodegas Weinert and Trapiche are fine producers and the main growing areas are Mendoza, in the shadow of the towering Andes and not far from Chile, along with Lujan de Cuyo, where the vineyards are cultivated at relatively high altitudes. Malbec is the traditional variety in Argentina, but Cabernet Sauvignon is making inroads, particularly in the premium end, as are Merlot and Chardonnay. Chandon is also making some noteworthy sparkling wines.

Both Chile and Argentina have tremendous promise as sources of inexpensive world-class wines—now and well into the next century.

SPAIN

This is a country of ancient traditions, backward practices and great potential. Until the mid-1990s, for example, it was illegal to irrigate vineyards in this hottest, driest of European winegrowing regions. This was to limit production and keep prices high as well as to avoid the costs of bringing water up to the vineyards. Now, by introducing irrigation and other commonsense measures, Spanish producers are pretty much bypassing the twentieth century and hurtling straight into the twenty-first.

Spain has a number of important geographical advantages, giving it possibly the best potential, of any other European country, to produce premium wines. It has the highest average elevation, some of the oldest vines and the largest area of vineyards planted.

"In the last ten years, Spanish winemaking has evolved more than in the previous fifty years," says importer Jorge Ordonez, a catalyst for the Spanish wine boom in the United States. "It's the biggest revolution in any winemaking country. The situation is incredible, really exciting. Things are happening really fast. The wine business has a tendency to be immobilized, but not now, not in Spain."

Not only is the quality and quantity of Spanish premium wines improving by leaps and bounds, but the prices are right. The majority sell in the $5 to $20 range while even the most sought-after Riojas go for $30 to $50.

Here are the areas to watch:

RIOJA: This is the old catchword for "Spanish wine," but it's about to reinvent itself. Jorge Ordonez refers to the new wines he's selling as Superriojas, Spain's answer to the Supertuscans. They're made primarily from the indigenous Tempranillo grape with some Grafiano and Garnacha and on occasion some Cabernet Sauvignon added to the blend. The top Riojan producers are practicing stricter grape selection, longer maceration and less filtering, and the result is better wines with more concentrated flavors.
RECOMMENDED PRODUCERS: Bodegas Muga, Remelluri, San Vicente, Bodegas Sierra Cantabria.
RIBERA DEL DUERO: In the late eighties and early nineties, following the lead of top producer Vega Sicilia, this region began to make great strides toward catching up with Rioja. The wines feature soft tannins, rich color, body and depth. The wines of Bodegas Reyes are highly recommended. After making his mark by working for Pesquera, where he was responsible for their excellent Condado de Haza, and others for years, Teofilo Reyes made the first wine under his own name in 1994 at the age of seventy. It is excellent.
PRIORATO: Typical of the best Spanish growing regions, this has an ancient tradition but just a sixteen-year modern history of growing premium wines. In the past, the co-ops accounted for about 60 percent of the approximately 100,000 cases made and the wine was relatively unknown, even in nearby Barcelona, where discerning natives still focus on wines from the nearby Penedes region, which is dominated by the world-famous Torres family firm.

SHERRY

THIS IS THE WONDERFUL, NUTTY, TANGY FORTIFIED WINE MADE IN SOUTHERN ANDALUCIA BY A COMPLICATED PROCESS THAT INCLUDES USE OF A SPECIAL YEAST CALLED *FLOR* AND A BLENDING SYSTEM CALLED *SOLERA* WHERE EACH AGING BARREL RECEIVES PORTIONS OF OLDER WINES. IT IS ONE OF THE WORLD'S GREAT APERITIFS.

BASIC SPANISH WINE TERMINOLOGY

BODEGA Winery.

CRIANZA Wines aged in oak up to about a year. The translation is similar to the French word *elever* and is also applied to the nursing or bringing up of children.

DENOMINACIÓN DE ORIGEN (DO) AND DENOMINACIÓN DE ORIGEN CALIFICADA (DOCA) Similar to the Italian DOC and DOCG system; quality and appellation guarantees.

GRAN RESERVA Aged the longest; the best vintages and selections.

JOVEN Young wines.

RESERVA Aged up to two or three years.

RECOMMENDED PRIORATO PRODUCERS: Clos de L'Obac and Finca Dofi.

NAVARRA: This region just east of Rioja saw its first major replantings at the end of the 1980s; before that, it was the kingdom of the cooperatives. The area stretches from the Ebro River to the Pyrenees, with altitudes from 350 meters up to 650 and a variety of soil conditions and microclimates, potentially hospitable to many different grape types. Bodegas Nekea makes an excellent Cabernet-Tempranillo (60–40) called Vega Sindoa. Concha Vecino is the winemaker at Nekea, one of the best in Spain and a woman, which is rare.

GALICIA: Again, it's only recently that this northwestern region has become renown for turning out the finest Spanish white wines, primarily the aromatic Albariño, which was virtually unknown even in Spain until about 1987. The grapes are grown in vineyards overlooking the sea and the wines are a tasty compliment to seafood dishes.

RECOMMENDATIONS: Godeval, made from 100 percent Godello, a revived local variety; Martin Codax, Bodegas de Vilarino-Cambados (100 percent Albariño); Borsao, Bodegas Borsao, (80 percent Garnacha, 20 percent Tempranillo).

SWITZERLAND

Switzerland has always been a quiet little powerhouse. It represents the confluence of three of the greatest winegrowing cultures in the universe: France, Italy and Germany. Although they're relatively unknown in international circles, there are a number of artisans making fine wines in the foothills and valleys of the Swiss Alps. There are also many wine lovers and connoisseurs in Switzerland, so its output of super-premium wines is rarely exported. Swiss producers are clever and versatile, using primarily two lesser-known varieties, Sylvaner and Chasselas, for whites, and relying on Merlot and Pinot Noir, which they call Blauburgunder, for reds.

UNITED STATES

American premium winegrowing has taken tremendous leaps forward since the first wine revolution in the 1970s. Nevertheless, there are many areas in California, Oregon and Washington with huge untapped potential. As we enter the twenty-first century, I believe we'll continue to see significant expansion. The result will be more and better wines across the entire spectrum of premium production.

CALIFORNIA

California's North Coast, which encompasses Napa and Sonoma Counties, is the epicenter of American premium winegrowing. In Napa, familiar winegrowing regions such as Oakville, Rutherford and St. Helena are joining the roster of established AVAs such as Mount Veeder, Stag's Leap and Howell Mountain. California encompasses America's breadbasket—the hot, fertile Central Valley—as well as hundreds of microclimates that are ideal for growing vines. Because of the influence of the Pacific Ocean, many of them are surprisingly foggy and cool, thus hospitable to varieties such as Pinot Noir and Chardonnay.

SOME PLACE-NAMES TO LOOK FOR: In Sonoma County, there will be exciting developments out of Russian River Valley, Alexander Valley, Knights Valley, Sonoma Valley and Sonoma Mountain. In Mendocino County, Anderson Valley is becoming a force to be reckoned with. The same is true of the Paso Robles and Arroyo Grande areas near San Luis Obispo; Salinas Valley near Monterey; the Santa Maria and Santa Ynez Valleys near Santa Barbara; Livermore Valley east of San Francisco and even Amador County in the foothills of the Sierra Nevadas in the interior. Expect continuing developments not only in the traditional varieties—Cabernet Sauvignon, Merlot, Pinot Noir, Chardonnay, Sauvignon Blanc—but also in the Rhône and Italian varieties.

ARAUJO ESTATE, Calistoga, Napa Valley: Bart and Daphne Araujo took over this property, built a new winery and began producing their Cabernet in 1991. Tony Soter is the consulting winemaker. Beginning in the mid-1970s, their Eisele Vineyard, one of the best in California, supplied grapes to Joseph Phelps for his Cabernets. A newer release is their sensational Syrah, which should quickly establish itself as a superstar. If their aim is to make a wine to rival Guigal's spectacular single-vineyard Rhône wines, they're on the right track.

MARK AUBERT, Napa Valley: Mark spent the majority of the 1990s tending the vines and making the wines at Peter Michael Winery. In early 1999, he left to become winemaker at two excellent Napa properties, Colgin Cellars and Sloan Vineyards, where he works closely with top vineyard manager David Abreu. Also, look for single vineyard–designated Chardonnay and Pinot Noir wines from the Sonoma Coast region, developed by Mark and his wife, Teresa, under their own label, Aubert Wines.

HEIDI PETERSON BARRETT, LA SIRENA, Calistoga, Napa Valley: For Heidi Peterson Barrett, winemaking is in the blood. Not only was her father, Dick, an important figure in the First Wine Revolution, but she married into another illustrious Napa Valley wine clan: her husband is Bo Barrett, the winemaker at Chateau Montelena just up the road. She became a "part-time winemaker" and consultant in 1988 with Gustave Dalla Valle as her first client. Together they developed his property and produced superb Maya wines. Gustave passed away in 1996 and Heidi has moved on. Her forte is in concentrated hillside Cabernet-based wines, elegant, emphasizing the fruit of the vineyard but with a good balance of ripe tannins and acidity. Under her own label, La Sirena, she is developing a hillside Cab and also makes one of the best Sangiovese varietals coming out of California. She oversees the winemaking for Paradigm, a fine Napa Valley Cab from Oakville (heavier soil, valley-floor fruit); Screaming Eagle, a neighbor of Dalla Valle that produces a very concentrated, rich, ripe Cab similar to Dalla Valle's Maya; Grace Family Vineyards and also Vineyard 29, along with the portion of the Hartwell lot that is made at the Grace winery.

BERNARDUS, Carmel Valley: Proprietor Bernardus "Ben" Pon is working with winemaker Don Blackburn to produce an excellent Monterey County Chardonnay, a Sauvignon Blanc and a Pinot Noir from Bien Nacido Vineyard in Santa Maria Valley. They also have a red table wine called Marinus, which blends Cabernet and Merlot.

ROBERT BIALE VINEYARDS, Napa Valley: Owned and operated by the father-and-son team of Aldo and Robert Biale and friends, this winery focuses on old-vine single-vineyard Zinfandels. Also look for small amounts of Petite Syrah, Sangiovese and Barbera.

BONNY DOON, Santa Cruz Mountains: The winemaker is Randall Grahm, a true individual who spearheaded the move into Rhône varietals ("Rhône Rangers") and has since branched out into Italians and others. Randall used to work for me, many moons ago. He puts out a witty, irreverent newsletter and also shows his literary bent not only as a master of puns but in the names of his wines, for example Old Telegraph, after the famous Châteauneuf-du-Pape Vieux Telegraphe, and Le Cigare Volant ("flying cigar," the French expression for flying saucer), after the town of Châteauneuf-du-Pape, which passed an ordinance in 1954 banning alien craft landings.

CAYMUS VINEYARDS, Rutherford, Napa Valley: Their Special Selection Cabernet has a well-deserved reputation as one of the best wines California has to offer. Call it what you want —the king of the blockbuster Cabs, the "textbook" Cab, the benchmark, America's answer to a first-growth Bordeaux, Caymus is something special. Chuck Wagner's family has been farming this area for nearly one hundred years. His father, Charlie, a legend in Napa, was born in Rutherford in 1912 and in 1943 he bought a dilapidated orchard with gravelly soil suitable for growing plums. By the mid-1960s, the fruit trees were succumbing to disease, so Charlie figured it was time to switch over to grapes. He planted three varieties, Johannisberg Riesling, Pinot Noir and Cabernet Sauvignon. The rest is history. The Wagners are among those plotting expansion to others areas of the state and to other grape varieties. They make Mer & Soleil, a Chardonnay, in Monterey. They are working with winemaker Chris Phelps, formerly of Dominus, to produce some wines out of Paso Robles. All of their projects bear close watching.

COLGIN-SCHRADER, Napa Valley: Ann Colgin and Fred Schrader are among Helen Turley's clients whose wines are made at Napa Valley Wine Co. They produce rich, dense Napa Cabs.

CORNERSTONE CELLARS, Napa Valley: Bruce Scotland, proprietor of the Highlands Wine Company, a retailer, is producing dark, intensely flavored Howell Mountain Cabernet from several distinguished vineyards. He is also making two Zinfandels and a proprietary blend of Howell Mountain and Rutherford Cabernet with Truchard Vineyard Merlot (from Carneros) called Tay, after his daughter.

ROBERT CRAIG, Napa Valley: A veteran winemaker who started his own brand in 1992, Craig is making Howell Mountain and Mount Veeder Cabernet Sauvignons as well as a Cabernet-Merlot blend called Affinity.

TOM EDDY, Napa Valley: Formerly winemaker at Château Souverain and Christian Brothers, Tom makes excellent ripe Napa Valley Cabernets with grapes from Diamond Mountain, Howell Mountain and Oakville.

VOLKER EISELE FAMILY ESTATE, Chiles Valley, Napa Valley: Volker Eisele has devoted his career to land preservation and to producing superior grapes in a beautiful little corner of Napa County. The estate of Volker and his wife, Liesel, is nestled in a secluded valley east of St. Helena. Volker was a sociologist at Berkeley during the 1960s and early seventies, his wife a landscape architect. They made the career change and he became a prominent grower. More recently, they began producing their own Bordeaux-style wine. In a typical vintage, 1992, it was 90 percent Cabernet Sauvignon and 10 percent Cabernet Franc.

ELYSE WINE CELLARS, Rutherford, Napa Valley: Proprietors Ray and Nancy Coursen are adventurous and talented winemakers with a wide and ever-expanding palette. They make superior Zinfandels; Jake's Cuvée, a Rhône blend; Nero Misto, a blend of Petite Syrah and a number of other red grapes including Zin, Grenache and Alicante; and a Cabernet Sauvignon from Morisoli Vineyard in Rutherford.

FIDDLEHEAD, Davis: Winemaker/proprietor Kathy Joseph had a background in biochemistry and microbiology but decided to pursue enology instead of her medical degree. She makes a Pinot Noir from the Santa Maria Valley (California) and one from Williamette Valley (Oregon) as well as a Santa Ynez Valley Sauvignon Blanc—all excellent.

GARY GALLERON, Rutherford, Napa Valley: Gary represents what the new generation is all about. He's as relaxed and loose as anybody I know, but when it comes to quality winemaking he is absolutely uncompromising, a hands-on artisan who's paid his dues. Gary worked at Whitehall Lane Winery from 1993 to 1999. In '98, he began working with Mario Perelli-Minetti and William Harrison, making Cabs, Chardonnays, Zinfandels, and Merlots. He also makes wines under his own name. All are delicious.

GRACE FAMILY VINEYARDS, St. Helena, Napa Valley: Dick Grace is the force behind America's most famous "cult Cabernet," a man who seems to possess endless reserves of energy and optimism. A recovering alcoholic, he judges his wines by color and aroma. Dick is a man of many trades: a former marine, a highly successful stock trader, a philanthropist and a practicing Buddhist. He and his wife, Ann, bought the property in 1976, restored it and planted a vineyard. The first Grace Family Vineyards harvest, bottled under the Caymus label, was in 1978. The Graces built a winery, and its first vintage was 1987. Their wine is 100 percent Cabernet, the cream of the California crop, a wine that is regularly described as opulent, brilliant, elegant, fruity and intense. The proceeds from all sales go to charities benefiting seriously ill children.

HARLAN ESTATE, Oakville, Napa Valley: Bill Harlan has been an influential presence in Napa Valley since the 1970s when he developed the Meadowood Resort in St. Helena, one of the premier small luxury resorts in America. He's developing his own winegrowing estate with the same type of long-term vision. Starting from scratch, in under fifteen years, he's built a legacy that will last for generations. His Harlan Estate proprietary red wine is a rich, balanced, incredibly well made Cabernet blend (with Cab Franc, Merlot and Petit Verdot, as needed). It zaps you with a laser beam of berry flavors and its aging prognosis is excellent. Hard to believe, but it's going to get even better.

HARTFORD COURT, Russian River Valley, Sonoma County: Owned by Jess Jackson of Kendall-Jackson fame, this winery produces Pinot Noirs and Zinfandels. Jackson owns a number of other premium producers including Robert Pepi, Edmeades, Kristone (Santa Maria Valley, for sparkling wines), La Crema and Cambria.

PAUL HOBBS, HEALDSBURG, Sonoma County: A highly respected veteran winemaker, Paul Hobbs worked at Mondavi, Opus One and Simi before he branched out on his own. He makes fine Pinot Noirs, Cabernets and Chardonnays from the Carneros, Howell Mountain and Sonoma Mountain appellations. He is also making Chardonnay, Cabernet Sauvignon and Malbec at Alamos Ridge in Mendoza, Argentina.

LAUREL GLEN, Sonoma Mountain: Patrick Campbell makes Cabernet Sauvignon–based wines of subtlety, balance and harmony, not flashy or over-oaked as many California wines tend to be. His wines are Laurel Glen, Counterpoint, Terra Rosa and Reds, "a wine for the people." Campbell put his 1990 Laurel Glen and Counterpoint up against the 1990 Ducru-Beaucaillou and Cheval-Blanc in a blind tasting. They showed extremely well, often being mistaken for Margaux.

LITTORAI, St. Helena, Napa Valley: Winemaker Ted Lemon and his wife–business partner, Heidi, are responsible for some of the best small-production Pinot Noirs (One Acre, Anderson Valley) and Chardonnays (Occidental) coming out of California (see page 44).

LEWIS CELLARS, Hillsborough: Randy Lewis is a guy who's used to pushing the envelope on the track, so it came pretty naturally for him to do it in the wine business. For twenty-three years, Randy raced cars. He started with Formula 3 in Europe, graduated to Formula 5000 in the United States, then raced successfully at Indianapolis for nine years. He and his wife, Debbie, started their winery in 1989 and he devoted his efforts full-time to it beginning in 1992 when he retired from racing. All of their grapes come from small, independent, quality-oriented producers. They are making a Cabernet Sauvignon–Cabernet Franc blend (typically 75 percent Sauvignon), a Chardonnay, a Merlot-based wine (about 75 percent Merlot, 20 percent Cabernet Sauvignon and 5 percent Franc) and, for the first time in 1996, a Syrah.

LONG VINEYARDS, St. Helena, Napa Valley: I admire Bob Long as someone who's willing to take chances to make better wines. He's got the passion for it, he's got a great site and he's a winegrower at heart, a big believer in *terroir*. Working closely with enologist Sandy Belcher, he produces a consistently superior Chardonnay along with smaller amounts of Cabernet Sauvignon, Sauvignon Blanc, Pinot Grigio (the first in Napa) and a late-harvest Johannisberg Riesling. A more recent project at Long Vineyards and one close to Bob's heart due to his Italian heritage is the creation of a Sangiovese.

PRIDE MOUNTAIN VINEYARDS, Spring Mountain, Napa Valley: With the help of winemaker Bob Foley, who put Markham on the map, Jim and Carolyn Pride produce elegant Cabernet Sauvignon and Merlot wines.

THE MALIBU ESTATE: Apart from Tom Jones's Moraga Vineyards, there is just one other premium winegrower in L.A. County: real estate mogul George Rosenthal. Beginning in 1987, George developed this property and lobbied for creation of an AVA. In 1996, it was granted by the BATF. It's called "Malibu–Newton Canyon." He produces an outstanding Cabernet Sauvignon with small amounts of Merlot and Cab Franc for the blend. He is also developing a Chardonnay vineyard.

MATANZAS CREEK WINERY, Bennett Valley, Sonoma: Matanzas Creek was founded in 1978 by Sandra MacIver and her husband, Bill. Many of the grapes are grown off-estate, but the MacIvers maintain close relationships with their growers. Matanzas is a model of high-quality production on a medium-sized scale (about 35,000 cases per year). Matanzas makes Sauvignon Blanc, Chardonnay and Merlot, which a small percentage of Cabernet Sauvignon. With its Journey program for Chardonnay and Merlot, Matanzas Creek has made a bold statement—for the winery and for California. The Journeys are true reserve wines, evolving from an intensive selection of the top 1 to 2 percent of the nearly 800 barrels in the winery. The first Journey Chardonnay was released in 1990. In its first six years, there were four Chardonnays and just one Merlot bottled.

PETER MICHAEL WINERY, Knights Valley, Napa: The estate was created in 1982 by British computer and media mogul Sir Peter Michael with a "hundred-year commitment" to developing a great winegrowing site. Mark Aubert, a protégé of Helen Turley and a firm believer in *terroir*, was both winemaker and vineyard manager at Peter Michael from 1991 until 1999. Peter Michael's vineyard-designated wines are Clos du Ciel ("Vineyard in the Sky"), Mon Plaisir ("My Pleasure"), Cuvée Indigène ("Indigenous Blend"), Belle Cote ("Beautiful Hill") and Le Carrier ("The Rock Quarry"), for Chardonnays; L'Après Midi ("The Afternoon"), Sauvignon Blanc; and Les Pavots ("The Poppies"), a blend of Cabernet Sauvignon, Merlot, Cabernet Franc. The reserve Chardonnays are called Point Rouge ("Red Dot") because their barrels are marked with a red dot.

CHÂTEAU MONTELENA, Calistoga, Napa Valley: Since 1982, Bo Barrett has been the winemaker of this Napa Valley institution founded in 1882 by Alfred Tubbs of San Francisco. The Barrett family took over in 1971 and their Chardonnay was one of the two California sensations of the famous 1976 Paris tasting. Their focus has always been on creating a Bordeaux-style estate winery. They also make excellent Zinfandels and Cabernets and in 1998 introduced an Italian-style wine—a Sangiovese-Primitivo-Zinfandel blend, called SV for St. Vincent.

MORAGA VINEYARDS, Bel Air: Sometimes you find great vineyards in the strangest places. Among my favorites is Moraga in Bel Air, one of the most elegant neighborhoods in America, just a few miles from The Wine Merchant, Beverly Hills. Tom Jones, the proprietor of Moraga, is the retired chairman of Northrup, where he developed the stealth bomber. He runs his estate like an R-and-D lab: There are thirteen different vineyards planted on the sixteen-acre property. Moraga produces a Bordeaux-style blend of about 80 percent Cabernet Sauvignon, 17 percent Merlot and 3 percent Cabernet Franc. They also produce a small amount of Sauvignon Blanc, which to me is reminiscent of Haut-Brion Blanc, its distant French cousin. Tony Soter is the winemaker. Superb wines, limited production.

NEWTON VINEYARDS, St. Helena, Napa Valley: Talented dynamic winemaker Su-Hua Newton turns out among the best Chardonnays, Cabernets and Merlots in the Napa area.

NIEBAUM-COPPOLA ESTATE, Rutherford, Napa Valley: The old Inglenook Estate has been bought and restored to its former glory by Francis Ford Coppola, who hired Tony Soter as winemaking consultant in 1988 to help bring out the best in its venerable *terroir*. The Cabernet-based flagship wine is called Rubicon.

OPUS ONE, Oakville, Napa Valley: A joint venture between Mondavi and Baron Philippe de Rothschild's daughter Philippine. The winery, built in 1992, is across Highway 29 from the famous Mission-style Mondavi Winery. True to Mondavi's formula, they have employed savvy marketing to popularize an excellent high-end Cabernet Sauvignon. Over 25,000 cases of the stuff go out the door in a hurry and it sells for about $125 per bottle at retail.

PARADIGM, Oakville, Napa Valley: Marilyn Harris, who along with her husband, Ren, owns and operates this winery, is the fourth generation of her family to farm in Napa Valley. They work with Heidi Peterson Barrett as consultant and Jason Fisher as winemaker to produce a Cabernet-based wine with some Merlot and Cab Franc. They also produce minimal amounts of Merlot and Zinfandel.

J. ROCHIOLI VINEYARD & WINERY, Healdsburg, Sonoma County: The Rochiolis are farmers first and foremost. Tom, who handles the winemaking and marketing duties, is the third generation. His grandfather Joe, an Italian immigrant, came to the property in 1938. The Rochiolis were strictly growers until the early eighties, supplying fine wineries such as Williams & Selyem, Davis Bynum and Gary Farrell. They generally produce up to five different Pinot Noirs, three Chardonnays, one or two Sauvignon Blancs and a Zinfandel. Their vineyard-designated Pinot Noirs are superb.

ROMBAUER VINEYARDS, St. Helena, Napa Valley: There are a lot of larger-than-life characters in the wine business, and I'd have to say Koerner Rombauer is at the top of the list. He is jovial, friendly and hospitable—a much-beloved character whose winery has been a stopping-off point for so many up-and-coming winemakers that Koerner calls it "The Wine University." The Rombauers built the winery in 1982; it has a 100,000-case capacity with room for expansion and is the host winery for many fine producers. Their house output is about 25,000 to 30,000 cases. They face all the challenges of sustaining the art of handcrafted winemaking on a medium-sized scale and yet they remain on the cutting edge of Chardonnay. Their wine is made in the classic style, with malolactic fermentation to soften the acid and stirring on the lees to give it depth of flavor. We pour plenty of Rombauer Chardonnay at our wine bar in Beverly Hills.

SEAVEY, Conn Valley, Napa: Conn Valley lies to the east of Napa with a climate that is slightly more extreme—hotter in the day and cooler at night. Seavey makes primarily Cabernet, some Merlot and a Chardonnay that does not undergo malolactic fermentation, relatively rare but something we may see more of in the future.

SELENE, Napa Valley: Mia Klein, who works with Tony Soter in his consulting business and is acknowledged to have one of the best palates among American winegrowers, makes Sauvignon Blanc and Merlot under this, her own, label. Try her wines and see if you agree with her palate.

SINE QUA NON, Ojai: Manfred Krankl is not only achieving great things at his L.A. restaurant, Campanile, and bakeshop, La Brea Bakery, but at his home winery in Ojai where he features Rhône varietals to match the restaurant's Mediterranean cuisine. Like children, every single release of wine is given its own name. The 1994 Syrah, released in 1996, was called The Queen of Spades. In 1997, they released a Chardonnay-Rousanne blend called The Bride, a Syrah called The Other Hand, and a Syrah-Grenache-Mourvèdre blend called Red Handed. All are excellent wines; Manfred's reputation as an innovator and purveyor of superior quality continues to blossom.

TONY SOTER, Napa Valley: Like Helen Turley, Tony Soter came of age during the first wine revolution and is a key player in the new revolution. Tony started working in the cellar at Stag's Leap when they were bottling the 1973 Cabernet that won the legendary Paris wine tasting in '76. He trained at UC-Davis, went on to become winemaker for Chappellet in 1977 and began his consulting business in 1980. Past clients have included Cain Cellars, Far Niente, Clos du Val and Robert Pepi. Since 1978, Tony has been making his own wines from various vineyard sources. In 1982 he launched his company Etude, which is French for "study." At Etude, he's made Cabernet Sauvignons, Pinot Blancs and Pinot Grigios, but his signature wines are the Pinot Noirs. Many consider Tony to have inherited the mantel as King of Wine Consultants from Andre Tchelistcheff when the great master died in the spring of 1994. He's recently begun to develop vineyards in Oregon. Tony and his associate Mia Klein are responsible for a star-studded list of client wineries, among them Viader Vineyards, Araujo Estate, Niebaum-Coppola, Dalla Valle, Moraga Vineyards and Spotswoode.

STEELE, Lake County: Proprietors Jed and Marie Steele took over the old Konocti Winery in Lake County. A veteran winemaker, Jed makes single-vineyard Chardonnays from various sites in Mendocino and Sonoma Counties as well as Bien Nacido in Santa Barbara and Sangiancomo Vineyards in Carneros; he also makes some Zinfandels and a small amount of Pinot Noirs.

SWANSON VINEYARDS, Oakville, Napa Valley: Swanson Vineyards produces a delightful rainbow of wines. The proprietor, Clarke Swanson, a familiar face around Napa as chairman of the Napa National Bank, made his vineyard and winery into a major player in under ten years. Swanson has two properties, one in Oakville, with distinguished neighbors including Silver Oak, Caymus, Opus One and Franciscan, and the other in nearby Yountville, among whose neighbors are Dominus and Martha's Vineyard (of Heitz fame). Andre Tchelistcheff was the consultant early on and he in turn hired twenty-six-year-old Marco Cappelli as winemaker in 1986. The Swanson philosophy is characterized by experimentation in the vineyard, close attention to the details of *terroir* and viticulture and the judicious blending of different grape varieties. They blend an average of eleven different lots of Merlot, for example, and sell bulk wine of those lots that don't make the cut. The Swanson wines are Estate Chardonnay, Rosato of Sangiovese, Estate Sangiovese, Estate Merlot and Cabernet Sauvignon. The flagship wine is Alexis, Napa Valley Red Table Wine, an unusual Meritage named after Clarke's eldest daughter. It's Cabernet Sauvignon based but with a high percentage of Syrah along with other varieties. It may be up to two thirds Cab and may contain as many as five other red grape varieties. The Alexis is a wonderful blend, front-loaded with fruit yet possessing a velvety smooth finish and great aging potential. Swanson also makes a Syrah, a late-harvest Sémillon (with 14.8% residual sugar) and a Pinot Grigio.

TRUCHARD, Carneros: Jo Ann and Tony Truchard have 169 acres of vineyards in the northern part of the cool Carneros region, which straddles Napa and Sonoma Counties. They sell most of their grapes to quality producers such as Cornerstone, but make about 10,000 cases of excellent wine under their own label, including Chardonnay, Merlot, Zinfandel and Cabernet Sauvignon.

HELEN TURLEY, Napa Valley: Helen Turley is the goddess of California winemaking. Her own label is Marcassin and she has a distinguished client list, including Colgin-Schrader, Bryant Family, Pahlmayer and La Jota. The somewhat reclusive Turley has shown her versatility with a number of varieties, although she's best known for her Chardonnays and Cabernets.

VIADER VINEYARDS, Howell Mountain, Napa Valley: If Randy and Debbie Lewis are a mom-and-pop operation, then Delia Viader is a mom operation. A single mother, she developed her property beginning in the late 1980s and has made her mark in a very short period of time. Superior vineyards aren't supposed to develop this fast. She works with winemaking consultant Tony Soter, vineyard consultant Richard Nagaoka and vineyard manager David Abreu. Her wine blends the characteristically rich Howell Mountain Cabernet Sauvignon with Cabernet Franc and is made "in the style of" the great Château Cheval-Blanc. Delia challenged the traditional model of hillside development, took a big risk planting Cab Franc and it's paid off. I see some of her character in her wine: There is a softness and sweetness, but also a very strong undercurrent of persistence and power. Great personality, great wine.

MORE CALIFORNIA FAVORITES

ALBAN VINEYARDS, San Luis Obispo: John Alban is doing exciting things with Rhône varietals Roussanne, Viognier, Grenache and Syrah.

AU BON CLIMAT, Santa Barbara: Jim Clendenen is the winemaker at this Central Coast winery known for its Pinot Noirs and Chardonnays.

CAFARO: A respected winemaker/consultant, Joe Cafaro makes Cabernets and Merlots.

CORISON: Cathy Corison was winemaker at Chappellet and this is her own label for Cabernet.

BRYANT FAMILY VINEYARDS, Napa Valley: A Helen Turley client for Cabernet; small production, very high quality.

DIAMOND CREEK, Napa Valley: Single-vineyard Cabernets from the Calistoga area: Gravelly Meadow, Volcanic Hill, Red Rock Terrace.

DOMINUS, Rutherford: The proprietor is Christian Mouiex from the family that owns Château Petrus; Jean-Claude Berrouet is his winemaker. Within a decade, Christian, an elegant gentleman farmer with no formal winemaking training but a strong family tradition, has built Dominus into a great wine.

DUNN VINEYARDS: Formerly winemaker at Caymus, Randy Dunn turns out some very fine rich, concentrated Howell Mountain Cabernet.

GARY FARRELL, Sonoma County: Known for his Russian River Pinot Noirs as well as Zinfandels and Chardonnays.

GROTH RESERVE: Medium-sized winery in Oakville, Napa Valley, making a reserve Cabernet that has many fans.

HEITZ CELLARS: Arguably the original "Cult Cab," a maverick of the first California wine revolution, Joe Heitz is known for his Martha's Vineyard and also Trailside wines.

IL PODERE DELL'OLIVOS: Jim Clendenen's label for Italian varieties such as Barbera, Nebbiolo, Arneis, Tocai Friuliano, Fiano.

JADE MOUNTAIN: Small Napa producer of Rhône varieties; they share a winery with White Rock, a small high-quality producer of a Cabernet-based red blend called Claret.

JARVIS: A thirty-seven-acre Napa vineyard on the proprietors' fourteen-hundred-acre estate; they make a fine Cabernet, a respectable Chardonnay and are developing their Cab Franc.

KALIN, Livermore Valley: They make fine Chardonnay, Sémillon and Pinot Noir.

KISTLER, Sonoma: Known for their classic California Chardonnays.

LA JOTA, Napa: A fine Howell Mountain Cabernet Sauvignon; also a Cabernet Franc.

ANDREW MURRAY: A young "Rhône Ranger" winemaker from Los Olivos; he makes a fine Santa Ynez Valley Syrah, among others.

PATZ & HALL: Try their Napa Chardonnays and their Russian River Pinot Noirs.

CHÂTEAU POTELLE: Known for its Chardonnay, Cabernet Sauvignon and Mount Veeder Zinfandel.

QUPE: Santa Barbara producer of Syrah, Pinot Blanc, Marsanne and Viognier; winemaker is Bob Lindquist. They also make good Chardonnay.

RIDGE: The winery is located in the Santa Cruz Mountains, south of the Bay Area. They make a fine Meritage from their own "Monte Bello" vineyard as well as a number of excellent Zinfandels from various Sonoma vineyards, including Sonoma Station, Lytton Springs and Geyserville. Paul Draper is the longtime winemaker.

SIDURI: Fine Pinot Noir from the Hirsch Vineyard and Rose Vineyard; they are also expanding to Oregon.

SILVER OAK: Classic Napa Cabs from Oakville; also from Alexander Valley.

STAG'S LEAP WINE CELLARS, Yountville: A landmark Cab of the first California wine revolution.

TALLEY VINEYARDS: Try the Arroyo Grande Valley Chardonnay; Brian Babcock is the winemaker.

LARRY TURLEY: Helen's brother makes a number of excellent vineyard-designated old-vine Zinfandels as well as a thick, intense Petite Syrah.

VINE CLIFF CELLARS, Oakville, Napa Valley: John Gibson, winemaker and general manager, makes Chardonnay and Cabernet Sauvignon with "balance, elegance and fruit."

CHRIS WHITCRAFT, Santa Maria Valley: A former retailer with a passion for Pinot Noir, Whitcraft makes Pinots from the Bien Nacido Vineyard in the Santa Maria Valley as well as from the Hirsch Vineyard, Sonoma Coast. He also makes Chardonnays from the Santa Ynez Valley.

WILLIAMS & SELYEM, Healdsburg, Sonoma County: Proprietors Burt Williams and Ed Selyem are known for their superb vineyard-designated Pinot Noirs; they also make Zinfandels and Chardonnays.

NEW YORK

New York State has two winegrowing regions, the Finger Lakes in the north-central part of the state and Long Island's North Fork. Because of the relatively chilly, damp climate, particularly in the Finger Lakes, premium winegrowing is truly a challenge. It involves a lot more spraying against mold and mildew than most premium winegrowers are comfortable with. One of the great viticultural research centers, Cornell University's Agricultural Experimental Station, is located in Geneva, in the middle of the Finger Lakes region. Traditionally, it was believed that only northern white wine varieties, such as Riesling or Chardonnay, could thrive in this area, but in August 1997 a Pinot Noir from Fox Run near Geneva was declared winner of a contest sponsored by the New York State wine trade association. There are some fine producers capable of making world-class wines in New York, including Bedell, Hargraves, Jamesport, Palmer, Lenz and Osprey.

OREGON

With its core of small "farm-style" producers, Oregon is America's answer to Burgundy, which is on roughly the same latitude. Pinot Noir is king and, while producing consistently good wine, has been a major challenge due to the humid climate and the possibility of early fall rains severely diluting the crop, a group of dedicated winegrowers are turning out world-class wines, many of them equal to their French counterparts. Among them are Argyle; Beaux Frères (owned by Robert Parker and his brother-in-law); Broadley; Chehalem; Cristom; Domaine Drouhin (Veronique, twenty-eight, daughter of Joseph, the famous Burgundian producer and *negociant*); Duck Pond; Fiddlehead; McKinlay; Ponzi; Domain Serene; WillaKenzie; Ken Wright. All highly recommended.

WASHINGTON

Washington State produces more wine than Oregon but receives less acclaim. Its producers have been turning out excellent Merlot since long before the Merlot craze hit California. Its principal growing regions are the Columbia Valley, the Yakima Valley and the Walla Walla area in the southeastern portion of the state. The Reserve Merlot from Leonetti, Walla Walla, is considered by many to be the finest red wine made in America. L'Ecole No. 41 also makes a superior Columbia Valley Merlot as well as a Cabernet. Another reliable producer for Merlot and also Chardonnay is Columbia Crest, in the Columbia Valley.

Michael Moore, whose Blackwood Canyon Winery is in Benton City near Yakima, is an intriguing figure on the Washington winemaking scene. The ultimate throwback, Moore is a "master of the barrel" who is making wines with pre–World War II methods, a true noninterventionist. He ages his wines for up to twelve years (that's right, *twelve years!*) in barrel before release and uses no preservatives, just the wine and the wood, which some would say is exactly what God intended. He makes Chardonnay, Sémillon, Riesling, Gewürztraminer, Merlot, Cabernet Sauvignon and Merlot-Cabernet blends. Moore was a pupil of Andre Tchelistcheff and he was also winemaker at Ventana in Monterey, California, before moving to Washington.

GLOSSARY

AC or **AOC** *Appellation Contrôlee,* or *Appellation D'Origine Contrôlée,* the French official guarantee of a wine's provenance and quality. AC wines are a notch above *vins de table* and *vins de pays*—table wines and country wines, respectively—and must qualify by coming from an official winegrowing region and following certain vinicultural and viticultural guidelines for that region.

acidity It is natural to grapes in their unripe stage, but as they ripen, the balance shifts from acids to sugars; nevertheless all wines have some acidity. There are two types of acid in wine: fixed and volatile, which comprise its total acidity (T/A). Fixed acids are malic, tartaric, citric and lactic. Volatile acid is acetic acid, which is produced by bacteria when the wine comes into contact with oxygen; too much acetic acid turns wine to vinegar.

appellation (*appellation* in French) An officially recognized winegrowing area.

aromatics The compounds in wine that provide the aroma.

barrel A generic term for an oak cask used in the aging of fine wines.

barriques Bordeaux-style oak casks holding 225 liters (about 60 gallons), or the equivalent of about 25 cases of wine.

berries An insider's term for grapes.

body A wine's weight as perceived by the palate, which consists mostly of the amount of alcohol and viscosity.

Botrytis cinerea A mold that grows on mature grapes in humid conditions, shriveling them; also known as "noble rot" when the grapes are made into fine sweet or dessert wines.

Brix A measure of the sugar content of grapes; used to determine whether they are ready to harvest.

bud wood The part of the vine that is grafted onto a rootstock and bears the fruit.

canopy A viticultural term for the leaf growth of a vine.

caves French for an underground or dugout cellar where wines are barrel-aged.

chai French for the storehouse where wines are barrel-aged.

château French for "castle," used to refer to wine-producing estates, primarily in Bordeaux.

clarification A general term for a process that clears the wine of particles or sediment; clarification includes fining and filtering.

classified growth This refers primarily to the 1855 ranking of the sixty-one premier châteaux (wine-growing estates) of Bordeaux in first, second, third, fourth and fifth growths. Burgundy has a three-tiered classification: *grand crus, premiers crus* and *village* or commune wines.

clone(s) Different varieties or species of grape vines that are grafted onto rootstocks to grow wine grapes.

clos French for "vineyard," specifically an enclosed vineyard in Burgundy.

complexity Descriptor indicating a wine that has multiple aromas and/or flavors.

côte French for "hill," often part of the name of a superior growing site, such as *Côte-Rôtie* along the Rhône River where Guigal, Jaboulet and other top producers make their excellent Syrah-based wines or Côte de Nuits in Burgundy.

coulure French term for the damage to flowers that prevents a vine from developing its full complement of fruit, usually caused by cold, wet and/or windy weather at flowering time, but can also be caused by overly hot conditions.

cru French for "growth," referring to a particular vineyard.

crush The processing of the harvested grapes.

custom crush When a producer or winemaker works in a winery he or she doesn't own.

267

véraison In the ripening process, when the grapes begin to change color.

cuvée French for "blend."

domaine French term used for a winegrowing property, especially in Burgundy. A particular _domaine_ may produce wines from different vineyards, either within its estate or from other lands, either bought or leased or from which grapes are purchased, for example the Domaine de la Romanée-Conti (DRC) in Burgundy produces wines from numerous vineyards, including La Tache, Romanée-Conti (the vineyard for which the entire estate is named), Echézeaux, Grands-Echézeaux, Richebourg and Romanée-St.-Vivant. In some cases, DRC is not the only _domaine_ or producer that makes wines from a particular vineyard, for example both DRC and Leroy makes wines from the Romanée-St.-Vivant vineyard. Many of these top vineyards are _grand cru,_ meaning they are the top Burgundy appellations.

elever French for "to raise."

enology (oenology in the U.K.) The science of wine and winemaking.

extraction This refers to winemaking processes that take the color, flavor and aroma compounds out of the grapes and put them into the solution that eventually becomes wine.

fermentation The process by which microorganisms called yeasts transform sugars into alcohol and carbon dioxide.

filtering The winemaking process that clears the wine of impurities by running it through a very fine filter. Often small enough to eliminate bacteria, it can also eliminate components of character.

fining Process of placing a neutral agent such as egg whites or bentonite into the wine to precipitate out solids such as lees and/or other unwanted sediment.

finish A wine's aftertaste.

fruit Insider's term for grapes.

grand cru French for "great growth"; in Burgundy it means the top vineyards, which have official status as separate _appellations contrôlées_ and are usually owned, leased or operated by more than one producer or _domaine._ In the Medoc area of Bordeaux it means the third tier of châteaus

after first and second growths; other Bordeaux regions have similar classification systems.

graves French for "gravelly soil"; _Graves_ is one of the Bordeaux appellations, although a great many of the vineyards all over the Medoc region of Bordeaux, north of the city, along the Gironde estuary, are covered with this type of soil, which works extremely well for the cultivation of superior wine grapes.

hectare A metric measure of surface area equal to 10,000 square meters or a plot of land 100 meters by 100 meters; equal to 2.471 acres.

hectoliter The metric measure equal to 100 litres or 26.418 gallons.

horizontal tasting Tasting and comparing many wines from a given vintage (_see also_ vertical tasting).

lees As in "on the lees" or "on their lees" (_sur lis_ in French); the dead yeast cells and other solid materials that settle to the bottom of the fermenter. Most wines are "racked off their lees"; others are aged on their lees, with stirring, which gives them more color, flavor and complexity.

liter The metric liquid measure equal to 1.0567 quarts; consists of 1,000 milliliters, the standard wine bottle size being 750 milliliters.

maceration The stage in the red winemaking process whereby the juice from the grapes is left in contact with the solid remnants of the grapes (the skins, pits and/or portions of stems). It encourages "extraction" of color and tannins from the grapes into the wine, particularly when the cap, the floating mass of grape remnants in the vat, is "punched down" into the liquid or when the liquid is "pumped over" the cap.

malolactic fermentation Part of the winemaking process, this is a secondary fermentation that takes place after primary or alcoholic fermentation (wherein the sugar from the grape juice is consumed by yeasts, yielding alcohol and carbon dioxide) in which malic acid, the tart compound present in green apples, is transformed into lactic acid, a mellower compound found in milk.

Meritage From California, a blend of primarily Cabernet Sauvignon with other Bordeaux components such as Merlot and Cab Franc from California.

moelleux French for "soft," refers to wines that are sweet, often late-harvest, such as Vouvray Moelleux.

must The crushed grapes and/or their juice that are in the process of becoming wine.

negociant Traditionally, in the French wine business, a wholesaler, merchant or middleman who buys wines from vintners and blends, bottles and markets them.

nose A wine's aroma.

oxidation Overexposure to oxygen, causing wines to taste flat and turn brownish; wine's equivalent to an apple turning brown or a nail rusting.

pH A measure of acidity in a liquid; the lower the number, the higher the acidity, so, for example, water has a pH of 7 while wines generally have between 3 and 4.

phenols (also known as phenolics) Complex chemical compounds found in wine that include anthocyanins and others responsible for coloring and tannins, they also preserve the wine and give it smoothness and complexity with age. Phenols are also antioxidants and probably contribute to the beneficial effects of steady consumption of small to moderate amounts of alcohol.

phylloxera A louse that gradually kills grape vines from the root up; the vinous equivalent of cancer. Some rootstocks are resistant to it, others are not. It is responsible for virtually wiping out the European vineyards in the late nineteenth century and for the replanting of large portions of California's vineyards beginning in the mid-1980s.

pomace The residue left over after the crushing of grapes and the extraction of grape juice to produce wine. Pomace can be distilled into a spirit—in France, it becomes *marc*, and in Italy *grappa*.

racking The winemaking term for moving the wine, as it ages, from one container, usually a wooden barrel, to another. Racking exposes the wine to air, which presents a certain risk of contamination or oxidation.

rootstock The part of the vine that is anchored in the ground, as opposed to the clone, which is the part that bears the fruit. Clones of different varieties can be grafted onto different rootstocks, which possess such characteristics as resistance to certain diseases or the ability to grow more or less fruit and vegetation in a given climate.

stabilization A general term for techniques that ensure clear wine—for example, chilling to precipitate out crystals of tartaric acid (*tartrates*).

TA Total acidity: fixed acidity and volatile acidity combined; *see* acidity.

tannins Chemical compounds that come from the seeds, skin and stems of grapes that can give wine a slightly bitter taste and/or astringent mouth-feel. They are traditionally believed to give a wine the potential to age and gain complexity by protecting it from oxidation.

terroir A French term denoting the combination of climatic and geographical factors that make each winegrowing site unique. Producers of the finest wines in the world all agree that a wine should "express its *terroir*"—that is, their job is to bring out the best of the distinct character of each site through viticultural and vinicultural techniques. Without *terroir*, wines risk "internationalization" and "homogenization."

triage French term for the sorting of grapes to select the best.

varietal A wine made entirely from a particular grape variety and named as such; for example, a Washington State Merlot or a New Zealand Sauvignon Blanc; often incorrectly substituted for "variety," which means a type of grape.

veraison The point at which grapes change color; warm afternoons and cool nights are required.

vertical tasting Tasting and comparing vintages from a given producer or region down through the years; *see also* horizontal tasting.

vigor The amount of energy a vine puts into growing shoots, leaves and grapes; dependent primarily on climate, water and nutrients available from the soil but also on the nature of the rootstock itself and on viticultural techniques.

Vin de Pays French for "country wine," the category above table wine and below the official appellations and *crus*.

Vin de Table French for "table wine."

vinification A fancy word for winemaking.

viticulture A fancy word for the cultivation of vines.

volatile acidity See acidity.

INDEX